Global Citizens

Australian Activists for Change

Against a backdrop of advancing neoliberalism and globalisation, this timely book examines nine prominent Australians from diverse backgrounds – 'global citizens' – who have each enhanced public life through promoting universal values and human rights.

The book charts over 50 years of campaigning, and espouses perennial causes such as peace, social justice, ecological sustainability and gender and racial equality. Ultimately, this inspiring volume sends a message of hope for Australian society and provides a benchmark for all proponents of change.

Geoffrey Stokes is Professor of Politics in the School of International and Political Studies at Deakin University, Melbourne.

Roderic Pitty is Senior Lecturer in Political Science and International Relations at the School of Social and Cultural Studies, University of Western Australia, Perth.

Gary Smith is Professor and Head of the School of International and Political Studies at Deakin University, Melbourne.

Global Citizens
Australian Activists for Change

Edited by
GEOFFREY STOKES, RODERIC PITTY AND
GARY SMITH

CAMBRIDGE
UNIVERSITY PRESS

CAMBRIDGE UNIVERSITY PRESS
Cambridge, New York, Melbourne, Madrid, Cape Town, Singapore, São Paulo, Delhi

Cambridge University Press
477 Williamstown Road, Port Melbourne, VIC 3207, Australia

Published in the United States of America by Cambridge University Press, New York

www.cambridge.org
Information on this title: www.cambridge.org/9780521731874

First published 2008

Cover design by Modern Art Production Group
Printed in Australia by Ligare

A catalogue record for this publication is available from the British Library

National Library of Australia Cataloguing in Publication data
Stokes, Geoffrey.
Global citizens : Australian activists for change / authors,
Geoffrey Stokes; Roderic Pitty; Gary Smith.
Cambridge ; Port Melbourne : Cambridge University
Press, 2008.
9780521731874 (pbk.)
Includes Index.
Bibliography.
World citizenship.
Globalization – Australia.
Australia – Politics and government – 20th century.
Pitty, Roderic.
Smith, Gary, 1950–
323.6

ISBN 978-0-521-73187-4 paperback

For April Carter.

Contents

Acknowledgments

The editors would like to thank Lucinda Horrocks for the excellent research and editorial assistance she provided for this project. Many thanks are due to those subjects of this study who gave up a portion of their valuable time to be interviewed, and respond to questions. We are also grateful to Deakin University, the Faculty of Arts, and the School of International and Political Studies for providing financial support for this project.

Cover photographs

We acknowledge permission to reproduce photographs for the cover, from left to right:

Top row:
Faith Bandler	© Newspix/Samantha Emanuel
Jack Mundey	Courtesy NSW Historic Houses Trust Members
Herb and Betty Feith	Courtesy David Feith and Australian Volunteers International

Middle row:
Bob Brown	Courtesy Peter Whyte
Michael Kirby	Courtesy Justice Kirby
Nancy Shelley	Courtesy Norman Ainsworth

Bottom row:
Margaret Reynolds	Courtesy Margaret Reynolds
Keith Suter	Courtesy Keith Suter
Thao Nguyen	Courtesy Thao Nguyen

Contributors

Peter Haeusler is Senior Lecturer in Politics and Policy Studies at Deakin University. His research interests include political thought and political culture in Australia. His recent work explores the nexus between Catholic social thought and Australian politics, with published papers in this field including 'Living with hope and fear: Advancing Catholic social ideals amid the spectre of communism', in B. Costar, P. Love and P. Strangio (eds) *The Great Labor Schism* (Scribe 2005). He is working on a book concerning the role of intellectuals in shaping Australian political culture.

Linda Hancock is Associate Professor in Public Policy at Deakin University. She has published widely in the fields of social and public policy analysis. Her books include (ed. with Brian Howe, Marion Frere and Anthony O'Donnell) *Future Directions in Australian Public Policy* (CEDA 2001); (ed. with Carolyn O'Brien) *Rewriting Rights in Europe* (Aldershot 2000); and (ed.) *Women, Public Policy and the State* (Macmillan 1999).

Lucinda Horrocks is Research Fellow in the Institute for Citizenship and Globalisation at Deakin University, where she has worked on numerous projects in the fields of politics, public policy, globalisation and citizenship. She also lectures in the disciplines of Politics and Sociology.

Michael Leach is Senior Research Fellow in the Institute for Citizenship and Globalisation, Deakin University. He has published on issues of national identity, immigration, Australian multiculturalism, and labour history. He is co-author (with Fethi Mansouri) of *Lives in Limbo: Voices of Refugees on Australia* (UNSW Press 2004). In 2000 he co-edited (with G. Stokes and I. Ward) *The Rise and Fall of One Nation* (University of Queensland Press). He is co-editor (with Fethi Mansouri) of *Critical Perspectives on Refugee Policy in Australia* (Deakin University 2003), and (with Damien Kingsbury) of *East Timor: Beyond Independence* (Monash University Press 2007).

Thao Nguyen holds degrees in Commerce and Law from the University of Sydney, and has worked at the New South Wales Legal Aid Commission. In 2004, Thao was the Australian Youth Representative to the UN General

Assembly. In the following year she was a member of the Australian non-governmental delegation to the UN Committee on the Rights of the Child in Geneva. Thao has been Youth Chair of the Ethnic Communities' Council of New South Wales, and a member of the National Community Advisory Committee to the Special Broadcasting Service (SBS).

Roderic Pitty is Senior Lecturer in Political Science and International Relations at the University of Western Australia. He has published articles on international law and Indigenous rights, written various works on Russia, and contributed chapters to *Facing North* (Melbourne University Press 2001, 2003), a history of Australian policies towards, and relations with, Asia. For some years, he was a contributing editor of the *Current Affairs Bulletin*. His current research interests focus on universal human rights and international justice.

Gary Smith is Professor and Head of the School of International and Political Studies at Deakin University. He was previously Head of the School of International Studies at the University of South Australia. He has also worked as Program Director at the Centre for Defence and Strategic Studies, Australia's senior defence college in Canberra. His research is on international relations in the Asia–Pacific region, global governance and civil society, and on Australian foreign relations. His publications include *Australia and Asia* (Oxford University Press 1997), *Australia in the World* (Oxford University Press 1996), and *Threats Without Enemies* (Pluto 1992).

Geoffrey Stokes is Professor of Politics at Deakin University. His recent research has focused upon the problems of transnational political thought. With April Carter he has co-edited *Democratic Theory Today* (Polity 2002) and *Liberal Democracy and its Critics* (Polity 1998). He has also edited *The Politics of Identity in Australia* (Cambridge University Press 1997) and *Australian Political Ideas* (UNSW Press 1994). In 1990–91 he was Senior Adviser to the Commonwealth Minister for Trade and Overseas Development.

Foreword

Carmen Lawrence

The stark division of community opinion in recent years over how to respond to people seeking asylum in Australia reveals a fundamental set of tensions in our society. As the numbers of asylum seekers increased in the late 1990s and the MV *Tampa*'s sorry human cargo was repelled by armed Australian soldiers, media coverage illustrated the chasm that exists between alternative visions of how Australia ought to be linked with the wider world. Some Australians strongly hold that there are fundamental principles of respect for human decency which transcend national boundaries. Others fiercely defend such boundaries against the uninvited. Those who are able to see beyond borders regard the needs of the asylum seekers as deserving humane consideration. Those who see only the borders condone the prolonged incarceration of refugees as a warning signal to others who might otherwise follow. This gulf reflects the varying respect for human rights standards in Australia. There is a divide between those who see Australia as part of a common humanity, and those who see Australia apart from the wider world, and who would also exclude others on the basis of race, religion, and culture.

As this book reminds us, there are and always have been a good many Australians, although probably not the majority, who have a strong sense of global citizenship, just as there are those who are proudly nationalistic and defensive of narrowly defined 'Australian values'. Many clearly appreciate that, in the age of global warming, resource depletion, and burgeoning population, the big problems we confront simply cannot be solved in splendid isolation. Those who espouse a global perspective have, until recently, found themselves on the receiving end of derision and abuse, accused of caring more about 'those people' than their own. *Ad hominem* attacks on critics of narrow parochialism were commonplace. The abusive epithet 'un-Australian' was often used to denigrate those who try to show how the world can be re-imagined and remade.

In such times, it is challenging to work toward a world in which the precarious aspects of our common humanity are reaffirmed. Yet the increased vulnerability felt by many people in western societies early in the twenty-first century offers a challenge, which the American writer Judith Butler

(2004: xii–xiii) has described as an opportunity. She says that this vulnerability 'offers a chance to start to imagine a world in which violence might be minimised, in which an inevitable interdependency becomes acknowledged as the basis for global political community'. What this book shows is that there are many strands of reason from which such a vision of an interdependent world can be created. Even during the Howard years, the voices of those who remained optimistic about Australia's links with the wider world were not silenced. There is a strong tradition, celebrated in this collection, of using universalist values to criticise and reform institutions and practices in Australia, and elsewhere. This tradition has clearly informed contemporary campaigns for racial equality, global peace, women's rights, environmental protection, and human rights more generally, as it did in the recent debate over asylum seekers.

The tradition of seeking to transcend parochial, nationalist, and populist politics drove Australia's active participation in the establishment of the United Nations. This was based on the recognition, after two catastrophic wars and the annihilation of millions, that such destruction was possible only because of the failure to accord basic human dignity and worth to all humans. The Nazis built the ideological campaign that led to the Holocaust upon a pre-existing political culture of anti-Semitism, onto which they grafted propaganda campaigns that depicted the Jewish people as vermin, and as threatening the fabric of German society. To those in the postwar era, the combination of this representation of the Jews as less than human, and the extreme nationalism of the Third Reich, seemed to demand a global remedy, namely an international framework for the protection of human rights.

Amongst the instruments devised was the UN Convention on Refugees. This was adopted in 1951, and ratified by the majority of nations, including Australia. The convention was designed to prevent a recurrence of the scandalous treatment of the Jewish people fleeing Nazi Germany, whose claims for asylum were rebuffed and who were returned to certain death in the gas chambers of occupied Europe. While many Jewish refugees escaped this horror, like the young Herb Feith who arrived in Australia with his parents in 1938, many others did not. The Refugee Convention has come under strain in recent years, but it continues to provide an essential framework for protecting the rights of people fleeing persecution. It is one of the many institutional threads linking Australian society with the wider world.

Australia has become an increasingly reluctant participant in protecting people from persecution. Many of the recent changes to migration legislation, which were presented in terms of protecting our borders from vulnerable people, arguably violate the Refugee Convention. In clear violation of our commitments under section 33 not to send people back to a place of persecution, asylum seekers from Iraq and Iran have been returned to danger. There is strong evidence that some of them may have been killed (Corlett 2005). The former UN High Commissioner on Refugees (Lubbers 2001) has observed:

> If refugees are sent straight back to danger – or are prevented from leaving their countries in the first place – then all the other measures designed to protect and assist them count for nothing. Under international law this should not happen, and blatantly ignoring international law is a dangerous path to tread.

By denying asylum seekers proper recourse to Australian law, while attempting to foist our responsibilities onto our impoverished Pacific neighbours, Australia has clearly reneged on its obligations and responsibilities under international law. If every country behaved in this way, there would be nowhere for people fleeing persecution to find peace, safety and security.

Australia's adherence to various UN declarations, conventions, and protocols has always been uneven, as has our willingness to subject ourselves to international norms and scrutiny. Indeed, in the past decade there was a fundamental reappraisal of our status within the international community. When he was Prime Minister, John Howard appealed to populist prejudice, and once referred to one UN human rights body as 'just a bunch of foreigners in Geneva'. Criticism from various UN human rights bodies has focused on Australia's failure to grapple satisfactorily with Indigenous injustice, the unprecedented turning away of some asylum seekers, and the indefinite detention of many others. In response to this criticism, the Howard government effectively banned cooperation with the UN Committee system, blocking future visits by UN inspectors, and further delaying routine reports. These defensive moves to protect Australia from adverse commentary attracted further UN criticism. In August 2000, the head of the UN Treaty section, Mr Kohona (quoted in Riley 2000), was openly critical of Australia:

> The moral authority Australia enjoys will be dissipated by this peevish attitude towards these UN committees. [It] should be doing its best to protect its good record and using it to advance the cause of human rights around the world.

Australia's obstructionist stance gave a green light to repressive regimes with far worse human rights records than ours. China, for example, congratulated the Howard government over its outburst against the UN in 2000 when our mandatory sentencing laws were criticised. In claiming that the UN should reserve its criticisms only for the most odious regimes, the Howard government failed to appreciate that Australia has a crucial role to play in setting an example, by protecting human rights within and beyond its borders. It failed to rise to the challenge of an interdependent world.

Changes in government policy in the past decade meant that Australia reached a low point in our implementation of international human rights obligations. On every major issue – except trade – the Howard government played down the idea of Australia as an international citizen: from the Refugee Convention to global warming and the Kyoto Protocol, from Indigenous self-determination to disarmament, from joining the attack on Iraq without UN approval to breaking UN sanctions against Iraq in the lead-up to the war. Such actions led many Australians to feel ashamed of their government, particularly when travelling abroad. While many of these actions are being repudiated by the new Rudd Labor government, one lesson of the last decade is that Australians must not rely only on governments to respond to the global challenges of the current era. Given the urgent need to imagine a world based on non-violence and responsibility for others, direct action by Australians to address global issues has become vital.

This collection of essays provides us with a timely reminder that Australia has a strong tradition of such action to draw upon. Citizenship for Australians does not require excluding others, whether refugees or other victims of injustice around the world. It is possible, and increasingly necessary, to be an Australian global citizen, concerned about universal human rights, and determined to enhance Australia's positive engagement with the wider world. This book reveals a tradition of global citizenship in Australia expressed in the lives of quite diverse people, some prominent and others less so. All have responded to the challenges of an interdependent world, seeking to resolve Australian problems in accordance with principles of our common humanity. In these vulnerable times, there is much to learn from these Australian activists, about how we can broaden our perspectives on our place in the world today, and practise an active citizenship that is limited neither by borders nor by timidity.

References

Butler, J. 2004. *Precarious Life: The Powers of Mourning and Violence*. London: Verso.

Corlett, D. 2005. *Following Them Home: The Fate of the Returned Asylum Seekers*. Melbourne: Black Inc.

Lubbers, R. 2001. Statement by UN High Commissioner for Refugees on the 50th anniversary of the Refugee Convention, 26 July, viewed 15 January 2008, http://www.unhcr.bg/briefing_documents/brfnote_26072001_en.htm

Riley, M. 2000. 'Australia warned: Grow up and stop sulking'. *Sydney Morning Herald*, 30 August.

1

Global Citizenship in Australia: Theory and Practice

Geoffrey Stokes[1]

> . . . our life should not be based on cities or peoples, each with its own view
> of right or wrong, but we should regard all men as our fellow countrymen.
>
> (Zeno cited in Baldry 1965: 159)

There exists in Australia a significant group of intellectuals whose distinguishing feature is their global outlook on politics and law. These are writers and activists who call upon universalist values to criticise and reform institutions and practices in Australia, and in other countries. By universalism is meant a doctrine, such as world peace, international human rights, or ecological sustainability, whose principles – moral and political – apply to all people whatever their gender, religion, culture, or political location. The Australians who hold such values are not the traditional kind of detached scholars or academics; they are engaged intellectuals who interpret, adapt and promote political ideas emphasising the global community to which all Australians belong. As 'global citizens', they attempt to enlarge Australian notions of political identity beyond the national. Contrary to certain nationalist and populist views, these intellectuals are not 'rootless cosmopolitans', unmindful of local concerns and affiliations, but strongly grounded in Australian society. Their ideas, life and work offer a new dimension to our understanding of globalisation, citizenship, and the scope for political action. This book draws out that important transnational tradition of political thought and action.

As engaged activists or publicists, such intellectuals interpret, adapt, promote, and creatively apply political ideas that are usually formulated by others. By articulating and transmitting social and political ideas to a broader public, they may be said to produce a form of Australian political thought.[2] These people rarely exert direct, formal political power, though they may

1

mix and meet with those who do. Thus, we may discern a category of public intellectuals who seek to extend our political perspectives beyond the local, and expand the traditional boundaries of national community and civic identity. Generally, their objective is to challenge, by words and deeds, the dominant public values, and establish new ones. Although they may adopt traditional political strategies, such as writing and lobbying for their cause, some have taken the more radical approach of protest and direct action. In a few cases, their tactics, such as the green bans, have been highly innovative.

This group of intellectuals comprises a distinct political tradition that seeks to transcend parochial, nationalist and populist politics in Australia. One of their guiding assumptions is that pursuing universalist political principles will benefit not only the people of Australia, whether or not they are citizens, but also those outside it. Just as important, they also work out of particular local and national historical contexts. Accordingly, in this book we consider those intellectuals situated in Australian institutions and organisations, and who grapple with and try to implement universal ideas. These public figures provide an alternative perspective upon, and contribution to, debates on citizenship in a world where social and economic problems increasingly transcend national boundaries, and where these boundaries are becoming more permeable.

Transnationalism, cosmopolitanism and internationalism[3]

There is no single tradition of thinking about and acting upon universalist principles and intuitions. Universalist ideas can be found in many religious, moral and political forms. A first task, therefore, is to distinguish between the different kinds of universalist political ideas and action, so that we may better categorise, understand and evaluate the contributions of this group of intellectuals. In this regard, the term transnationalism may usefully be deployed to describe those normative traditions of political theory and practice on issues, events and conditions that are not limited to the nation-state. Familiar examples from the nineteenth and twentieth centuries include communist, socialist, liberal, and feminist internationalism. Nonetheless, there are significant differences of origin, principle and strategy among these transnationalist ideologies. We distinguish here between two types of transnationalism, namely cosmopolitanism and internationalism, both of which share a number of common features, including the advocacy of universal principles, but which diverge over how these principles may be put into practice.

Perhaps the original form of transnationalism is *cosmopolitanism*, which is a philosophy of life and morality based upon universal values (Heater 2001: 179). Its origins lie among the philosophers of ancient Greece and Rome, though similar ideas about the essential unity of all people are discernible in non-western cultures, most notably Hinduism in India and Confucianism in China (Heater 1996: x). The Cynics of the fourth century BC saw cosmopolitanism as a moral way of life in which one lived according to the universal natural law and rejected values set by human decisions and convention (Kleingeld and Brown 2002: 2). The primary moral emphasis was upon individuals and their obligations to others, not on states or polities. The principal task for a Cynic was to set an example of the virtuous life.[4]

The later Stoics of the third century BC, however, while recognising the universal law of the divine cosmos, did not entirely reject political engagement.[5] Accordingly, cosmopolitan morality has been extended into political theories of cosmopolitan, or global, or world citizenship involving notions of civic identity, values, rights and responsibilities that transcend national boundaries, as well as institutions appropriate to them. The term 'cosmopolitan citizenship' conveys the notion of a moral *and* political community whose members share, or ought to share, a number of basic human values such as the equal moral worth of each person, mutual respect and tolerance of differences, and even the promotion of justice and non-violence. The cosmopolitan citizen maintains a global perspective upon obligations owed to others, whatever their race, religion, ethnicity, social status, or their connection to a nation-state.

David Held (2003) has distilled these observations into four fundamental principles of cosmopolitanism. The first two are essentially moral while the second two are political. He first sketches an individualist moral ontology, namely, that 'the ultimate units of moral concern are individual people, not states or other particular forms of human association' (Held 2003: 470). Held's (2003: 470) second principle of 'reciprocal recognition' is the ethical requirement that every person should accord equal respect to every other person. Held then articulates two cosmopolitan political principles, which he calls 'consent' and 'inclusiveness and subsidiarity'. The principle of consent 'recognises that a commitment to equal worth and equal moral value requires a non-coercive political process through which people can negotiate and pursue their interconnections, interdependence and differences' (Held 2003: 470). Finally, the principle of inclusiveness and subsidiarity recognises that '[t]hose affected by public decisions ought to have a say in their making' (Held 2003: 471). Thus, at a minimum, the cosmopolitan or global citizen is bound to be a participatory democrat. That is, global citizens do not just delegate responsibility for political decision making to their parliamentary representatives, but seek to participate in making decisions that affect them.

Cosmopolitans may differ over the means considered best able to promote universal values and principles. Within cosmopolitanism, therefore, we may discern differences of emphasis and implementation in which various dimensions may combine. As we have seen above, one type focuses more upon the moral role of the *individual* and the person's relations with other human beings. Here, cosmopolitanism emphasises a broad *moral* stance that gives priority to the autonomy and dignity of individual humans, and the principle of mutual respect (Vertovec and Cohen 2002: 10). This stance may extend into a *legal* cosmopolitanism that specifies and codifies universal rights and obligations. There is also a third form of *political* cosmopolitanism dedicated to creating institutions, national and transnational, to protect universal rights and fulfil global responsibilities.[6] A common concern is the promotion of peaceful relations between people and states. In the creation and maintenance of international legal institutions such as the International Criminal Court, the legal and the political types of cosmopolitanism tend to merge.

In practice, moral individualist cosmopolitanism seeks to protect and promote the values of individual autonomy and human dignity. Particularly since the formation of the United Nations (UN), the rationale for such values derives from ideas and codes of universal human rights. This form of cosmopolitanism is expressed both through individual action and collectively, through groups in global civil society, such as international non-governmental organisations (INGOs). Moral cosmopolitanism, as I have outlined it, may have a purely private dimension, but it becomes public and political when it takes either a critical or constructive form in seeking to change policies or modify institutions of domestic government or transnational governance. We may legitimately call this latter activity a form of citizenship and specifically categorise its civic ideology as one of *cosmopolitan citizenship, world citizenship* or *global citizenship*.

Modern global citizenship requires the individual to be actively concerned about issues that impact on global society. Those who see themselves as global citizens engage in political activism to compel governments and corporations to abide by commonly acknowledged international values such as those embodied in the UN Charter and the Universal Declaration of Human Rights. Global citizenship values are also evident in many INGOs and transnational social movements that are less constrained by the formal rules of the inter-state system than governments, and may criticise and try to shape that system (Falk 1994; Ghils 1992; Korten 1990, Tarrow 2005). There is a strong tradition of INGOs, such as the Red Cross and Amnesty

International, that are often able to influence national governments when their citizens are powerless to do so. Other global citizens aim to establish political institutions of global governance, global democracy or world federations to give substance to citizens' rights and duties (e.g. Kerr 2001; Suter 1981). Coming from below, as it were, these institutions are not based upon the current system of nation-states. Cosmopolitan ideas are not just relevant to global problems; they provide a perspective in which critics can scrutinise particular problems such as abuses of human rights within their own society.

By contrast, the second form of transnationalism, *internationalism*, is based upon what Hedley Bull (1977: 25–7) has called an 'international society' of nation-states. Internationalism is the principle that 'in the interests of greater prosperity and security, nation states must collaborate in international organizations' (Northedge 1966: 53).[7] Internationalism offers a vision of a global order based upon nation-states that are bound by their respect for state sovereignty, and an obligation to participate in international institutions (Bull 1977: 42; Carter 2001: 2; Pogge 1992: 48–9). The guiding principle is that of inter-state order, supplemented where feasible by international justice. Internationalists reject the traditional 'realist' interpretation of international politics as one of a state of anarchy in which conflict is inevitable, and in which order and security can only be maintained by stronger states exercising their superior power. Internationalists specify a strong role for the nation-state, but within a framework of cooperation for mutual benefit based upon limited and voluntarily agreed-upon restrictions on sovereignty. Examples include the League of Nations, the United Nations and their associated agencies, such as the International Court of Justice. Nonetheless, these liberal international institutions may or may not have a global reach. Wherever liberal institutionalism is at work, we may categorise its civic ideology as one of *international citizenship*.[8]

This form of transnational citizenship often arises out of serious problems – war, global poverty, natural disaster relief, environmental degradation or financial collapse – that threaten the security of sovereign nation-states. Ideally, as international citizens, nation-states agree to cooperate under a system of international rules and institutional regimes bound by common principles of conduct (such as those set out in international law and multilateralism). Here, international citizenship is largely the province of national governments working within the many international and regional institutions formed under the auspices of international organisations such as the UN. Except under the most extreme circumstances, international citizenship is usually limited by the mutual respect for sovereignty of other states. Within international society, the civic actors or 'citizens' are states and their officials or representatives. Furthermore, these institutions can create their own problems. For example, the role of powerful international organisations like the World Bank and the International Monetary Fund, as well as the regional polity of the European Union, has raised issues about their infringement upon national sovereignty and the erosion of national citizenship. Nonetheless, on such problems, Kofi Annan (1999), when he was the Secretary-General of the UN, suggested that the notion of state sovereignty was being redefined to take account of infringements upon 'individual sovereignty', such as where there are mass violations of human rights. He noted, for example, a 'developing international norm in favour of intervention to protect civilians from wholesale slaughter'. Annan (1999) saw this norm as sanctioned by the UN Charter: 'When we read the charter today, we are more than ever conscious that its aim is to protect individual human beings, not to protect those who abuse them'.

Both cosmopolitanism and internationalism share a number of common features, including the advocacy of global cooperation. Yet 'global' and 'international' forms of citizenship part company over the different kinds of political actors involved, the different priorities given to the nation-state and national sovereignty, and in assumptions about what is politically possible within a particular context. Whereas internationalism is concerned primarily with promoting peaceful relations and security between states, cosmopolitans approach such problems with a greater focus upon the role of the individual and their rights and obligations to others. Internationalism is associated with the theory and practice of international citizenship, and cosmopolitanism is generally expressed through global or world citizenship.[9] Nonetheless, cosmopolitanism and internationalism may be understood as two poles of a political continuum, and particular individuals may operate at different times as either global citizens or, when working for nation-states, as international citizens.

Political identity and obligation

Our discussion above raises important theoretical and practical questions about political identity and obligation. On the first issue, a common question is whether any citizen can maintain more than one primary civic identity and loyalty. In response, Martha Nussbaum (1996: 9) sketches the Stoic view on the matter:

> The Stoics stress that to be a citizen of the world one does not need to give up local identifications, which can be a source of great richness in life. They

suggest that we think of ourselves not as devoid of local affiliations, but as surrounded by a series of concentric circles.

These concentric circles begin with the family and progressively include extended family, neighbours, local groups, fellow city dwellers, and fellow countrymen, to name but a few possibilities. She continues: 'Outside all these circles is the largest one, humanity as a whole'. Nonetheless, this understanding does not require us to abandon our other affiliations.

> We need not give up our special affections and identifications, whether ethnic or gender based or religious. . . . But we should also work to make all human beings part of our community of dialogue and concern, base our political deliberations on that interlocking commonality, and give the circle that defines our humanity special attention and respect.

Historically, dual identities, loyalties and obligations are evident among the Roman Stoics, such as Cicero and Seneca, who maintained that a citizen had obligations to both the cosmos and the *patria*, or homeland (Kleingeld and Brown 2002: 3). For them, political engagement ought not to be confined to one's own polis.[10]

In an age of globalisation, such concerns have become more vital, for it is widely considered that the political identity of many citizens has become more fluid, hybrid, and multi-layered. As we have seen, such features did not just arise in the late twentieth century. Wherever there have existed multinational empires, citizens have maintained more than one political identity. Even in more recent centuries, where the primary allegiance of citizens to the nation-state has been an important source of civic identity, this has not excluded other usually complementary identities. We may therefore conclude with Alonso (1995: 585) that:

> The idea that citizenship in a nation-state should be a person's primary identity is a recent one on an historic scale. In many cases it is only a hopeful fiction, although sometimes a useful one. For most people, this form of identity competes with, or complements, several other forms of identity such as race, tribe, language, ancestry, religion or ideology.

The Earth Charter formulated in March 2000 (cited in Dower 2003: 166) recognises just such multiple identities: 'We are at once citizens of different nations and of one world in which the local and global are linked'. Multiple affiliations and obligations have become the condition of, and possibility for, modern political life.

Yet one may still ask whether it is possible to undertake the possibly conflicting ethical obligations associated with different civic identities. Can citizens combine both a universalist commitment to cosmopolitan values *and* respect for national allegiances? Here too, the possibility of maintaining multiple ethical commitments, with certain provisos, has been demonstrated. Charles Jones (1999: 169) affirms, for example, that 'no nation-based ethical commitments can ever constitute the entire sphere of a person's legitimate obligations'.[11] Such possibilities have been referred to in the American literature as 'rooted cosmopolitanism' (e.g. Ackerman 1994; Cohen 1992).[12] Here, the qualifying adjective needs to be understood as meaning 'grounded in particular political context', rather than the less respectable meaning commonly given it by Australians. The term 'cosmopolitan patriots' (Appiah 1996) also conveys the aspiration to combine local affiliations with universal values.[13]

Recognising these conditions of political life, however, does not dispense with debate over the limits and requirements of a cosmopolitan political identity.[14] One vexed question is which identity and obligation has primacy for the individual and the state. National governments, predictably, tend to assert the primacy of a national political identity over more cosmopolitan and internationalist ones. Tan (2005: 165), among others, however, requires that the commitment to cosmopolitanism must have primacy, for it is arguable that this ethic gives meaning to all subsidiary ones. Nonetheless, there remain many other practical issues to be determined, including the rights and duties that citizens should accord to strangers, or to those outside the nation, or to future generations.[15] Intense political dispute and conflict has occurred over such issues. It is not just their symbolic value that is significant, but also, as in the case of immigration, whether individuals and groups can gain access to material resources and physical space.

The process of constructing any political identity is an inherently selective one, in which certain memories of the past are brought to prominence, and others are forgotten. For nation-states like Australia it is the nationalist heritage that usually receives most attention, and this often obscures the disparate and often fragmented history of 'transnationalist' achievements. This book aims to recover that transnationalist tradition of Australian political thought and action. The intention is to provide a way of interpreting, and confirming the legitimacy of, a distinctive set of political ideas and experience. But in this project too, choices must be made.

Scope, limits and qualifications

As this is primarily an interpretive task, we do not seek to evaluate in any systematic way the political success or failure of its subjects. Furthermore, this study of cosmopolitanism in Australian political thought focuses on its legal and political dimension. It does not include the meaning of cosmopolitanism as an attitude or disposition that enables one to travel widely, and be familiar with different cultures (Vertovec and Cohen 2002: 13). Nor does it include aesthetic cosmopolitanism that represents the cosmopolitan as one who holds an appreciation of beauty that reaches beyond criteria commonly accepted within a particular society. Similarly, we have little interest in consumerist cosmopolitanism exemplified in the expansion of global fashions and styles or the global spread of consumer goods. Most importantly, the book does not encompass the pejorative use of 'cosmopolitan' in Soviet and post-Soviet bloc countries to signify lack of patriotism and allegiance to international capital, or as a racist political code word for 'Jew'.

Though neoliberalism is eminently worthy of examination in its own right, we also put to one side this 'economic' form of cosmopolitanism. This is because neoliberalism's emphasis upon universal economic principles that promote freer markets and global free trade is an unduly narrow or reductionist form of cosmopolitanism. By recommending significant limits on government intervention in economy and society, neoliberalism rules out too much that would be of political interest to those in the larger tradition of cosmopolitanism. Specifically, neoliberalism tends to give primacy to a limited range of economic freedoms over other kinds of human rights. For this reason, it may be claimed that although neoliberalism meets the first moral criterion of cosmopolitanism, it does not sufficiently adhere to the second principle of equal mutual respect. Furthermore, its advocates tend not to follow the two political principles outlined by Held above. Because of neoliberalism's minimalist approach to democracy and citizenship, which gives preference to a strong centralised state governed by representative and elitist forms of democracy, it falls short of the participatory ethos required by political cosmopolitanism.[16] Further, it is arguable that most transnational corporations are not subject to sufficient democratic controls, either externally by the state or internally through participatory and inclusive forms of management.[17] It is for these reasons that contemporary global citizenship may be considered a direct critic and opponent of neoliberalism. It may be argued further that the globalising power of neoliberalism gives global citizenship one of its most powerful rationales.

Given the discussion above, we are also not concerned with those who may be called 'internationalists' and whose careers have largely occurred within the official circles of government and the public service. There is a long and distinguished list of Australian prime ministers, foreign ministers and public servants who have espoused and acted upon internationalist principles. A notable example was H. V. Evatt, whose work in and support for multilateral institutions led an American dean of law to bestow upon him the title of 'citizen of the world' (Tennant 1972: 220). One former Labor foreign minister, Gareth Evans (1989), even attempted to give conceptual and policy substance to the idea of Australia as an 'international citizen' in world affairs.[18] Our focus, however, is largely upon those who have pursued a cosmopolitan agenda outside the system of states, or who have been on the fringes of government, or who have worked both inside and outside government. Because of their idealism and critical bent, such cosmopolitans have often been in disagreement with the official Australian internationalists.

The book is not intended to be comprehensive. It aims simply to provide a representative range of examples of cosmopolitan thought and action in Australia. This has meant that we had to leave out a few subject areas and people that may rightly be considered cosmopolitan. For example, although we discuss one person of South Sea Islander descent, there are no Aboriginal or Torres Straits Islanders. Certainly, Indigenous activists have engaged in transnational activism for their cause, such as by their participation in the World Council of Indigenous Peoples and forums of the United Nations.[19] Nor is the Indigenous quest for self-determination incompatible with cosmopolitanism, since most arguments for Indigenous self-determination tend to invoke universal values. Nonetheless, Indigenous appeals to international law and justice serve two main functions. Like the cosmopolitans, Indigenous activists and writers have used such principles to show up the structure of discrimination and oppression suffered by Indigenous people, and provide grounds for the reform of policies and institutions. Where the principles support programs of democratic inclusion, there can be an accommodation with cosmopolitanism.

Yet, reference to international law has also buttressed calls for Indigenous self-determination that go beyond inclusion. In this discourse, the primary goal is to promote self-government and the freedom of Indigenous people to make their own choices over issues that concern them. Although Indigenous people may choose to build their political campaigns for self-determination upon international principles, this is not the primary aim, which is to enable authentic forms of political autonomy. By its very nature, this quest for self-determination puts Indigenous values to the fore, and these may conflict with the principles contained in such documents as the Universal Declaration of Human Rights. A Kombummerri elder and Queensland Aboriginal activist, Mary Graham (cited in Ivanitz 2002: 129), points out the source of the problem:

The notion of individual rights at all is a very new notion, a very western notion. We talk about responsibilities, not rights.

Taking account of such views does not automatically refute philosophical arguments that the pursuit of self-determination *ought* to imply universal rights. The aim is simply to concede that in practice, Indigenous people have other priorities, and may legitimately choose to give primacy to a different set of principles. To foreclose that option would be to limit the scope of Indigenous self-determination. Indigenous politics therefore has an ambiguous and uncertain relationship to cosmopolitanism.[20]

There are many other individuals, such as professional philosophers and social theorists, who warrant attention.[21] These include Peter Singer, who has written widely on animal liberation and global ethics, and who once stood for the Senate as a Green. The political theorist Alastair Davidson, who has consistently taken a critical stance on citizenship issues, would also qualify. Both have attempted, in different ways, to establish an intellectual basis for global citizenship. There have also been strong feminist traditions of cosmopolitan and transnational theory and practice that have focused upon the position of women in Australia and the world.[22] Overall, however, our subjects are united by their concern to apply cosmopolitan principles rather than to formulate them.

This book

This book directs our attention to Australians who have taken a global perspective on the social and political problems confronting Australia. It therefore contrasts markedly with previous volumes, such as Margaret Bowman and Michelle Grattan's *Reformers* (1989) and Mark Thomas's *Australia in Mind* (1989). Although both books examined the lives, ideas and achievements of leading Australian intellectuals and political activists, little consideration was given to any of their international or global concerns. Indeed, in his 'Foreword' to Bowman and Grattan's book, Geoffrey Robertson (1989) noted a tendency towards insularity among the 'reformers' chosen for inclusion.[23]

Each chapter in this book, however, focuses upon a particular Australian thinker, writer or activist, and discusses their contribution to the larger cosmopolitan tradition. A major criterion of selection is their work of political action, speaking and writing in attempting to reshape public perceptions, values and political agendas in ways that draw out the importance of a global context for Australian politics and law. Who, then, are these Australian global citizens and what have they done to merit this title and attract our attention? A number of prominent activists and writers seem to fit the criteria for cosmopolitanism outlined above. They include Faith Bandler, Herb Feith, Jack Mundey, Nancy Shelley, Bob Brown, Keith Suter, Margaret Reynolds, and Michael Kirby. Also included is an interview with a younger Australian, Thao Nguyen, who sees herself as a global citizen. It must be said, however, that most took up their political vocations well before the concepts of cosmopolitanism and global citizenship became fashionable.

Most of those studied have worked in and around non-governmental organisations, trade unions and radical social and political movements. Nevertheless, two of them, Margaret Reynolds and Bob Brown, have been elected to the national parliament, and another, Justice Kirby, is a High Court judge. Although Reynolds was a parliamentarian for sixteen years, she is probably most well known for her activism on human rights through local, national, and international non-governmental organisations. Bob Brown is the leader of a small political party, yet what is significant about his work is his critical stance on environmental and human rights issues, rather than his contribution to government or legislation. For Kirby, it is his many public speeches and writings on international law and justice, as much as his High Court judgments or earlier work on law reform, that support our claim to include him as a cosmopolitan.

Faith Bandler (b. 1918) has been a high-profile advocate of human and civil rights for Indigenous people for half a century. Born in Tumbulgum in northern New South Wales, Bandler is the daughter of a South Sea Islander. In 1883, her father was kidnapped from his home in Vanuatu and taken to Australia to work on the Queensland sugar cane fields. Bandler was one of the founders of the Aboriginal Australian Fellowship and was a prominent figure in the decade-long campaign for full constitutional recognition of Aboriginal citizenship. She was later involved in campaigns for land rights, reconciliation and the recognition of Pacific Islanders. Bandler has also been active in the movement for women's rights in Australia. Throughout her life, she has articulated strong commitments to universal values of human dignity and equality, and emphasised modern Australia's historical connections with other cultures. Roderic Pitty examines Bandler's lifetime of activism as an expression of cosmopolitan political thought in action.

Herb Feith (1930–2001) has at least two main claims to inclusion as a global citizen; first as a pioneer of cross-cultural engagement, and second as a public intellectual who taught about and campaigned for global peace and justice. In the 1950s, he was Australia's first 'volunteer abroad' in Indonesia, and initiated what was to become Australian Volunteers International.

As an academic, Feith later wrote *The Decline of Constitutional Democracy in Indonesia* (1962), and established himself as one of the world's leading scholars of Indonesian government and politics. During the second half of the 1960s, however, Feith shifted to a larger intellectual and activist (and spiritual) plane. He expanded his frame of interest to the global problems of peace and war, and overcoming poverty, injustice, and western parochialism. In his regional activism he aimed to generate global civil society networks in both Indonesia and Australia around these issues. He also campaigned against repression, especially in East Timor and West Papua. A particular characteristic of Feith's work was his primary concern with the plight of the worst off in society. Both his intellectual and political work was motivated by a profound belief in the possibility of human agency. Gary Smith's chapter maps the political thinking and activism of an extraordinary Australian.

Jack Mundey's (b. 1929) contribution to global citizenship has occurred through his work as a trade unionist, environmentalist and urban activist. As a member and Secretary of the NSW Builders Labourers Federation in the 1960s and 1970s, he promoted the idea of the 'social responsibility of labour'. By this he meant that industrial struggles should be linked to issues beyond wages and conditions. For Mundey, these issues included ecological sustainability, cultural heritage and expanding the scope for participatory democracy. Through these ideas and his activism, he set a model for connecting local actions with global problems. Fundamental to his core philosophy was the view that all economic classes and social strata in western societies share interests in an ecologically sustainable future, particularly in the context of rapid global urbanisation. Michael Leach examines the significance of Mundey's work from the perspective of cosmopolitanism.

Nancy Shelley (b. 1926) is a Quaker community activist who has worked full-time for peace for over twenty years since ceasing employment as a mathematics educator. Throughout this time she insisted on the centrality of non-violence as a principle of peace activism. Her contribution to peace education was also based on a belief that much can be learned from diversity. Influenced by her experience as an educator and the Quaker practice of 'speaking truth to power', Shelley sought to promote a paradigm shift in understanding peace as a positive process. She addressed issues concerning the economics of sustainable peace, the problem of overcoming conflict in multi-ethnic states (with special reference to Sri Lanka), and also the impact of militarisation on Australian defence and foreign policy. Building on her analyses of militarisation, Shelley also formulated an innovative critique of neoliberalism. Roderic Pitty reviews Shelley's work in these areas, focusing on disarmament, the need for non-military diplomacy, and her concern to develop 'other ways of seeing the world' based on non-violence (Shelley 1990: 116).

Dr Bob Brown (b. 1944) is an environmental, peace, and social justice activist who stands as the public face of the environmental movement in Australia today. He combines his global ideals with political action at the grassroots, and in national parliamentary institutions. Brown came to prominence in the late 1970s through his participation in the successful campaign (1978–83) to stop the construction of a dam across the Franklin River in southwest Tasmania. Since then, Brown's election to the Tasmanian parliament, his role in the formation of the Australian Greens party, and his subsequent election as a senator for Tasmania in the Australian Parliament have given him a high level of political prominence. Focusing on the period since the Franklin River campaign, Peter Haeusler examines Brown's political ideas and the wellsprings of his commitment. Attention is given to his holistic, global view of the relationship between 'ecology, economy, equality and eternity' (Brown 1990).

Keith Suter (b. 1948) has been a writer and activist for peace, disarmament and human rights in Australia in a number of political forums. He represents a particular Christian approach to local and global politics that has been influential in and around progressive social movements in Australia. Whereas Suter has recently written on globalisation, the nation-state and corporate power, earlier in his life he was concerned with Aboriginal rights, international law, East Timor, the environment and disarmament. While advocating a strong role for NGOs, including the churches, he also supports the UN, and for twenty years was either national or state president of the United Nations Association of Australia. He is also an advocate of world federation. Lucinda Horrocks sets out Suter's contribution to a Christian cosmopolitanism in Australia.

Margaret Reynolds (b. 1941) is a human rights campaigner and feminist activist. She has worked on a wide range of international campaigns directed towards improving respect for human rights in Australia and overseas. After being a campaigner for cross-cultural education in north Queensland in the 1960s and 1970s, she was elected to the Senate in 1983. Reynolds subsequently became Minister for Local Government from 1987–90, and Minister Assisting the Prime Minister on the Status of Women from 1988–90. Most recently, she has lobbied for human rights through the United Nations Association of Australia, and also through non-governmental Commonwealth organisations. Linda Hancock reviews her diverse record of political activism to demonstrate the nature of her commitment to international human rights. Particular attention is directed towards her efforts for women in Australia and overseas, as well as her support for Indigenous peoples and refugees.

Michael Kirby (b. 1939) has been a prominent proponent of legal reform since the 1970s and is institutionally embedded in a way that the others are not. He became an influential leader in generating respect for universal human rights in Australia, well before his appointment to the High Court in 1996. Roderic Pitty critically reviews Kirby's efforts to apply cosmopolitan ideas of fundamental human rights, and hasten what he has called 'the slow pace of change in the Australian democracy' (Kirby 2002: 55). Although consideration is given to the early period of Kirby's influence as head of the Australian Law Reform Commission, the main focus is on his advocacy of the relevance of human rights for Australian law and society since his conversion to cosmopolitan justice at an international meeting of judges in Bangalore, India in 1988.

Thao Nguyen (b. 1980) was born to Vietnamese parents in a Thai refugee camp, and came to Australia with her family. She grew up in western Sydney, and has initiated and coordinated a number of community and cultural development projects focusing on youth and ethnic communities. Thao has spoken at numerous national and international conferences where she has addressed issues such as generational change, youth political participation, and multiculturalism. In 2004, she was selected to be the Australian Youth Ambassador to the UN. In her interview with Roderic Pitty and Gary Smith, Thao Nguyen explains how she and many other young Australians are becoming global citizens.

These cosmopolitan figures often share a number of concerns. Most have wanted the institutions of Australian democracy to become more inclusive of those on the margins of society, and to adopt regimes based upon international human rights. Mundey and Brown are particularly linked by their work for ecological and social sustainability. A constant theme for Feith, Shelley and Suter, for example, is their advocacy of global peace and justice. The Christian religion is a central motivation for both Shelley and Suter, and also Kirby. Bandler, Reynolds, and Nguyen are connected by their activism to overcome discrimination on the basis of race or gender. All of them have looked outward from Australia to larger global problems, as well as inward to local and national issues.

This group of individuals epitomises an important but neglected part of Australian political culture. They portray Australians as part of a larger transnational community with common global aspirations. Such cosmopolitans also demonstrate how it is possible to maintain multiple political identities and commitments. These thinkers and activists embody a kind of practical utopianism that offers significant models for those wanting alternatives to the traditional nationalist approaches to global problems.

Conclusion

With a few notable exceptions, such as Alastair Davidson (e.g. 1994; 1996; 1997a; 1997b), the dominant assumption in Australian citizenship studies has been that the nation, or state and local communities within it, provides the most relevant political context for understanding citizenship.[24] Yet, within both the official and unofficial arguments defending universalist perspectives on human rights and obligations can be discerned the growth of a cosmopolitan political theory and practice that is both national and transnational. Although generally not formulated in philosophically precise terms, these ideas mark an increasing recognition of Australia as a more open and inclusive moral community. Cosmopolitan discourse has been brought to bear upon issues both within and outside Australia. For example, universalist norms and values are used to criticise policies on immigration, asylum seekers and refugees, environmental protection, Indigenous and women's rights, social justice and free trade. The people considered above have contributed much to building greater awareness of the possibilities for global citizenship in Australia.[25]

This is not to say that cosmopolitan ideas are widespread, understood, or appreciated by the majority of Australian citizens. In fact, the intrusion of universalist and internationalist ideals into public debate and policy has attracted hostility, both from Liberal–National Coalition governments and populist political movements such as One Nation. It has been suggested that such cosmopolitans are part of an elite that disdains the majority opinion, and are therefore antidemocratic. But this would be to take a restricted liberal definition of democracy as simply the aggregation of votes. Certainly, cosmopolitans tend to be against the simple prejudices characteristic of populism, but they counterbalance this attitude with a more critical and transformative view of Australian democracy. At a minimum, they would argue for a greater inclusivity of different opinions in the liberal democratic institutions. More radically, however, they hold a broader vision of an Australian democracy that is more participatory and deliberative.

For all the criticisms directed against it, however, cosmopolitanism is *not* the dominant political tradition, but nor is it an insignificant one. Cosmopolitan thinking offers the potential for bringing about important shifts in Australian political culture. It operates as a political lens for viewing and understanding many difficult local, national and international issues. Such a lens is important because it allows discussion of options and action towards goals that were previously unthinkable. Cosmopolitanism encourages us to entertain what historically some have regarded as odd, if not dangerous, notions: that women ought to be accorded equal rights with men, or that gays and indigenous peoples ought to be treated with respect, or that democracy need not be limited to institutions of the nation-state. One of its further advantages lies in providing intellectual resources for resisting other, arguably divisive, ideologies, such as neoliberalism, populism and religious fundamentalism. Wherever cosmopolitan values come into play, Australians are given permission to recognise their common bonds with many others, whether or not they hold formal citizenship status in the nation.

Notes

1 A number of people have offered valuable comments on this chapter. I would therefore like to thank not only my co-contributors to this volume, but also those who participated in the panel session on 'Cosmopolitanism and Australian Political Thought' held at the 2003 annual meeting of the Australasian Political Studies Association in Hobart. I am especially indebted to the criticism and advice offered by Roderic Pitty and Lucinda Horrocks.

2 See Melleuish and Stokes (1997).

3 Parts of the following discussion draw upon material in Stokes (2000a and 2004).

4 Thus, the philosophical doctrine of 'Cynicism' must be distinguished from its more contemporary popular, pejorative meaning where a cynic is held to be one who has little faith in human goodness, and is distrustful of any human motives other than personal interest.

5 Kleingeld and Brown (2002: 2) explain: 'the Stoics do not believe that living in agreement with the cosmos – as a citizen of the cosmos – requires maintaining a critical distance from conventional polises. Rather, ... the Stoics believe that goodness requires serving other human beings as best one can in the circumstances, that serving all human beings equally well is impossible, and that the best service one can give typically requires political engagement'.

6 Some writers, such as Beitz (1999: 287), distinguish somewhat differently between moral and institutional, or political, cosmopolitanism on the grounds that the moral kind does not justify the creation of global institutions, but simply provides 'the basis on which [international] institutions should be justified or criticized'.

7 For a more radical historical interpretation, see Anderson (2002).

8 See the overview in Williams (2002).

9 On this account, Singer's (2002) book *One World,* which aims to set out 'the ethics of globalisation', makes arguments for global citizenship, though the term itself does not appear in the book. Where he does use the term in a co-authored book with Tom Gregg (2004), *How Ethical is Australia? An Examination of Australia's Record as a Global Citizen,* the authors are clearly referring to the actions of governments and what should be called 'international citizenship'.

10 The issue of dual identity and duties is also evident in Christian philosophy where the Christian is advised to distinguish between responsibilities to Caesar and those that are to God (Matthew 22: 21).

11 Jones refers initially to 'nationalist attachments' but then more precisely to 'national attachments'.

12 See also the discussion and examples in Tarrow (2005: 35–56).

13 See the discussion of the tension in cosmopolitanism between 'universal concern and respect for legitimate difference' in Appiah (2006: xv ff).

14 See e.g. Linklater (1999; 2004); Miller (1999); Neilsen (1999); Nussbaum (1996); and Stokes (2004).

15 In such debates, cosmopolitans often take the lead in rejecting what Alastair Davidson (2003: 135) has called 'exclusionary communitarian nationalism' and argue for more open and inclusive immigration policies.

16 See also the discussion in Kleingeld and Brown (2002: 10–11).

17 For an extensive discussion of such problems and what may be needed to meet cosmopolitan 'social standards', see Held (2002).

18 See also the critical discussion by Goldsworthy (1995).

19 See the account of Indigenous internationalism in de Costa (2006).

20 For a discussion of self-determination in Aboriginal political thought, see Stokes and Gillen (2004).

21 A number of Australian philosophers and political theorists have distinguished an Australian 'national identity' marked by commitments to universalism and cosmopolitan ideals rather than to parochial values (see e.g. Kamenka 1993; Melleuish 1993, 1997).

22 See e.g. the surveys in Caine (1998b), Curthoys (1998) and Pettman (1998).

23 This fault may have been the result of the authors' interests rather than the result of any inherent insularity on the part of the subjects.

24 See e.g. Galligan and Roberts (2004).

25 Especially among intellectuals concerned with immigration (e.g. Castles 2000; Davidson 1994; 1996; Hogan 1996), but also more broadly (Kostakidis 2006), there has been a growing tendency to refer to the need for Australians to take up global citizenship.

References

Ackerman, B. 1994. 'Rooted cosmopolitanism.' *Ethics* 104:516–35.

Alonso, W. 1995. 'Citizenship, nationality and other identities.' *Journal of International Affairs* 48(2):585–99.

Anderson, P. 2002. 'Internationalism: A breviary.' *New Left Review* 14, March/April:5–25.

Annan, K. 1999. 'Two concepts of sovereignty.' *Economist* 18 September, viewed 1 December 2006, http://www.un.org/News/ossg/sg/stories/kaecon.html

Appiah, K. A. 1996. 'Cosmopolitan patriots.' In Cohen (ed.) *For Love of Country*, pp. 21–9.

Appiah, K. A. 2006. *Cosmopolitanism: Ethics in a World of Strangers*. London: Allen Lane.

Baldry, H. C. 1965. *The Unity of Mankind in Greek Thought*. Cambridge: Cambridge University Press.

Beitz, C. 1999. 'Social and cosmopolitan liberalism.' *International Affairs* 75:515–30.

Bowman, M. and M. Grattan 1989. *Reformers: Shaping Australian Society from the 60s to the 80s*. Melbourne: Collins Dove.

Brown, B. 1990. 'Ecology, economy, equality, eternity.' In C. Pybus and R. Flanagan (eds) *The Rest of the World is Watching: Tasmania and the Greens*. Sydney: Sun, pp. 245–57.

Bull, H. 1977. *The Anarchical Society: A Study of World Order in Politics*. London: Macmillan.

Caine, B. (ed.) 1998a. *Australian Feminism: A Companion*. Melbourne: Oxford University Press.

Caine. B. 1998b. 'International links.' In Caine (ed.) *Australian Feminism*, pp. 158–68.

Carter, A. 2001. *The Political Theory of Global Citizenship*. London: Routledge.

Castles, S. 2000. 'The future of citizenship in a globalising world.' In K. Rubenstein (ed.) *Individual, Community, Nation: Fifty years of Australian Citizenship*. Kew: Australian Scholarly Publishing, pp. 119–34.

Cohen, J. 1996. (ed.) *For Love of Country: Debating the Limits of Patriotism*. Boston: Beacon Press.

Cohen, M. 1992. 'Rooted cosmopolitanism.' *Dissent* 39:478–83.

Curthoys, A. 1998. 'Cosmopolitan radicals.' In Caine (ed.) *Australian Feminism*, pp. 39–48.

Davidson, A. 1994. 'Citizenship, sovereignty and the identity of the nation state.' In P. James (ed.) *Critical Politics*. Melbourne: Arena, pp. 111–25.

——1996. 'Towards international citizenship.' *Australian Journal of Politics and History* 42(1):70–2.

——1997a. *From Subject to Citizen: Australian Citizenship in the Twentieth Century*. Melbourne: Cambridge University Press.

——1997b. 'Globalism, the regional citizen and democracy.' In B. Galligan and C. Sampford (eds) *Rethinking Human Rights*. Sydney: Federation Press, pp. 215–33.

——2003. 'The politics of exclusion in an era of globalisation.' In L. Jayasuria, D. Walker and J. Gothard (eds) *Legacies of White Australia: Race, Culture and Nation*. Crawley: University of Western Australia Press, pp. 129–44.

De Costa, R. 2006. *A Higher Authority: Indigenous Transnationalism and Australia*. Sydney: UNSW Press.

Dower, N. 2003. *An Introduction to Global Citizenship*. Edinburgh: Edinburgh University Press.

Evans, G. 1989. 'Australian foreign policy: Priorities in a changing world.' *Australian Outlook* 43(2):1–15.

Falk, R. A. 1994. 'The making of global citizenship.' In B. van Steenbergen (ed.) *The Condition of Citizenship*. Thousand Oaks CA: Sage, pp. 127–40.

Feith, H. 1962. *The Decline of Constitutional Democracy in Indonesia*. Ithaca, NY: Cornell University Press.

Galligan, B. and W. Roberts 2004. *Australian Citizenship*. Melbourne: Melbourne University Press.

Ghils, P. 1992. 'International civil society: International non-governmental organizations in the international system.' *International Social Science Journal* XLIV(3): 417–31.

Goldsworthy, D. 1995. 'Australia and good international citizenship.' In S. Lawson (ed.) *The New Agenda for Global Security: Cooperating for Peace and Beyond*. Sydney: Allen & Unwin, pp. 171–87.

Heater, D. 1996. *World Citizenship and Government: Cosmopolitan Ideas in the History of Western Thought*. London: Macmillan.

——2001. 'Does cosmopolitan thinking have a future?' In K. Booth, T. Dunne and M. Cox (eds) *How Might We Live?: Global Ethics in the New Century*. Cambridge: Cambridge University Press, pp. 179–97.

Held, D. 2002. 'Globalization, corporate practice and cosmopolitan social standards.' *Contemporary Political Theory* 1(1):59–78.

——2003. 'Cosmopolitanism: Globalisation tamed?' *Review of International Studies* 29(4):465–80.

Hogan, T. 1996. 'Citizenship, Australian and global.' *Thesis Eleven* 46:97–114.

Hutchings, K. and R. Dannreuther (eds) 1999. *Cosmopolitan Citizenship*. Macmillan: Houndmills.

Ivanitz, M. 2002. 'Democracy and indigenous self-determination.' In A. Carter and G. Stokes (eds) *Democratic Theory Today*. Cambridge: Polity, pp. 121–48.

Jones, C. 1999. *Global Justice: Defending Cosmopolitanism*. Oxford: Oxford University Press.

Kamenka, E. 1993. '"Australia made me" . . . But which Australia is mine?' *Quadrant* 37(10):24–31.

Kerr, D. 2001. *Elect the Ambassador! Building Democracy in a Globalised World*. Sydney: Pluto Press.

Kirby, M. 2002. 'Surface Nugget.' *Quadrant* 46(10):53–6.

Kleingeld, P. and E. Brown 2002. 'Cosmopolitanism.' In E. N. Zalta (ed.) *The Stanford Encyclopedia of Philosophy*. (Fall 2002 Edition) The Metaphysics Research Lab, Stanford University: Stanford, viewed 16 September 2003, http://plato.stanford.edu/archives/fall2002/entries/cosmopolitanism/

Korten, D. C. 1990. *Getting to the 21st Century: Voluntary Action and the Global Agenda*. West Hartford CT: Kumarian Press.

Kostakidis, M. 2006. 'Aussies turning inwards.' *Australian* 22 November: 17, viewed 29 November 2006, http://www.news.com.au/story/0,23599,20801270-5007146,00.html

Linklater, A. 1999. 'Cosmopolitan citizenship.' In Hutchings and Dannreuther (eds) *Cosmopolitan Citizenship*, pp. 35–59.

——2004. 'Cosmopolitan citizenship.' In E. F. Isin and B. S. Turner (eds) *Handbook of Citizenship Studies*. London: Sage Publications, pp. 317–32.

Melleuish, G. 1993. 'The case for civilization: An Australian perspective.' *Thesis Eleven* 34:156–64.

——1997. 'Universal obligations: Liberalism, religion and national identity.' In G. Stokes (ed.) *The Politics of Identity in Australia*. Melbourne: Cambridge, pp. 50–60.

Melleuish, G. and G. Stokes 1997. 'Australian political thought.' In W. Hudson and G. Bolton (eds) *Creating Australia: Changing Australian History*. Allen & Unwin, pp. 111–21.

Miller, D. 1999. 'Bounded citizenship.' In Hutchings and Dannreuther (eds) *Cosmopolitan Citizenship*, pp. 60–80.

Neilson, K. 1999. 'Cosmopolitan nationalism.' *Monist* 82(3):46–68.

Northedge, F. S. 1966. 'Internationalism.' In M. Cranston (ed.) *A Glossary of Political Terms*. London: The Bodley Head, pp. 53–7.

Nussbaum, M. 1996. 'Patriotism and cosmopolitanism.' In Cohen (ed.) *For Love of Country*, pp. 2–17.

Pettman, J. J. 1998. 'Transnational feminisms.' In Caine (ed.) *Australian Feminism*, pp. 330–7.

Pogge, T. 1992. 'Cosmopolitanism and sovereignty.' *Ethics* 103:48–75.

Robertson, G. 1989. 'Foreword.' In M. Bowman and M. Grattan, *Reformers: Shaping Australian Society from the 60s to the 80s*. Melbourne: Collins Dove.

Shelley, N. (ed.) 1990. *Whither Australia? A Response to Australia's Current Defence Policy*. Sydney: Commission on International Affairs of the Australian Council of Churches.

Singer, P. 2002. *One World: The Ethics of Globalisation*. Melbourne: Text.

Singer, P. and T. Gregg 2004. *How Ethical is Australia? An Examination of Australia's Record as a Global Citizen*. Melbourne: Australian Collaboration with Black Inc.

Stokes, G. 2000a. 'Australia and global citizenship.' In W. Hudson and J. Kane (eds) *Rethinking Australian Citizenship*. Melbourne: Cambridge University Press, pp. 231–42.

——2000b. 'One Nation and Australian populism.' In M. Leach, G. Stokes and I. Ward (eds) 2000. *The Rise and Fall of One Nation*. St. Lucia: University of Queensland Press, pp. 23–41.

——2004. 'Transnational citizenship: Problems of definition, culture and democracy.' *Cambridge Review of International Affairs* 17(1):119–35.

Stokes, G. and K. Gillen 2004. 'Self-determination in Aboriginal political thought.' In P. Boreham, G. Stokes and R. Hall (eds) *The Politics of Australian Society: Political Issues for the New Century*. 2nd edn, Frenchs Forest: Pearson Education Australia, pp. 62–78.

Suter, K. 1981. *A New International Order: Proposals for Making a Better World*. Sydney: World Association of World Federalists.

Tan, K-C. 2005. 'The demands of justice and national allegiances.' In G. Brock and H. Brighouse (eds) *The Political Philosophy of Cosmopolitanism*. Cambridge: Cambridge University Press, pp. 164–79.

Tarrow, S. 2005. *The New Transnational Activism*. New York: Cambridge University Press.

Tennant, K. 1972. *Evatt: Politics and Justice*. Sydney: Angus and Robertson.

Thomas, M. 1989. *Australia in Mind: Thirteen Influential Australian Thinkers*. Marrickville: Hale & Iremonger.

Vertovec, S. and R. Cohen 2002. 'Introduction: Conceiving cosmopolitanism.' In S. Vertovec and R. Cohen (eds) *Conceiving Cosmopolitanism: Theory, Context, and Practice*. Oxford: Oxford University Press, pp. 1–22.

Williams, J. 2002. 'Good international citizenship.' In N. Dower and J. Williams (eds) *Global Citizenship: A Critical Reader*. Edinburgh: University of Edinburgh Press, pp. 41–52.

Faith Bandler

Faith Bandler is an author and campaigner for racial equality and women's rights. She was a founding member of the Federal Council for the Advancement of Aborigines and Torres Strait Islanders (FCAATSI) in the 1950s, and through her leadership was instrumental in bringing about the 1967 referendum, a milestone in the recognition of Indigenous rights in Australia. In the 1970s she campaigned for government recognition of the injustices imposed on South Sea Islanders like her father, who had been 'blackbirded' or coercively taken from his native Vanuatu and forced to work in colonial Queensland. She was a founding member of the Women's Electoral Lobby and the Australian Republican Movement. She has received many honours, including the Order of Australia in 1984, being named one of Australia's National Living Treasures in 1997, and being presented with a Sydney Peace Foundation Award by Nelson Mandela in 2000.

Faith Bandler, New South Wales campaign director for the Federal Council for the Advancement of Aborigines and Torres Strait Islanders, toasted by members of the Aboriginal-Australian Fellowship a fortnight after the 1967 referendum, for her efforts in gaining enormous publicity for the 'Yes' vote. (Courtesy Australian Women's Weekly and Jack Horner Collection, AIATSIS.)

2

Faith Bandler: Campaigning for Racial Equality

Roderic Pitty[1]

> I see it as a human being's duty to get involved in raising people to be equals
> in society.
>
> (Bandler 1993)

Few, if any, Australians other than Faith Bandler could stand beside Nelson Mandela in 2000 as a historical equal. Mandela presented Bandler with an award to honour her life of courageous advocacy for justice and human rights for Indigenous people (Lake 2002: 208). A photograph of the occasion was celebrated by the radical Aboriginal activist Gary Foley (2002) as a 'great moment in indigenous history'. He described Bandler as a living legend. She is of South Sea Islander, not Aboriginal, heritage, and is best known for her leading role in the 1967 referendum campaign for Aboriginal rights. Over 90 per cent of Australian voters gave the Commonwealth Government the power to pass special laws to benefit Aborigines, who they said must be counted in the census (Bandler 1989: 114). The referendum challenged Australia to meet global standards of racial equality. It enlarged Australia, by extending both democracy and active citizenship to potentially include Indigenous peoples, who had previously been largely excluded.

Bandler is a legend because of what she enabled others, including Foley, to become. She once wrote in the guest book for an exhibition of twenty-five years of Aboriginal struggle, photographed by Juno Gemes: 'Worth making it happen' (Bandler 2004). She was a formidable lobbyist, and has been described as 'one of the top twenty Australians of the twentieth century' (Moore 2004: 126). In 1970 Bandler called for the release on parole from prison of the Aboriginal poet and playwright Kevin Gilbert. She lobbied the New South Wales Minister of Justice, J. C. Maddison, who was her local member. He felt obliged to meet her, given her national standing as a campaigner for Indigenous rights. After his release, Gilbert wrote many plays, poems and calls for Indigenous self-determination (Gilbert 1973;

23

1977). Bandler helped to create the space for an erudite Wiradjuri warrior like Gilbert to get new Indigenous voices heard, in anthologies such as *Inside Black Australia* (1988). Later, Gilbert (1990: 7) wrote that Aboriginal children marching for justice also became legends who will 'never die'. This showed the success of Bandler's long campaign for justice.

Bandler's campaigning for racial equality was inspired by the black American civil rights leader and singer Paul Robeson. He visited Australia in 1960, and after a film about Aboriginal malnutrition in the Warburton region of Western Australia moved him to tears, he told a Sydney audience that it is not races of human beings who are backward, but rather societies based on racial discrimination (Lake 2002: 86). Bandler shared this core belief in equality. She encouraged many white Australians to become aware of the social causes of Aboriginal suffering, to see their responsibility before the world to end Indigenous misery, and to challenge the indifference of others. In the 1950s, Bandler's Aboriginal friend and mentor, Pearl Gibbs (quoted in Bandler and Fox 1983: 41), once told Len Fox that, for victims of racism, 'it's not an Aboriginal problem. It's a white problem'. Gibbs asked Bandler to get the white people involved in fighting for Aboriginal human rights, insisting: 'while I'm not free, you're not free' (quoted in Bandler and Fox 1983: 3). Bandler helped to change the attitudes of many white Australians towards Aborigines, leading the 1967 referendum campaign together with her friend, the poet Oodgeroo Noonuccal. Both were great speakers, sharing 'a shrewd grasp of what needed to be said on behalf of indigenous Australians' (Cochrane 1994: 63).

To understand how Bandler helped to change Australia, it is vital to see the inclusive nature of her activity. This chapter first reviews the sources of Bandler's commitment to extending freedom in Australia. It then explains how Bandler argued for the 1967 referendum as part of a cosmopolitan vision of racial equality, including a special role for Aboriginal citizenship in Australia. It then discusses Bandler's subsequent focus in the 1970s and later on gaining substantive equality for her South Sea Islander people. Finally, the historical implications of the 1967 referendum are considered, explaining how Bandler's activity can be seen to have linked the Australian Constitution with the wider world of international campaigning against all forms of racial discrimination.

The awakening of an activist for freedom

Bandler was forced to leave school early by the poverty of the 1930s Depression. Her openness to struggles for freedom as a child sprang from three

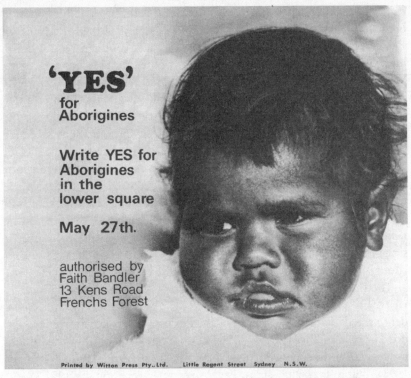

'YES'
for
Aborigines

Write YES for
Aborigines
in the
lower square

May 27th.

authorised by
Faith Bandler
13 Kens Road
Frenchs Forest

Printed by Witton Press Pty., Ltd.   Little Regent Street   Sydney   N.S.W.

As New South Wales campaign director for the 1967 referendum, Faith Bandler was responsible for much of the publicity, such as this poster. (Courtesy Faith Bandler and Jack Horner Collection, AIATSIS.)

family sources. The first was her father's heritage. He was captured as a slave from Ambrym Island in present-day Vanuatu when aged just thirteen, and indentured in Queensland's cane fields for twenty years before gaining freedom in 1903 (Lake 2002: 2–4). Like about 1200 other Melanesians in Australia, he escaped deportation, but 'resentment still boiled in him as he recalled' the 'hard years' of service to the sugar industry (Bandler 1984: 26). This meant that independence was prized in Bandler's family, since her father fought for it himself, as retold in stories of 'the long road to freedom' (Bandler 1977: 144; Moore 1979: 37). The second source was Faith's mother's determination to get her children educated. This was vital after Faith's father died when she was five years old. He had said that education is good, but 'other people need help and comfort' too (Bandler 1984: 124). When Faith had to leave school early, she had a thirst for knowledge and a feeling for compassion. The third source was Faith's brothers, who introduced her to Robeson's songs and radical politics. Under their influence,

25

Faith's horizon widened when, with her sister Kath, she saw Robeson star in the film *Showboat* in 1936 (Lake 2002: 21).

These family influences made Faith into a woman concerned about global justice even before she worked with Kath in the Women's Land Army in World War II. Then she saw Aboriginal workers segregated from other workers, and 'paid very much less per basket' (Bandler and Fox 1983: 2). After the war, living in the 'cosmopolitan world of Kings Cross', she gave talks about Aboriginal rights to peace activists (Lake 2002: 29). At such meetings she got to know her future husband, Hans, a Jewish refugee from Vienna who showed films, and shared her passion for classical music. Meeting him changed her life. He provided a firm anchor for her activism. Bandler's experience 'spending her young adulthood in a cosmopolitan environment gave her the added confidence' to become an inspiring role model for other black women (Darling 1996: 98). While she did this, her husband maintained a supportive role, as New South Wales state coordinator of local campaign committees in the long build-up to the 1967 referendum (Taffe 2005: 96).

There was more to Bandler's growing cosmopolitan awareness than familiarity with various cultures. What made her a great speaker was the confidence she drew from her mother, together with the belief in freedom she drew from her father and the deeper cosmopolitanism of universal human rights, which was expressed in her commitment to helping others (Bandler 1993). Before marrying Hans, Faith went to Europe for the 1951 World Youth Festival in Berlin. Knowing that fascism had horribly exacerbated racism (Bandler 1989: 2), she went to see the aftermath of the Dachau concentration camp in Germany. As it happened, Hans had not yet told her that he had been sent there before the war (Lake 2002: 50). Seeing Europe in ruins after the war also confirmed Bandler's strong belief in the need for a peaceful world, in which children can grow with a hopeful future (Bandler 1993).

When Bandler returned to Australia in late 1951, her passport was confiscated, along with the books and records of Robeson she had brought back (Lake 2002: 47). She was unable to travel overseas for ten years. She was seen as subversive in the vicious atmosphere of Cold War hysteria that affected Australia. Despite losing her job because of her political activity, she was not intimidated. Experiencing repression contributed to her resilience, and her belief in the need to create a different Australia, open to the best that the world had to offer, including scrutiny and criticism from outside. Yet she spent the early 1950s 'insulated from that other life – the life of racism borne by other people'. She later recalled that her 'lifestyle kept me more informed about what was happening in Europe than what was happening right here in my own country' (Bandler 1989: 6).

Bandler had seen and learnt much on her trip abroad about poverty and struggles for political equality. In India and Sri Lanka soon after their independence, she had seen great misery and hunger, but she noted that 'at least those people had the freedom of their own streets in their own cities', in contrast to Aborigines kept away on reserves (Bandler 1989: 82). Her knowledge of the wider world, combined with her family's heritage, ensured that, when Gibbs repeatedly came to ask her for support to help end the injustices facing Aborigines, Bandler knew what to do. Together they created the Aboriginal-Australian Fellowship (AAF) with a few supporters in Sydney in 1956. This organisation was the first to campaign for the constitutional change that occurred in May 1967. Bandler (1989: 69) later said about the Aboriginal advancement movement that it began to grow as it attracted people with energy and commitment to share, when 'the time was ripe' for change. As someone combining social mobility, charisma and a lot of hard work, Bandler herself attracted many people to the cause.

In campaigning for racial equality, Bandler was inspired by the 'unique relationship' that Gibbs had with Jessie Street, a feminist married to the NSW Chief Justice, and a woman who had befriended Aborigines since her childhood. Bandler (1989: 69, 72) says that these women, from very different backgrounds, were the 'hands that rocked the cradle' of commitment which led to the 1967 referendum. They showed her that politics was the business of women (Gilbert 2005: 121). Later, when Bandler (1997: 5) reflected on what would best describe Street in action, she said: 'I saw her as an important citizen of the world'. Street had argued for equality at the UN, and she conceived the idea of the referendum. It was Street who 'used such force in such a gentle way' to get Bandler committed to accept the challenge of a referendum (Bandler and Fox 1983: 11–12). Yet the idea was so daunting that initially Bandler didn't tell the AAF executive about it, for fear of being unable to explain it (Lake 2002: 68–9). While she was brimming with enthusiasm, Bandler (1989: 80) wondered how politicians were 'going to let a straggly bunch like us change the law by which they run the entire country'.

There was little reason for optimism in April 1957, when Bandler and her colleagues in the AAF organised a public meeting in Sydney Town Hall. Yet it was attended by over a thousand people, 'about half of whom were Sydney-based Aboriginal people cajoled there by Pearl Gibbs' (Horner 2004: 22). This meeting launched the first of the petitions calling for constitutional change to create a 'New Deal for Aborigines' (Bandler 1989: 88). The petition reactivated a political campaign for Commonwealth action promoted two decades earlier at the 1938 Day of Mourning and Protest held in Sydney. That 1938 meeting had been attended by Doug Nicholls, who chaired the 1957 meeting (Ferguson and Patten 1995; Palma 2002: 79). Despite the meeting's

27

size, it was hardly reported by the mainstream media (Bandler and Fox 1983: 13–14).

Bandler soon got the petition launched by a Labor MP, Les Haylen. He presented the first petitions to parliament in May 1957, ten years before the referendum. Bandler spent most of that decade advocating for the referendum to all sorts of community groups. She protested on the streets (often with her daughter Lilon), such as in Martin Place, Sydney, in 1965, exposing the exclusion of Aborigines from the census. She spoke regularly at meetings, and used the new media of television very effectively. Her biographer, Marilyn Lake (2002: 90), says that Bandler's 'brilliance as a public advocate of Aboriginal rights rested on her ability to always relate specific instances of injustice to general principles'. This ability to link a 'particularist social movement' with a commitment to global values such as equality is a feature of global citizenship (Dower 2003: 47). Bandler says the idea of equality 'inspired me to get the movement going' (Bandler and Fox 1983: 5). For Bandler, equality did not require uniformity, but rather an inclusive view of Australian citizenship, in which Aboriginal people could become equal without losing their distinct cultural heritage and identity.

Cosmopolitan aspects of Aboriginal citizenship

The 1967 referendum was significant because it highlighted Australia's responsibility to change itself as a society, to accept the global objective of ending all forms of racial discrimination outlined in a 1965 UN Convention that was eventually ratified by Australia in 1975. Harry Penrith, an AAF activist later known as Burnum Burnum, saw the referendum as a key part of a process of social and political change, as a sign of 'the emerging cosmopolitan nature of Australian society' (quoted in Attwood and Markus 1997: 137). He saw the referendum as 'a definite turning point in modern Australian political history and the conscience of the nation' (quoted in Attwood and Markus 1997: 136). Bandler titled her history of the social movement that created the referendum *Turning the Tide*, referring to the great change in public opinion that occurred over a decade.

Bandler's key role in helping to change public attitudes about Aborigines is confirmed by Ray Peckham, another Aboriginal activist with the AAF in New South Wales. He had travelled with Bandler to Europe in 1951 with the Margaret Walker Dance Group. Peckham (2005) recalls that, among the small group of three dozen or so activists who often met three or four times a week for a whole decade from 1957, Bandler stood out clearly:

There was no one, man or woman, who could have handled it as well as Faith did. She had everything – she had the charisma, the politics, she could sing, she was beautiful and she could debate. Look what she did with politicians such as Dunstan and Whitlam, she had them wrapped around her finger! No one could have done what she did at that time. And at meetings, she always said: 'I'm not an Aborigine'. But she was a wonderful fighter for our cause, with great stamina.

Bandler's formal position in 1967 was as NSW Secretary of the Federal Council for the Advancement of Aborigines and Torres Strait Islanders (FCAATSI), but her role in the referendum campaign was a national one. She was the AAF's publicity officer, and much of the media work was coordinated from Sydney. On 26 May 1967, the eve of the crucial vote, Bandler (quoted in Attwood and Markus 1997: 46) warned that a failure to pass the referendum would be 'a disastrous step backwards for Australia'. She argued for the referendum in cosmopolitan terms, as Australia's responsibility to the world.

The idea that the Commonwealth Government had an international responsibility to achieve Aboriginal justice had been raised before, such as by William Cooper and Bill Ferguson in the 1930s (Attwood and Markus 2004: 43; Horner 1974). By the 1960s, two new circumstances made the arguments of Bandler and others effective. First, the creation of the United Nations provided a new context for international influence on Australia, particularly with decolonisation in Asia and Africa. Second, comparisons with apartheid in South Africa exposed Australia's own racism. During the decade of FCAATSI's campaigning for various reforms before the referendum, comparisons were made between racial discrimination in Australia and South Africa, particularly after the 1961 conference of that body. Bandler was included in the all-Aboriginal session at that conference which called for action to 'abolish apartheid in our own country before the next Commonwealth prime ministers conference' (Horner 2004: 63). In May 1961, when the Australian Government refused to give Aborigines full voting rights, Bandler said directly that this 'strongly resembled the South African policy of apartheid' (Bandler and Fox 1983: 106). Such international comparisons troubled the Australian Government, which feared growing international scrutiny from the UN (Clark 1997; Chesterman 2005: 43–4). This was why all Aborigines were reluctantly granted federal voting rights in 1962. Even in very conservative times, appealing to universal standards of equal human rights enabled Australians to change their society.

During and after the long haul of the referendum campaign, Bandler spent seventeen years going to FCAATSI conferences at Easter time. At the tenth

FCAATSI conference in March 1967, she spoke about the looming referendum vote, reminding delegates how long the campaign had been going and how vital it was (Horner 2004: 120). Despite her optimistic media role, she was not hopeful on the day of the vote. She 'feared the worst', afraid the disappointment of a failure would be too difficult to face (Bandler 1993). This feeling arose not just from her strong personal commitment, but because she knew what was at stake. The vote was for an inclusive idea of citizenship rights for Aborigines and Torres Strait Islanders, in which their need for special, beneficial laws could be recognised. It was only a limited recognition, since it lacked a proper legal acceptance of their status as the original owners of Australia. Yet, knowing well the pervasiveness of racism in Australia, Bandler realised that achieving even this limited hand of friendship was by no means assured.

The referendum campaign was successful because it became a vote about Australia's international image. Bandler (quoted in Attwood and Markus 1997: 107) said often that 'the eyes of the world are on Australia and her handling of black Australians. Not only Asia is watching but Africa and the whole Western world'. In 1960, at FCAATSI's annual conference, Whitlam had told Bandler 'you'll never get a referendum', but she had replied 'we will' (Bandler 2005a; Horner 2004: 57–9). In 1967, Whitlam was a strong advocate of the constitutional change, saying 'the people of Australia should and must, *in all humanity* and for their own honour, support it overwhelmingly' (quoted in Attwood and Markus 1997: 109, emphasis added). He had fully accepted Bandler's essential claim that the Commonwealth Government had a universal obligation to assume responsibility for Aboriginal affairs. The referendum was more than a legal matter of extending the Commonwealth's power to pass laws to benefit Aborigines and Torres Strait Islanders, and counting them in the census. It raised the question of Australia's treatment of Indigenous peoples before the eyes of the world. This global aspect of the referendum's significance is vital to understanding what its achievement means for a cosmopolitan and inclusive vision of Aboriginal citizenship.

A common theme in the referendum campaign was the need to include Aborigines and Torres Strait Islanders as culturally different equals within Australian society. This aim had been expressed as a demand for 'full citizenship rights' by Aboriginal leaders such as Doug Nicholls, who had appealed to the UN in 1963 for an inquiry into assimilation policies (Attwood 2003: 163; Harvey 2003: 231). The discourse of citizenship was crucial to FCAATSI's campaign for both legislative and constitutional change (Taffe 2001: 16; 2005: 98). Creating an *inclusive* form of citizenship for Aborigines would overcome the discriminatory laws of different legal regimes across Australia. The effect of such laws was, as Nicholls told Whitlam, that an Aboriginal person travelling interstate 'really needed a surveyor, a lawyer, and a politician with him to advise of when and where he was breaking state laws' (quoted in Horner 2004: 59). In Queensland and Western Australia, a Certificate of Citizenship or 'Dog Licence' was granted by magistrates to Aboriginal individuals only if they did not associate with, and identify with, their own communities (Attwood and Markus 1997: 17). Aborigines saw Australian citizenship as discriminatory, separating them from their communities. This is why the grassroots Aboriginal activist Mum Shirl, a helper for Aboriginal prisoners in New South Wales, said being a citizen 'wasn't even a word I even thought about' (Attwood and Markus 1997: 53). Having experienced exclusion, Bandler knew the importance of creating a new form of citizenship that recognised difference.

A major purpose of the referendum campaign was to alter the restrictive, official view of citizenship. In this view, Aborigines and Torres Strait Islanders were mere 'citizens without rights' (Chesterman and Galligan 1997) or 'invisible citizens', as Chicka Dixon, an Aboriginal activist who worked with Bandler promoting the referendum in NSW, recalls (quoted in Attwood and Markus 1997: 116). By contrast, Aboriginal citizenship was seen by activists for the 1967 referendum as opposed to assimilation. It required a new recognition by politicians and the wider Australian community that Indigenous peoples will retain their own cultural heritage (Horner 2004: 115). Bandler saw the benefits of the referendum as being an 'acknowledgement of Aboriginal citizenship and *the rights inherent in this status* as well as funding from the Commonwealth government' for Aboriginal needs (Bandler 1989: 161, emphasis added). Proponents of the referendum saw Aboriginal citizenship not in nationalist terms, but rather in what we would now call a cosmopolitan way. Dixon put this clearly in a newspaper article a week before the vote. He wrote: 'We don't mind accepting our responsibilities, but in return we want White Australia to recognise officially that we exist. We want to be human like everyone else' (Attwood and Markus 1997: 117). For Bandler and her colleagues, this meant having a respected culture, not being treated as inferior.

The referendum affirmed Aboriginal citizenship in a double sense, both as Australian citizens and also as Indigenous citizens. This was the meaning of the double change to the Constitution, removing section 127 so as to count Aborigines in the census, and deleting the exclusion in section 51(xxvi) so special laws could be made for Aborigines. Under Prime Minister Menzies, the government had agreed to hold a referendum only about section 127 (Attwood and Markus 1997: 32). Bandler strongly pressured Holt, who succeeded Menzies, to hold a referendum including special laws for Aborigines (Bandler 1989: 99–103). The government said that 'the best protection for Aborigines is to treat them, for all purposes, as Australian citizens'. Nonetheless, Bandler kept on lobbying until it relented. She thought it vitally 'necessary for the Commonwealth to be able to legislate for the benefit of Aborigines thus making available large allocations of funds, which state revenues could not meet, to make amends for almost 200 years of neglect and dispossession' (Bandler 1989: 100; 1993). This double dimension of Aboriginal citizenship, affirmed by the referendum, enabled the Whitlam government to start 'the beginning of the process of finding and implementing solutions' (Bandler 1989: 164).

Action to overcome Aboriginal injustice was seen by Bandler not as an act of charity, but as an act of reciprocity. This was seen as a human duty to the original land owners, who had been forcibly dispossessed. As Mary Bennett (quoted in Bandler 1989: 61) said in her 1957 book *Human Rights for Aboriginal Australians*, such a duty was 'merely paying a long overdue debt'. The referendum, which affirmed Aboriginal citizenship, was based on this crucial idea of reciprocity. Reciprocity involved accepting, not denying, that Indigenous peoples determine their own identity. Through the referendum, it was white Australia that finally had to change. Aborigines did *not* change to become citizens. Instead, Australian society had to change, to *include* Indigenous peoples' own visible citizenship.

Because of that inclusion, aspirations that Aborigines had held for generations, such as ending the forced separation of children from their families, were easier to pursue. Bandler cared very much about protecting Aboriginal cultural identity, having fostered an Aboriginal boy named Peter for ten years from 1959. Realising 'how he pined for his own people', she found his real parents in Mt Isa, and ensured that he could return to them (Lake 2002: 87; Bandler 1993). The Aborigines Welfare Board, which controlled the Stolen Generations in New South Wales, was finally abolished in 1969, as Gibbs had demanded decades earlier (Bandler 1994: 32). The referendum had helped some of those affected, like Burnum Burnum, to become proud of their Aboriginality (Attwood and Markus 1997: 137). It also led to international contacts. In 1971, Bandler and her colleagues in FCAATSI invited UN agencies and indigenous representatives from Oceania and Africa to Australia to monitor Indigenous rights (FCAATSI 1971). This followed the split in FCAATSI in 1970, with Bandler's old friend Oodgeroo Noonuccal estranged from her, just days after reading a poem at Parliament House about coming 'with sorrow in our hearts' (Taffe 2005: 258–60).

Bandler was the National Secretary of FCAATSI from mid-1970 until 1973. That was a time of intense Aboriginal political agitation, most emphatically expressed in the 1972 Tent Embassy (Smith 1981). During that time, Bandler kept in touch with what was happening around the country, seeking to support local initiatives. In early 1973, Aboriginal cotton chippers in Wee Waa, New South Wales, went on strike to protest their low pay and awful working conditions (e.g. being sprayed with pesticides while having lunch). Bandler contacted unions in Sydney urging immediate support, in one letter informing the Trades and Labour Council of a meeting to be held later that day (Bandler 1973). She was also a Council Member for the Aboriginal Legal Service when it was first set up, and pressured the new Whitlam government to keep its promises on land rights (Lake 2002: 150). With more activity happening in support of Aboriginal justice after the Tent Embassy in 1972, she could finally consider ways of helping her own people.

Ending discrimination against South Sea Islanders in Australia

Bandler saw the referendum as 'a turning point in Australian history', but she knew its potential would not be realised quickly. She thought that when a Labor government finally returned to office, the pace of policy reform 'would be quickened, and the process of change, once begun, could not be stopped' (Bandler and Fox 1983: 111). Yet when the Whitlam government initiated policies to include Indigenous peoples within Australian society, one consequence was to complicate the social position of South Sea Islanders in Australia. Bandler lobbied the government on what became the 1975 *Racial Discrimination Act*, arguing that her own people suffered from a history of racism and exclusion (Lake 2002: 159). She told the 1975 Royal Commission on Human Relationships that public servants of Islander descent were needed to provide appropriate social services (Lake 2002: 168). She was worried that some of her people were identifying as Aborigines or Torres Strait Islanders, and losing their heritage, just to get the assistance they needed (Lake 2002: 185). This is why she wrote stories about South Sea Islanders who struggled to make Australia a home for their people, while keeping in contact with their ancestral islands (Bandler and Fox 1980: 112).

For two decades from the early 1970s, Bandler lobbied politicians to help South Sea Islanders in Australia overcome racial discrimination, with little success. Her people had suffered a legacy of dispossession from their island homes, but this was less well known than the emerging history of Aboriginal Australia. She later called these Islanders 'truly the forgotten people of this country' (Bandler 1993). It was thus harder to campaign for compensatory assistance on the premise of reciprocity, and get governments to accept responsibility for overcoming discrimination against Islanders. Eventually, an inquiry by the Human Rights and Equal Opportunity Commission in the early 1990s recommended a formal recognition of the unique status of Australian South Sea Islanders, and the provision of appropriate educational and other social services (HREOC 1992: 71–2). It suggested that special laws could help the Islanders in Australia overcome continuing racial discrimination (HREOC 1992: 70).

Because Bandler had devoted so much effort to the task of including Aborigines and Torres Strait Islanders as equals by changing Australian society, the exclusion of her South Sea Islander people from opportunities that arose in the 1970s disappointed her. Her prominence in the referendum campaign meant she became very well known in Australia, and overseas. With the recognition of Aboriginal rights under Whitlam, Bandler felt able to explore her heritage. In 1974, she visited her father's island of Ambrym for the first time, getting a lift on a boat from Vila, the capital of Vanuatu, because someone recognised her from all her 'coming and going to Canberra' (Bandler 1985: 58). Despite her public prominence, it still took a long time before she gained official recognition of the Islanders' contribution to Australia. After that, new challenges arose.

At the end of the twentieth century, Bandler (1999a) spoke of a new task facing ordinary people in this country: to save Australia 'from isolation as a nation' separating itself from the world. She stressed that, 'in moving forward, old certainties must be reclaimed' and 'old definitions must not be lost'. This attitude reflected her respect for old Aboriginal writers, such as Oodgeroo Noonuccal and Jack Davis, who 'wrote when it was tough' about Aboriginal hopes before the Commonwealth had accepted its national responsibility for Aboriginal affairs (Bandler 1999b: 107–8). For Bandler, that responsibility had a vital cosmopolitan dimension, expressed in the efforts to increase global scrutiny of the plight of Indigenous peoples in Australia. She says that her extraordinary commitment to the struggle for the referendum 'had to do with basic human rights'. She recalls having 'seen in Europe what had happened when the Jews were deprived of those rights and I was aware that the Aboriginal people were deprived of those rights here in Australia, because they were shut away' (Bandler 1993). Ending that oppression meant overcoming Australia's practice of shutting itself off from outside scrutiny.

Bandler had been optimistic in the early 1970s, but she knew there was no guarantee that inclusive change would be easy. As a strong Whitlam supporter, she was pleased when he declared, in his 1972 election campaign launch, that 'Australia's treatment of her Aboriginal people will be the thing upon which the rest of the world will judge Australia and Australians – not just now, but in the greater perspective of history' (quoted in Bandler 1989:

164). This encapsulated why she had acted, thinking that Australians must become responsible before the world for what happens in their own country, not just leave all action to the government. The travesty of Whitlam's dismissal led her to get involved in another petition campaign in May 1977, decrying the Constitution and calling for its replacement 'by a democratic constitution' through a 'directly elected people's convention' (Lake 2002: 192). This failed to occur. The later movement for an Australian republic, which she supported, lacked the clear focus and commitment of the referendum campaign for Aboriginal citizenship. Two key differences were that the successful movement was a grassroots one, and inspired by cosmopolitan values, whereas the republican movement became elitist, captured by nationalists and opportunists.

Bandler's struggle to gain official recognition for her own people in Australia after the referendum raises important questions about formal and substantive equality, and the Commonwealth's power to pass special laws for racially designated groups under section 51(xxvi) of the Constitution. These issues are considered in the section below, but a major irony about Bandler's achievement must be noted. The whole purpose of her activity, throughout the long referendum campaign and later seeking recognition for her own people, has been to stop anyone from 'putting one group down against another on the grounds of race', as she stressed in a TV interview (Bandler 1993). Yet that was the initial purpose of section 51(xxvi). It was directed in 1901 against Pacific Islanders, including Bandler's own people. They were seen as temporary Australians, an 'introduced race' able to be deported (Attwood and Markus 1997: 2). How could a provision that was clearly racist in origin later be reshaped to enable Commonwealth action to eliminate racial discrimination, not just against Pacific Islanders in Australia, but also against Aborigines and Torres Strait Islanders after the 1967 referendum? The answer is through a fundamental shift in the meaning of the Constitution itself, which can be seen as the key legacy of Bandler's campaigning for racial equality.

Reorienting Australia's Constitution towards humanity

In 1968, Bandler (1989: 121) summarised the referendum's key successes, saying it had turned public opinion around, 'enlightened backward thinking politicians', and also 'brought the Aboriginal people to tread the corridors of power in this country'. One of her Aboriginal friends, the activist Ken Brindle, recalled that: 'the whole thing was, we had faith in you and your lot because the government didn't like you, and anyone the government didn't like, well, we thought they must be all right' (quoted in Bandler 1989: 136). What Bandler and FCAATSI did was to persuade the government, which didn't like them, to put the Constitution in line with the changing values of the wider world, through the referendum. This was seen as a test for Australia. Its success created space for Aborigines to become equals, within an inclusive Australian society.

Two views of the 1967 referendum, one literal and the other metaphorical, understate the significance of the constitutional changes that Bandler and her colleagues won. The significance was not obvious to everyone in the movement at the time, although Brindle later said he would have been more enthusiastic in the 1960s if he 'could have foreseen' then all the benefits that Aborigines would later derive from constitutional change (quoted in Bandler 1989: 135). Yet some historians claim that the referendum enabled only the *possibility* of Commonwealth responsibility for Aboriginal affairs to increase in the future. They say it had nothing to do with citizenship at all. They also say Street misled her followers, such as Bandler, by thinking that section 127 of the Constitution (which excluded Aborigines from the census) denied citizenship rights for Aborigines (Attwood 2003: 165). According to this literal view, the 1967 referendum involved 'mundane' constitutional changes, unsupported by 'references to grand principles such as "equal rights" or "citizenship", let alone "freedom"' (Attwood 2003: 163). If this were true, Bandler's activity agitating for the referendum was misconceived. She certainly was inspired by these universal ideals, and by the desperate need for Aboriginal access to the resources controlled by the federal government. On these points, there was no basic difference between Bandler's understanding of what the referendum meant and that of her FCAATSI colleagues (see Bandler 1993). She believed that winning the referendum vote meant that, under the Constitution, the government now had to treat Aborigines as human beings, accepting their distinct cultures, not imposing assimilation on them.

Bandler's biographer, Lake, puts forward a metaphorical response to this literal view. She points out that it ignores 'the symbolic significance of the referendum', which included Aborigines in the 'imagined community' of the Australian nation, as distinct from the Australian state (Lake 2002: 67–8). According to her interpretation, changing section 127 (on the census) 'related not to Aborigines' rights as citizens of the state, but to their status as national subjects' (Lake 2002: 67). This view accepts that Street was mistaken in believing the Constitution itself prevented legislative change to grant Aborigines citizenship rights like the vote. It shifts the focus towards understanding the broader social change that accompanied the referendum, which Bandler (1989) stressed in her history of FCAATSI. The petition campaigns conducted in 1958 and 1962 by FCAATSI certainly contributed to many legislative reforms that occurred before 1967 (Horner 2004: 74). Yet the metaphorical view implies that legislative reform to gain equality for Aborigines was dependent on the *national symbolism* of counting Aborigines, just like others, in the census. This ignores the change to section 51(xxvi), which Bandler pressed so hard for, in order 'to protect Aboriginal culture, identity and land' (Lake 2002: 113). This change was essential for achieving substantive equality, by overcoming the structural inequalities resulting from colonial dispossession (Bandler 1993). Without such change, Aboriginal citizenship, as Kevin Gilbert said in 1971, is only 'a Bill of no value, without substance or honour' (quoted in Stokes 1997: 165).

The metaphorical view downplays the significance of Aboriginal citizenship as a core idea of the referendum, which Bandler (1989: 161) stressed. Real citizenship implies a certain relationship to the state, or to a broader political community, not just a national identity (Walter and MacLeod 2002: 1–5). The idea of equal citizenship was crucial in the referendum campaign, but what was most important was the complementary idea of Aborigines and Torres Strait Islanders having a *special place* in Australia. This was clearly stated in FCAATSI's principles. These recognised that Indigenous peoples are 'distinct cultural groups' who must be guaranteed the retention of 'their own customs, languages and institutions', together with ownership of their traditional lands, as well as 'special assistance' to overcome dispossession, *plus* 'the same rights, privileges and responsibilities as other Australians' (Bandler 1989: 167–8). Ideas about special Aboriginal citizenship rights were easier to advance after the referendum's success (Rowse 2000: 21). A 1968 FCAATSI petition saw the referendum as giving 'a clear mandate' for accepting 'common justice and international standards' (Attwood 2003: 293–5). As an act of *inclusion*, the referendum's core justification was cosmopolitan. It was *not* primarily 'an appeal to national sentiment' about including Aborigines as citizens just like white Australians, as some historians claim (Attwood and Markus 1997: 44; Attwood 2003: 176; compare Attwood and Markus 2007: 46). Rather, it recognised that *Australia itself now had to change*, to follow the world's standards.

It is the global context of the referendum campaign that the literal and metaphorical views of its significance both understate. A proponent of the literal view suggests that, in the late 1960s, Aborigines shifted from political campaigning which had stressed 'a common humanity' to a new discourse of Aboriginality that now emphasised 'cultural or historical differences' (Attwood 2003: 316). Yet it is false to see these discourses as inconsistent. The rhetoric used in the referendum campaign combined them both. The metaphorical view is insufficient in suggesting that the referendum's symbolism involved changing only Australian *nationalism* to include Aborigines. The inclusion that occurred was mediated mainly by a concern about Australia's image *abroad*, as Bandler highlighted effectively, not by a reshaping of Australian nationalism. It was not just the empathy of the Australian nation that was crucial for the referendum's success, but the view that Australia had to be accountable to the world for Aboriginal human rights. This cosmopolitan view linked the Constitution to fundamental human rights, well before the emergence of discussion about a bill of rights in Australia (Bandler 1993).

The implications of this linkage may not be readily apparent, because the Constitution is, at face value, an old document that seems to command what Justice Michael Kirby (2000: 1) has described as mistaken 'ancestor worship'. This reverence takes the form of an assumption that 1901 is the latest date that matters when judges, or any other citizens, read the Constitution, since its meaning was fixed then (Kirby 2000: 4). This approach obviously has difficulty mastering any words of the Constitution that have been changed by referendum, as in 1967. Kirby points out that section 51(xxvi) of the Constitution, as it now exists, cannot be understood without an awareness of how the world changed in the first two-thirds of the twentieth century. He argues that the Constitution's words may remain largely the same, but 'the meaning and content of the words take colour from the circumstances in which the words must be understood and to which they must be applied' (Kirby 2000: 11). Those circumstances include Australia's obligations under international human rights law, and the reasons for the 1967 referendum. For Kirby, section 51(xxvi) cannot *now* authorise racist legislation directed against Indigenous peoples, as it once did against Bandler's own people. The world has changed so much since 1901 that racism, which breaches international treaties ratified by Australia, is unlawful unless the Constitution permits it, which it does not clearly do (Kirby 1998: 417; see Chapter 9 for further discussion).

Kirby's view of the Constitution helps us to see how Bandler has helped change Australia. Kirby's legal view is inconsistent with the literal view of the referendum expressed by those historians who see it as merely a mundane change not linked to citizenship. A constitutional change to permit special laws to benefit Indigenous peoples, supported so overwhelmingly by the electorate after a decade of lobbying, should not be dismissed as mundane, regardless of its context. Kirby's view of constitutional interpretation, and his understanding of the Constitution as now forbidding racist legislation *because of* the referendum, was not supported in a 1998 case by a majority of the High Court. Yet it was not rejected by a majority either, as that *Kartinyeri* case was resolved using different principles. When assessing Bandler's contribution to changing Australia, it is worth noting that, if Kirby's view is subsequently adopted, the referendum will need to be seen in retrospect as having eliminated, in principle, racial discrimination from the Constitution and so potentially from Australian law.[2] That is what Bandler and most Australians, including the Liberal politician W. C. Wentworth, who insisted on the change to section 51(xxvi), thought was done in 1967 (Bandler 1989: 110; Attwood and Markus 1997: 98–9). Racial discrimination was already forbidden then by the international law of nations, although Australia formally incorporated that law into its domestic law only with the *Racial Discrimination Act* in 1975.

Conclusion

Bandler's activism is a historic example of global citizenship in action in Australia. The 1967 referendum campaign promoted cosmopolitan values of human rights and cultural diversity. It was a struggle to get Indigenous peoples treated with full respect as peoples with their own cultures. The lack of a treaty with Indigenous peoples in Australia means this struggle has become harder than in countries like Canada and New Zealand, but this is no reason for doubting that the referendum opened a big door for change. Historians who reject Bandler's transformative view of the referendum as merely 'a comforting fiction' still accept her basic thesis that the tide really did turn. They agree that the referendum changed an old 'political discourse which refused to countenance Aboriginal rights, the rights of Aborigines as indigenous peoples, rather than the rights of Aborigines as Australian citizens' (Attwood and Markus 1997: 66, 71; compare Attwood and Markus 2007: 71, 84, and Behrendt 2007: 29). By creating a space for Aborigines to demand recognition of Indigenous rights, the referendum prepared Australians to confront the future political challenges of cultural diversity. Bandler (1989: 163–4) says many white Australians 'became bewildered' when faced with the need to respond reciprocally to a radical Aboriginal political presence. She thinks many white Australians still tend to put people into separate boxes, instead of seeing what they have in common, but she believes this does not diminish the inclusive potential of the referendum (Bandler 2006).

Bandler and her colleagues were able to include Indigenous peoples within Australian democracy by facilitating their involvement in a campaign to change the Constitution so it had a place for them. The change was momentous, although its full potential has yet to be realised. Only two sections of the Constitution were revised, so the place is very limited, but the limits must not be overstated. The place is defined by the positive idea of Aboriginal citizenship. This did not include Aborigines within an old national definition of citizenship. Instead, it recognised cultural diversity and affirmed the historical position of Indigenous peoples in Australia. Understanding this does not depend on the Constitution itself referring to ideas of equality, citizenship, or freedom (after all, it does not refer to the prime minister's role). The section on special laws for Aborigines must simply be read in the light of realities in the contemporary world. Those realities now include the long-awaited UN Declaration on the Rights of Indigenous Peoples, endorsed by the General Assembly in September 2007 despite opposition from Australia.

Constitutional recognition of the need for special laws to benefit Aborigines remains limited by political realities. Yet, since these can change, that section retains potential for advancing Aboriginal rights. When seen in conformity with international law, that section could be a foundation for Australia becoming a society in which Aboriginality is prized, not diminished. If that section is taken in isolation as merely rendering the Constitution 'silent' on Indigenous rights, then the rhetoric of Bandler and so many others in 1967 is assumed to have fallen on deaf ears (Brennan et al. 2005: 57). Yet it did not.

The real focus of criticism must be not the limits of the referendum, but the limits of what followed in later decades, when Australian governments fooled 'the world into thinking that something positive was being done for Aborigines' (Gilbert, quoted in Attwood and Markus 1997: 132). Such criticism implies a continuing relationship between Australia (and Australians) and the wider world over the issues of Aboriginal justice, as Whitlam recognised in 1972. It implies the possible revival of the cosmopolitan perspective. Bandler (2006) says that Australians have suffered 'a very sluggish time' in the past decade. In her view this has increased the impact of the people who she once called 'bloody yuppies', those who 'think about no-one's future other than their own' (Bandler 1993). Yet, remarkably, she has not lost her optimism. She says: 'We can change anything. Nothing is set in concrete. We can have a peaceful world' (Bandler 2005b: 264). It is Bandler's achievement to have made a humane, cosmopolitan, and inclusive future for Australia possible.

Notes

1 I would like to thank particularly Faith Bandler and also Jack Horner for their comments on this chapter, as well as Geoff Stokes for editorial advice. Readers interested in more details about how Bandler put ideas into action should consult her biography (Lake 2002) and also the extended transcripts of several hours of interviews by Robin Hughes for the *Australian Biography* TV program (Bandler 1993).

2 Jack Horner, a long-time colleague of Bandler's in the AAF and FCAATSI, commented about this point: 'this is what we thought we had accomplished'.

References

Attwood, B. 2003. *Rights for Aborigines.* Sydney: Allen & Unwin.

Attwood, B. and A. Markus, with D. Edwards and K. Schilling 1997. *The 1967 Referendum, or When Aborigines Didn't Get the Vote.* Canberra: Aboriginal Studies Press.

Attwood, B. and A. Markus 2004. *Thinking Black: William Cooper and the Australian Aborigines' League.* Canberra: Aboriginal Studies Press.

——2007. *The 1967 Referendum: Race, Power and the Australian Constitution.* 2nd ed., Canberra: Aboriginal Studies Press.

Bandler, F. 1973. Letter, as FCAATSI General Secretary, to the Secretary of the NSW Trade Unions Council, 23 January. Australian Institute of Aboriginal and Torres Strait Islander Studies Library, Papers of FCAATSI, MS 3759, series 25, item 11.

——1977. *Wacvie.* Adelaide: Rigby.

——1984. *Welou, My Brother.* Sydney: Wild and Woolley.

——1985. 'The role of research.' In J. Davis and B. Hodge (eds) *Aboriginal Writing Today.* Canberra: Australian Institute of Aboriginal Studies, pp. 55–62.

——1989. *Turning the Tide: A Personal History of the Federal Council for the Advancement of Aborigines and Torres Strait Islanders.* Canberra: Aboriginal Studies Press.

——1993. 'Faith Bandler: Civil rights activist.' Interview with Robin Hughes, 24 and 25 March, *Australian Biography* series, Film Australia, for SBS TV. Full interview transcript (from eight separate tapes) viewed 7 January 2008, http://www.australianbiography.gov.au/bandler/interview1.html. The TV script, viewed 7 January 2008, is at http://www.australianbiography.gov.au/bandler/script/html

——1994. 'The debt we owe Lionel Murphy.' 1988 Lionel Murphy Lecture. In V. G. Venturini (ed.) *Five Voices for Lionel.* Sydney: Federation Press, pp. 29–37.

——1997. 'Jessie Street Trust annual launch address.' Sydney: 11 April, viewed 3 December 2004, http://www.isis.aust.com/afnt/jessie.htm

——1999a. 'Inaugural speech to the Brisbane Institute.' Brisbane: 1 March, viewed 3 December 2004, http://www.brisinst.org.au/resources/bandler_faith_Inaugural.html

——1999b [1993]. 'Paving the way: A tribute to black Australian writers.' In N. James (ed.) *Writers on Writing.* Sydney: Halstead Press.

——2004. Remarks in visitors' book for Portraits from the Movement 1978–2003: Juno Gemes, an exhibition at Macquarie University Art Gallery, dated 5 April.

——2005a. Interview with Roderic Pitty. Turramurra: 2 April.

——2005b. Entry in 1000 Peace Women Across the Globe. Zurich: Kontrast.

——2006. Interview with Roderic Pitty. Turramurra: 11 January.

Bandler, F. and L. Fox 1980. *Marani in Australia.* Adelaide: Rigby.

——(eds) 1983. *The Time Was Ripe: A History of the Aboriginal-Australian Fellowship (1956–69).* Chippendale: Alternative Publishing Co-operative.

Behrendt, L. 2007. 'The 1967 Referendum: 40 Years on.' In N. Gillespie (ed) *Reflections: 40 Years on from the 1967 Referendum.* Adelaide: Aboriginal Legal Rights Movement, pp. 25–9.

Brennan, S., L. Behrendt, L. Strelein and G. Williams 2005. *Treaty*. Sydney: Federation Press.

Chesterman, J. 2005. *Civil Rights: How Indigenous Australians Won Formal Equality*. St Lucia: University of Queensland Press.

Chesterman, J. and B. Galligan 1997. *Citizens without Rights: Aborigines and Australian Citizenship*. Melbourne: Cambridge University Press.

Clark, J. 1997. '"Something to hide": Aborigines and the Department of External Affairs, January 1961 – January 1962.' *Journal of the Royal Australian Historical Society* 83(1):71–84.

Cochrane, K. 1994. *Oodgeroo*. St Lucia: University of Queensland Press.

Darling, E. 1996. 'They spoke out pretty good: The leadership of women in the Brisbane Aboriginal rights movement, 1958–1962.' *Melbourne Historical Journal* 24:87–103.

Dower, N. 2003. *An Introduction to Global Citizenship*. Edinburgh: Edinburgh University Press.

FCAATSI 1971. *Memorandum to the General Assembly of the United Nations Re Racism and Racial Discrimination in Australia*. Australian Institute of Aboriginal and Torres Strait Islander Studies Library, Papers of FCAATSI, MS 3759, series 14, item 4, International Year for Action to Combat Racism.

Ferguson, W. and J. Patten 1995 [1938]. 'Cries from the heart: *Aborigines claim citizen rights!*' In I. Moores (ed.) *Voices of Aboriginal Australia: Past, Present, Future*. Springwood: Butterfly Books, pp. 54–60.

Foley, G. 2002. 'Great moments in indigenous history: Have faith in Nelson!' Photograph, Faith Bandler and Nelson Mandela, September 2000. *Koori History Website*. Kooriweb: viewed 3 December 2004, http://www.kooriweb.org/foley/great/grt11.html

Gilbert, K. 1973. *Because a White Man'll Never Do It*. Sydney: Angus & Robertson.

——1977. *Living Black*. Ringwood: Penguin.

——1988 (ed.) *Inside Black Australia: An Anthology of Aboriginal Poetry*. Ringwood: Penguin.

——1990. *The Blackside: People are Legends and Other Poems*. Melbourne: Hyland House.

Gilbert, S. 2005. '"Never forgotten": Pearl Gibbs (Gambanyi).' In A. Cole, V. Haskins and F. Paisley (eds) *Uncommon Ground: White Women in Aboriginal History*. Canberra: Aboriginal Studies Press, pp. 107–26.

Harvey, K. and The Aboriginal Community Elders' Service 2003. *Aboriginal Elders' Voices: Stories of the 'Tide of History'. Victorian Indigenous Elders' Life Stories and Oral Histories*. Melbourne: Aboriginal Community Elders' Service.

Horner, J. 1974. *Vote Ferguson for Aboriginal Freedom: A Biography*. Sydney: Australia and New Zealand Book Company.

——2004. *Seeking Racial Justice: An Insider's Memoir of the Movement for Aboriginal Advancement, 1938–1978*. Canberra: Aboriginal Studies Press.

HREOC 1992. *The Call for Recognition: A Report on the Situation of Australian South Sea Islanders*. Sydney: Human Rights and Equal Opportunity Commission.

Kirby, M. 1998. 'Reasons for judgment in *Kartinyeri v Commonwealth*.' [1998] HCA 22, 195 *Commonwealth Law Reports* 337, pp. 386–422.

——2000. 'Constitutional interpretation and original intent: A form of ancestor worship?' *Melbourne University Law Review* 24(1):1–14.

Lake, M. 2002. *Faith: Faith Bandler, Gentle Activist*. Sydney: Allen & Unwin.

Moore, C. 1979. 'Oral testimony and the Pacific Island labour trade to Queensland: myth and reality.' *The Oral History Association of Australia Journal* 1:28–42.

——2004. 'Review of Marilyn Lake, *Faith* (Lake 2002).' *Australian Journal of Politics and History* March, 50(1):126–7.

Palma, B. 2002. 'Save our site: The story of the campaign to save the Australian Hall, site of the 1938 Aboriginal Day of Mourning and Protest.' In A. Heiss (ed.) *Life in Gadigal Country*. Sydney: Gadigal Information Service, pp. 78–84.

Peckham, R. 2005. Interview with Roderic Pitty. Dubbo: 8 June.

Rowse, T. 2000. *Obliged to Be Difficult: Nugget Coombs' Legacy in Indigenous Affairs*. Melbourne: Cambridge University Press.

Smith, Shirley. 1981. *Mum Shirl: An Autobiography*. With Bobbi Sykes. Melbourne: Heinemann.

Stokes, G. 1997. 'Citizenship and Aboriginality: Two conceptions of identity in Aboriginal political thought.' In G. Stokes (ed.) *The Politics of Identity in Australia*. Melbourne: Cambridge University Press, pp. 158–71.

Taffe, S. 2001. 'Witnesses from the conference floor: Oral history and the Federal Council for the Advancement of Aborigines and Torres Strait Islanders.' *Journal of Australian Studies* 67:10–21.

——2005. *Black and White Together*. St Lucia: University of Queensland Press.

Walter, J. and M. MacLeod 2002. *The Citizens' Bargain: A Documentary History of Australian Views since 1890*. Sydney: UNSW Press.

Herb Feith

Herb Feith was a scholar, teacher and peace activist. He started his career as an Indonesian specialist, and wrote a treatise on the development of the Indonesian state. One of Australia's first international volunteers, he worked as a volunteer in Indonesia in the early 1950s. He was a supporter of peace research, and initiated peace think tanks and forums in Australia, in addition to supporting and publicising many international causes. He campaigned vigorously for self-determination in East Timor. Throughout his career he built up a large network of contacts with scholars, politicians and activists around the world. He was known as a generous mentor and teacher, influencing many now-prominent international relations experts both in Australia and internationally. Herb died in 2001.

Herb Feith (right) with his adopted Indonesian family, including Ibu Kromodiharjo (seated far left) and Bapak Kromodiharjo (seated middle), in Pedoworedjo, Yogyakarta, when Herb was an Australian Volunteer translator with the Indonesian Ministry of Information, early 1950s. (Courtesy Australian Volunteers International and David Feith.)

44

3

Herb Feith: Working for Peace across Cultures

Gary Smith[1]

Herbert Feith escaped the Holocaust as a seven-year-old boy, and came to Australia as a refugee. His parents, Arthur and Lily Feith, fled with him from Vienna in 1938, just ahead of the Nazi pogroms, not expecting to find passage on a ship to Australia. Herb (as he would always be called) spent the rest of his childhood in the relative security of Melbourne during World War II, and attended university in the immediate postwar years. He then set off on an extraordinary path of intellectual and political activity, analysing and acting on challenging global problems, their manifestations in Australia's region, particularly in Indonesia, and their implications for Australians.

From his youngest days as an activist/scholar, Feith sought to make intellectual sense of some of the largest problems facing humanity. He understood these in global rather than national terms, and devoted attention to mass poverty, the gap between rich and poor, and the profound cultural differences within and between states. He sought to understand and challenge violence, militarism, repression and war as persistent features of political life. His activism was in turn based on human rights and global values rather than national values. These agendas included the alleviation of poverty, inter-cultural dialogue and understanding, peace and conflict resolution. Feith became Australia's leading scholar of Indonesia, and the Australian best-known there for his knowledge and understanding of that country. He sought to advance an agenda of cooperative Australian–Indonesian relations at both the inter-governmental and people-to-people levels. He went on to address the difficult circumstances of groups who sought more autonomy in the international system. He mapped out the moral and practical dimensions of self-determination claims, seeking new UN mechanisms for conflict resolution, and he supported East Timorese self-determination campaigns over the quarter-century of Indonesian occupation.

Unlike many notable refugees in Australia who became successful in business, law and medicine in the conventional national context, Feith's life was deeply informed by a cosmopolitan perspective. This derived from his personal immersion in the understanding of other cultures and wider international forces, and from the values that he developed to guide his research and action. 'Success' for Feith might be a problematic idea when the bar he set was so high, but he had extraordinary achievements as an Australian thinker, educator and activist who maintained a vibrant cosmopolitan outlook. His life's activity had a major impact in Australia and abroad, as can be readily seen in a brief review of his main activities.

Founder of Australian overseas volunteer movement. Shortly after Indonesia's independence, the young Herb Feith went to work in Indonesia alongside Indonesians, as a volunteer working in the new Ministry of Information. He lived and worked in Indonesia for a total of four years in the early 1950s. By personal example and through his lobbying in Australia, Feith became the driving force behind the new Australian overseas volunteer movement, later known as Australian Volunteers International (AVI). AVI, more than fifty years on, has about 1000 Australians currently working under its auspices overseas and with Indigenous Australians.

Australia's leading scholar of Indonesia. Feith's deep engagement with Indonesia continued and was combined with brilliant academic work. He completed a Masters at the University of Melbourne, and a PhD at Cornell University on Indonesian politics in the 1950s. His studies were undertaken in a period when the new democracy conducted its first major elections and then faltered into governmental instability. His book *The Decline of Constitutional Democracy in Indonesia* (1962), with its unparalleled use of local sources, and his subsequent writings, established him as one of the world's foremost Indonesia scholars, and the Australian academic most well known within Indonesia. He became Professor of Politics at the relatively new Monash University in 1968, as Monash became a hub of knowledge and expertise about South-East Asia. He remained committed to the idea of the federal democratic Indonesian state as an appropriate political community for the former Dutch East Indies.

Peace educator and activist. The extensive anti-communist massacres in Indonesia in 1965–66, and the turbulent 1960s student protests in western countries over the Vietnam war, shifted Feith's focus in the 1970s and 1980s to peace and justice issues. He developed peace education courses at Monash University, and was a major force behind the Labor government's decision to establish the Peace Research Centre at the Australian National University.

He was the leading figure in the creation of the Victorian Association for Peace Studies and then the Secure Australia Project as academic/activist organisations.

The problem of self-determination. The great wave of decolonisation after World War II led to the creation of many new states, large and small, with political independence. Feith celebrated the emancipatory nature of these dramatic events, but he was immediately alert to problems generated by the artificial nature of new political communities, in particular the problem of self-determination of groups disaffected with their minority status, and seeking to retain and develop a separate identity. For Feith, the question was framed by concern for human suffering: how to mitigate the brutality that new states often used against claims to self-determination by minority groups. He sought to engage the UN in assessing such claims, and proposed that federalist political solutions be pursued rather than centralist military solutions. He also identified Indonesian–Australian joint approaches to global crises, campaigned against excessively military tactics in Australia's approach to the world, and expressed concern about the possibility of an Australian–Indonesian arms race.

In the firing line. Feith applied this global thinking to the case of East Timor, and contributed to keeping the idea of options for self-determination alive after the Indonesian invasion and occupation of 1975. At the same time he sought to educate not only Australians about Indonesian thinking, but also Indonesians about the strength and validity of the self-determination claims by the East Timorese. Over two decades later, in 1999, Feith was an observer of the independence ballot in East Timor. The ballot was followed by an intensified period of orchestrated militia violence and killings, until the UN-authorised and Australia-led military intervention brought the country under control. Angus MacIntyre, friend and fellow Indonesia scholar, recounts a series of events at a house in East Timor that he and Feith were visiting during the period of violence. The day before, militia had entered the house and issued a threat to return and kill the inhabitants. The militia returned while Feith and MacIntyre were present. MacIntyre recounts that 'a raging argument ensued at the front door' (Encounter 2003):

> Herb had come forward through the house to the front and these militia men I think were a little taken aback to see this very old and frail man with flashing eyes and perfect Indonesian condemning them for their behaviour and while this was going on the people in the house actually escaped, ran away out the back door and so in the end it was just Herb arguing with the militia on the veranda with an empty house behind him.

47

This chapter reviews Feith's impressive legacy across these diverse areas of activity. 'Herb was an ideas man', said one of his Australian colleagues (Mackie 2002: 19), and this chapter explores some of his key ideas, taking us through the sweep of half a century of international politics. But Feith was also an activist, from the perspective of an Australian deeply concerned with the wider issues of common humanity in the region and the world at large.

Feith's journey is tracked from his pioneering role as an Australian volunteer in Indonesia; a world-renowned scholar of Indonesia; a writer and teacher on global peace and justice; a supporter of the project of Indonesian democracy through its forty-year suppression by authoritarian forces; an activist on East Timorese self-determination, and also against tendencies to militarism in the Australian Government's approach to the region.

Early days: founder of Australian volunteers movement

Contemporary discussions of cosmopolitanism often seek to identify the current reality and future prospects of an emerging global civil society (Anheier et al. 2006). This concept describes emerging phenomena of non-governmental organisations and social movements that address common global problems. These organisations are creating, in uneven and haphazard ways, a new set of positive 'people-to-people' forces in international politics, cutting across and influencing inter-governmental relations. Those same discussions will often identify two of the harsh and persistent constraints on the development of a sense of global community: deep inequalities in wealth between (and within) nations, and the enduring difficulties of cross-cultural communication and understanding.

As a young graduate, Feith was a pioneer in this new frontier of global cooperation, creating elements of civil society across national boundaries where none had existed. With no organisational structure to assist in the task, he arranged to work in post-independence Indonesia as a volunteer in 1951, in the Ministry for Information. He returned for a second period, spending a total of four years in Indonesia as a larger volunteer movement began to follow his example. Feith described his interest in volunteering as a way of addressing global divides: seeking culturally appropriate ways for people in a rich and mainly western country to assist those in a poor and non-western country, with both enriched by the experience. His personal example and engagement provided impetus to the establishment of the Australian overseas volunteers movement, based on these ideas of accepting local living conditions and extensive periods of involvement.

Volunteering is part of the Australian community fabric, and part of 'civil society'. Feith was tapping into and extending this important Australian tradition. Australians volunteer locally to fight fires, to provide emergency services and ambulance services, and to assist international sporting events. To be a volunteer is to perform a service to a community wider than one's family, of one's own free will. This is a double freedom: from the market and from the state. It is a freedom from performing a service for the purpose of financial reward, and from performing a function required by law, although there may be a structure of basic financial support, and the legal frameworks of the state may play an important enabling role.

Feith's originality was to take this tradition into the international sphere after the debilitating world wars of the twentieth century. Internationally, Australians in the first half of that century volunteered in large numbers to fight in major wars. Mostly this involved signing a contract with the state, and the free will of the volunteer became compromised. After World War II, this kind of volunteering, to fight for country and wider cause, had lost its appeal. But new international challenges reshaped the concept of volunteering, and Herb Feith played a key role in this process.

The unravelling of European colonialism was the great historical drama in Asia, on Australia's doorstep. New, independent but very poor states were being created in South and South-East Asia as the force for decolonisation became unstoppable. The Indonesian nationalist revolution, for example, had secured independence from Holland. Australia's official response to these developments in the 1950s was characterised by the poor leadership of British Empire loyalists such as Liberal prime minister Robert Menzies, who had once dismissed the Indonesian nationalist leader Sukarno as a collaborator with Japan. Whereas the Labor governments at the time of Indonesian independence had facilitated and welcomed the process of decolonisation, for many Liberals of that era, there was an overriding concern about new insecurities, a fear of communism in Asia, and fear of 'Asia' itself, as China aligned with Moscow in the Cold War. It was in the conservative climate of Liberal governments in Australia that Feith volunteered to assist in administration in the new state of Indonesia in the 1950s.

Feith and the early volunteers in Indonesia were an important group in Australian political life in this early Cold War period (Diprose 2002). They brought back to Australia a sense of Indonesia as neighbour, an understanding of the complexity of the neighbour's society, and enjoyment in the challenge of cross-cultural understanding. These perspectives worked against the dominant official and popular tendency to stereotype and fear the Asian region. Their influence endured as the international volunteering movement grew in size and complexity to become an established part of Australian community life. Herb Feith was, by imagination, determination and example, to initiate a movement that would in time propel many thousands of fellow Australians into experiences that would give them a wider sense of global community.

Understanding Indonesia

Herb Feith established a worldwide academic reputation as a pre-eminent 'Indonesianist', widely respected outside the country as one of a handful who were the best in the field, but also inside Indonesia as one who had a deep understanding of Indonesian social and political life. His work clearly benefited from what was unmatched access to Indonesian local publications and newspapers, but also access to intellectuals, political figures – a network which he had developed from his time as a volunteer – and the everyday life and perspective of Indonesian families and villagers. He was able to integrate his deep experience of life in Indonesia with the intellectual currents emanating from North America's most prestigious centre of research excellence on South-East Asian Studies, Cornell University. Out of this inter-cultural experience he produced a unique body of work.

Two key dimensions of Feith's work that are of particular interest in the context of cosmopolitanism are his approach to the questions of human agency versus historical determinism, and the response to the murderous crisis that engulfed Indonesia in 1965.

Herb Feith's worldwide reputation as a scholar of Indonesia rests on his book about the fate of Indonesian democracy in the 1950s, and on a series of articles and chapters on the Guided Democracy period under Sukarno that began in 1958 and continued until the tragic events of 1965–66 (Feith 1962; 1967). His book *The Decline of Constitutional Democracy in Indonesia* (1962) examines the various cabinet governments that formed and re-formed in the lead-up to the first parliamentary election in 1955, the elections that year, and the character of the four major political parties that emerged at the election and the diverse social forces they represented. It further analysed the subsequent political instability in Indonesia as 'Western type political institutions . . . worked unsatisfactorily and finally crumbled' (Feith 1982a: 50). President Sukarno's decision to create Guided Democracy curtailed the evolution of constitutional democracy, a path not resumed until forty years later in 1998.

From a cosmopolitan perspective, the most significant dimensions of Feith's book are revealed in the far-reaching debate which it generated. The debate began between Feith and Yale University Professor Harry Benda, an eminent Jewish-Czech historian, and continued with new contributions for over thirty years (Benda 1964; Feith 1965). Benda charged Feith with asking the wrong question: it should not be 'why did Indonesian democracy fail?', but why did anyone think it had a chance of succeeding given Indonesia's divergent social currents and historical experience. Concerning the course of the 1950s, Feith (and his supporters) would assert that it was quite conceivable that instead of an emerging presidential authoritarianism, alternative democratic forces could have prevailed. These forces were led by those who saw the value in constitutional democracy as an Indonesian solution for its problems as a modern, emerging independent state. On this account, it was touch and go, and the outcomes could have been very different (Feith 1994).

For some this was a debate about the particular times of the 1950s, to be won or lost, and indeed recontested, as fresh perspectives and new research weighed in on each side. But there was a much larger question at stake. Feith's own self-assessments were somewhat complicated by his later disaffection with the 'political science' categories that he used in his early writing, and its overstated claims to objectivity. Nevertheless, he regularly reasserted his conviction about his general position in the debate. For him, this was as much a key assumption about the fundamental nature of politics as it was a statement about a particular time. Feith believed in the possibility of human agency, in the potential for people (as citizens, national or global) to take control of difficult courses of events, and steer them to more just and humane outcomes. In all his intellectual work, Feith would resist the construction of deterministic pictures of politics that allowed no scope for human agency.

The decline of constitutional democracy in Indonesia became a catastrophic fall, destroyed by the extremely violent events of 1965–66 through which General Suharto took power. At the peak of its academic success, the political science project for Feith became unhinged. The Indonesia that Feith knew and admired, even as it lurched from democracy to authoritarianism, was all but destroyed by the mass killings of many hundreds of thousands of people seen as communists and communist supporters in 1965–66, following the coup attempt against army leaders, and the counter-coup led by General Suharto. The scale of these killings made it one of the most violent events of the second half of the twentieth century. By virtue of his expertise, Feith was called on to explain and interpret what was going on to Australians, and indeed a wider global community of concerned observers.

These bloody events shook Feith's conviction in the value of studying and interpreting Indonesian political life. His optimistic spirit for the new nation, in which 'administrators' might balance the work of 'solidarity makers', within a democratic framework, seemed inappropriate to the world after 1966. At the same time, the wider social currents in western societies, triggered particularly by the reactions to the deepening US involvement in war in Vietnam, stimulated Feith to look for more comprehensive analyses of wider forces affecting the developing world as a whole. He also began to search for ways of thinking and writing which could be grounded in realities but also identify with progressive forces for change.

Feith returned to Indonesia in 1968, and wrote for the *New Republic* a detailed account of the state of political prisoners who he observed and visited, which led the government to ban him from Indonesia for several years. In it he wrote: 'The Suharto government has . . . done much less than it could to live down the shame that surrounds its birth, the slaughter of probably well over half a million people in the anti-communist holocaust which followed the abortive coup of October 1965' (Feith 1968a: 17). To use the term 'holocaust' was to make a direct comparison with the mass murder of Jews from which Feith himself had narrowly escaped, and implied the strongest possible condemnation. Yet, in that same year he also wrote an article on the early Suharto period which acknowledged the benefits of economic stability, compared with the downward spiral of poverty of the last years of Sukarno (Feith 1968b). With this ambiguous signature on two decades of intense application to understanding Indonesia, Feith shifted his intellectual focus to a wider canvas, and did not return to Indonesia for a decade.

Peace, justice, development

In the 1970s and 1980s, Herb Feith became much less an Indonesianist and more a social thinker, activist and educator preoccupied with the major themes of peace, justice and development – wider, global paradigms. His cosmopolitanism would be derived less from his far-reaching inter-cultural experience and would be based more on the writings of others on global issues. At the same time, he shifted his intellectual identity from that of a 'professionally political scientist kind of person' (Feith 1972: 1) to that of an engaged intellectual who could champion human rights and take political stands, firmly aligning himself with the traditions of value-oriented social inquiry. Developing an activist style, he also explored and refined a reflective approach to his values.

Feith came to be strongly influenced by a radical thinker on poverty and development, Ivan Illich, who established the Center for Intercultural Documentation in Mexico as a forum for discussion of the meaning of development in areas of public health, education and transportation. Illich had been born in Central Europe and went to the US after World War II as a Catholic priest in Harlem. He then became president of a Puerto Rican University before establishing the Center. Feith described it as a centre 'for thinking about new ways of tackling problems of poverty, unemployment and inequality . . . in ways which look to simple technology and human ingenuity'. Feith was greatly impressed by Illich's ideas, stating that his 'three page piece called "Outwitting the developers" . . . did more to turn my thinking on this whole subject upside down than all the learned articles I had been reading for years for my course' (Feith 1972: 5).

With these new frameworks, Feith wrote a major article on the phenomenon of 'repressive developmentalist' regimes, as a Third World regime type, which then included Brazil, Iran, South Korea and Indonesia (Feith 1982c). In these countries, highly authoritarian regimes, often militarised, presided over rapid economic growth and growing inequalities. These regimes created a degree of political legitimacy from the scale of growth, but at the same time undermined that legitimacy with the unequal distribution of costs and benefits. In an empirically open analytical style, Feith would list the 'case for' as well as the 'case against' these regimes, but the latter would weigh more heavily on his mind, and his argument. 'Growth' could no longer be seen as the same as 'development', and he became sharply critical of conventional assumptions that celebrated economic growth. He was shocked by the deepening corruption that came with the acquisition of massive wealth by key individuals close to these regimes, and analysed the narrowing basis of regime legitimacy and potential for legitimation crisis. In the case of Indonesia, Suharto's longevity as ruler confounded the analysis, as he remained in power until 1998, when the East Asian economic crisis finally drove him from office, leaving behind an economic ruin.

In the first half of the 1980s, the resurgence of Cold War tensions between the US and the Soviet Union, and the emergence of the European peace movement, created the context where Feith would become both a peace activist and peace educator. He was greatly concerned that the escalating nuclear arms race might lead to nuclear war, and he was one of the drivers behind the formation of the Victorian Association for Peace Studies (VAPS) in the early 1980s. He wrote with prescience in February 1980 about an emerging social movement (Feith 1980: 3; see also 1982b):

If I am right that we are all going to be seeing greater connections between global-level militarization and our own week-to-week lives, and that anti-militarism and survival will become the basis for new coalitions comparable to the anti-Vietnam war one and the anti-nuclear power one, and the anti-fascist one of the 1930s, we . . . are likely to find ourselves charged with a new range of common tasks.

VAPS established itself as an important component of the re-emerging Melbourne peace movement, the People for Nuclear Disarmament coalition, and undertook a range of activities that developed into a style of social activism for which Feith helped to set the model. These included calling public meetings; publishing 'dossiers' on key peace issues, and a newsletter that developed into a national peace magazine; building links with professional associations such as the Medical Association for the Prevention of War and church peace groups; and issuing 'Statements of Concern' to the media signed by a broad range of community leaders. At Monash University, Feith offered a highly innovative course entitled Peace: Theories, Strategies and Movements (Bretherton, Burns et al. 1989).

Cold War tensions eased in 1986 with the Reagan–Gorbachev talks, and within three years the nuclear threat of massive casualties from an 'East–West' conflict had disappeared. Conservatives would claim the US and Reagan 'won' the Cold War through economic and military strength. For Feith, the peace movement in Western Europe had played a crucial role in ending this confrontation of nuclear-armed powers. The massive display of international solidarity had demonstrated to the leaders of the Soviet Union that they had an exaggerated sense of the expansionist ambitions of the West, and to western leaders that the citizens of Europe were not prepared to be the passive pawns in a nuclear war.

Feith shared in the general mood of optimism over the prospects for a new world order after the Cold War. He saw this not just as an opportunity to address the continuing issue of potential inter-state violence, but to focus in a renewed way on the intractable issues of *intra-state* violence and injustice in many regions. Many of the crises of the twentieth century, and in particular the two world wars, took the form of inter-state violence, and the Cold War was an inter-state conflict between the two superpowers and their allies. Yet it was a conflict that often involved tight constraints on the behaviour of allies. Intra-state problems across the various continents were certainly not new (witness the massacres in Indonesia), but they appeared to increase in number and scale as the constraining settings of the Cold War vanished. In Africa, there was the Rwandan genocide of Tutsis by Hutus. In the case of Europe, the focus was on the violent disintegration of Yugoslavia. In Asia, the problems were often connected to the artificiality of the entities that became the successor states to the colonial order, with disaffected and often repressed minorities yearning for much greater autonomy and possibly secession. The pattern of violence was linked directly to the politics of repression and self-determination.

Feith had already shown an interest in this larger problem. In the early 1970s, for example, he closely followed the situation of the Pakistan civil war, and took on a public education role in Australia, arguing that the case for an independent state of Bangladesh was strong (Feith 1971). The Bangladeshi case was based on their sense of identity and legitimate representation, the repressive practices of the Pakistani government, and the impossibility of holding together a Pakistani state in two vastly separated halves.

Rethinking self-determination

In the 1990s, Feith ambitiously sought to engage the United Nations in a set of new processes to assist in the recognition of legitimate claims to self-determination. This would lead to much greater accountability for the treatment of regional and ethnic minorities by governments (Feith and Smith 1994). Writing with colleague Alan Smith, he framed the issue in an original and insightful fashion: the UN had played a critical role in the resolution of 'first generation self-determination claims', or the decolonisation of the world once controlled by European powers. Now there was a critical role in assessing and resolving 'second generation self-determination claims', by groups unreconciled to their place within the current state borders. He put out proposals for UN reform in a decade in which new hopes for the UN were often expressed, now that the superpower standoff that once permanently crippled the Security Council had ended. Of course, such proposals challenged the fundamental principle of sovereignty as 'non-interference', and yet they intersected with the new debates about humanitarian intervention, and the limits on sovereignty of those states that failed in their responsibility to protect their citizens.

To a number of groups seeking self-determination, Feith would elaborate a range of options, and often suggest a preference for seeking greater autonomy *within* states, for new kinds of federalism, rather than challenging the symbols of state sovereignty directly through demands for secession. He was strongly opposed to the idea that every claim of self-determination was a case for secession, and this led him into conflict with some sections of the social justice movement who might on principle champion a group's claims where there was an authoritarian government. His main reason for seeking accommodations along a spectrum of possibilities was pragmatic and informed by an essentially realist conception of international politics. Changing borders is often one of the hardest and most bloody struggles of international politics. Bangladesh was seen by Feith as very much the easy exception on separatism that confirmed the hard rule. After all, Pakistan was geographically in two parts, with its arch-rival India controlling the extensive territory in between.

Interestingly, Feith was relatively unconcerned with the dilemmas that would preoccupy many European cosmopolitan thinkers – over their distaste for the very idea of 'ethnic self-determination'. These European perspectives were in turn influenced by the Yugoslav experience of the 1990s, where there was far-reaching concern over the prospects of 'ethnic cleansing' by minorities who now found themselves free from repressive majorities. Feith was more willing to champion the cause of an oppressed group to secure a political space and reduce its exposure to violence, than to worry over how, in their ethnic particularism, once-oppressed groups would behave, if and when faced with their own minorities. But in addressing such groups, who may have thought little about their struggle as expressing global values, he was in turn also a counsel of accommodation, of new arrangements within states, of living in a better but less than perfect world. He wrote his own script on this complex global issue, with a focus on minimising violence, unimpressed by dogmas on the left or right of those who may romantically elevate the 'people' or the state as the agent of universal values. He was at times criticised by opponents and supporters of separatist groups alike for being too radical and for being too conservative.

Indonesia and East Timor

These explorations of a wider world canvas of intra-national conflict, from the global surveys of repressive developmentalist regimes to the proposals to reform the UN so that it may assist in the resolution of self-determination claims, did not stray that far from Feith's lifelong interest in Australia's neighbour, Indonesia. The sprawling archipelago of Indonesia was beset by a range of centrifugal forces, by claims by regional and ethnic groups for autonomy, and indeed for secession. The major claims were made in Aceh by Muslim separatists, in West Papua by the OPM (*Organisasi Papua Merdeka*, or Free Papua Movement), and by the East Timorese resistance. How should the validity of these claims be judged? Who was worthy of support?

These are difficult questions from a cosmopolitan perspective. Feith sought to develop principles and make political proposals on these questions, aware that his opinions and arguments carried considerable influence in academic circles, among NGOs in Australia and Indonesia, and among wider civil society networks mobilised behind the claims of particular groups. An important part of Feith's views was an abiding commitment to the idea of the Indonesian state as the expression of a larger community purpose. For him, it was an 'eminently reasonable' view that the Indonesian state 'rooted in eight decades of common endeavour and struggle, should not be allowed to founder' (Feith 1992a: 77). How, then, to balance this view against the claims of more particular ethno-nationalisms, in a context of conflict and oppression?

Feith took the following positions on issues of ongoing importance (Feith, Bell et al. 1986; Feith and Smith 1994).

Aceh had only a weak claim to secession from the Indonesian state. In the international norms of decolonisation, which was in effect the new international law, Indonesia was the successor state to the Dutch East Indies, and Aceh an integral part of it. If Aceh were to break away, the disintegrative forces would multiply. On the other hand, Aceh had serious complaints against the repression of the central government over many years, and of exploitation of resources, and there was clearly a case for substantial autonomy. This autonomy was eventually confirmed in 2005–06 after the devastation wreaked by the 2004 tsunami.

West Papua had a more protracted history of incorporation into Indonesia, as a Dutch holdout until a switch in US policy saw Indonesian control achieved through a 1962 agreement ending Dutch rule. West Papua was part of the Indonesian nationalist imagination from the beginning, and in international law its status is arguably similar to Aceh. This legality is qualified by the contrived act of incorporation conducted under UN auspices in 1969. Having allowed such an inadequate and manipulative process to take place, the UN remained open to the criticism that the outcome was invalid. The OPM emerged as an organisation seeking independence from Indonesia for West Papua. A distinct Melanesian identity is a core part of the OPM ethno-nationalism. Nevertheless, for Feith, West Papua should have substantial autonomy within Indonesia. He told a dialogue in East Jakarta about Aceh and West Papua (reported in *Jakarta Post* 2001):

> In the long run there should be a new formulation on the autonomy given to both provinces. For example, like those implemented in Hong Kong, which is part of Mainland China, or those imposed in England. Both provinces must be given greater authority and bargaining positions so that they can fully accommodate their needs.

When interviewed by the *Jakarta Post* in October 1999, Feith pointed out that one of the founders of the Indonesian state and later a vice president,

57

Mohammad Hatta, was a federalist by principle, and it was 'a greater degree of federalism' that Feith urged as a solution to secessionist struggles in Indonesia in both Aceh and Papua (King 2004: 74).

East Timor, however, was in another category, principally because it had not been part of the Dutch East Indies, and was not part of the Indonesian nationalist project that led to Indonesian independence. After the 1975 Indonesian invasion of the former Portuguese colony, Feith joined the attempts the following year to get the Indonesian Government to withdraw, and to lobby the Australian Government to refuse to condone the occupation. These efforts were unsuccessful, and the Australian Government became the first in the world to recognise Indonesia's claim to sovereignty over the area. Subsequently, the Hawke Labor government in 1984 formally abandoned the ALP's commitment to support an act of self-determination in East Timor. Feith campaigned assiduously to keep East Timorese self-determination alive in international forums, as well as in Indonesia and Australia, once the policy door in Australia had been shut.

Feith's activism was based on an argument about global decolonisation norms, and he presented alternatives which he thought may be accommodated by the international system even if they offered less than the East Timorese were entitled to (Feith 1992a). He argued this was essentially an unresolved 'first generation' self-determination claim where the East Timorese were entitled to be the successor state to Portuguese colonialism. However he proposed international solutions based on far-reaching autonomy, notionally within Indonesian sovereignty, which he thought might appeal to a post-Suharto leadership. This approach appealed to the East Timorese leadership at one time. Such ideas were attacked, however, by international supporters of East Timorese independence who were sometimes less interested in the possibility of a political compromise than the recognised leadership of the resistance.

In his campaigning, Feith drew attention to Indonesia's inability to carry the Non Aligned Movement with it on this issue (due especially to the influence of ex-Portuguese colonies), and how the occupation of East Timor continued to damage Indonesia's standing in world affairs. He publicised this damage to audiences in Indonesia in an attempt to build on the currents of independent thinking that existed under the authoritarian regime. He then mapped these currents of opinion inside Indonesia on the issue, and alerted non-Indonesian audiences about the possibilities of a change in policy after Suharto. In the 1990s, he wrote a series of incisive papers on the situation in East Timor, on Indonesian political turbulence and on the global NGO and state activities in support of East Timor (Feith 1992a; 1992b; 1992c; 1993). At the same time, he was also working against those in

Australian public life who represented 'Indonesia' itself as a threat to Australia rather than attributing responsibility to the nature of the specific Indonesian regime.

A less militarist approach for Australia

In addition to seeking a solution to East Timor's oppression, Feith was more generally interested in making the most of the post-Cold War opportunity in Australia's international diplomacy. He accepted that from governments, the best that may be expected was an internationalist rather than a cosmopolitan approach, as they were constrained by the system of 'sovereign' states and the idea of the 'national interest' in such a system. But the constraints were not absolute and there was an opportunity for governments to pursue 'good international citizenship' if they were supported in doing so. He encouraged the diplomatic rhetoric and activism of Australia's foreign minister, Gareth Evans, along with his emphasis on the UN, and UN reform.

One of Feith's major concerns, building on his knowledge and life experience of Australia and Indonesia, was the potential for an emerging arms race between Australia and Indonesia. He was apprehensive that the Indonesian armed forces and their political supporters would find additional reasons for maintaining their special status in Indonesian politics by pointing to the 'Australian threat'. He believed that the excessive military spending and modernisation program that Australia was embarking upon under the leadership of Labor's defence minister, Kim Beazley, in the late 1980s would contribute to this dynamic. These concerns led to his involvement in the Secure Australia Project (SAP) in the late 1980s and early 1990s. The Secure Australia Project, formed just as the Cold War was ending, sought to restrain the 'new militarism' which came to the fore briefly in the Labor Party. The project sought to reassert the primacy of foreign policy and diplomacy in regional relations. Feith hoped the existence of the project would be noticed in Indonesia and would help restrain some of the impulses to militarism in that state.

Beazley responded to the critique and rejected its argument, but he later acknowledged that his attempts to reassure Indonesian leaders had met 'with some scepticism' from them (Andrews 2001: 291). In an essay in a 2005 *Quarterly Essay* on 'Australia as a military power', writer John Birmingham (2005) paid tribute to the prescience of aspects of the 'new militarism' critique – and also to the fact that the Labor government of the time was willing to enter into an intellectual engagement with the arguments. Feith's concerns about the excessive military dimension to Australian foreign relations

59

are of continuing relevance in the contemporary situation. The Howard government's enthusiasm for a US military intervention in Iraq contributed to a spiral of violence in the Middle East, and was associated with a lack of interest or influence in wider areas of international citizenship (Cheeseman 2006).

Conclusion

In the midst of these energies, engagements and writings, Feith was also doing things that many other Australians might more easily relate to. He was married to Betty for almost fifty years, a father, then a grandfather, lived in suburban Glen Iris, held down a job at Monash University, paid the bills. He had less familiar qualities: a demanding and restless intellect, which Betty Feith put down to coming from a Central European Jewish background (at the time of the Holocaust). He lived out an anti-materialist lifestyle in an era of unprecedented boom in economic affluence. He was deeply interested in the spiritual, and deeply disaffected with the selective passions and narrow politics of mainstream Judaism, and organised religions generally. Betty Feith said she thought of him as a Christian. They met in the Student Christian Movement, and he went to church regularly. Feith wrote in his later years that he thought of himself as a 'syncretistic Jew', who added elements onto Judaism from other religions, in the way that many nominal Muslim Indonesians (*abangan*) added elements from other religions and cultures to fashion a personal syncrestic religious view (Feith 2002).

Contemporary research on the cross-cultural learning associated with the acquisition of a second or subsequent language and embedded cultural experiences emphasises that every person comes to occupy their unique hybrid inter-cultural space. Feith's cross-cultural engagement was so profound that he was seen by many as authoritative in the insights that he might offer to European Australians about their region. Feith was admired as a person who provided leadership to Australians, as to how they might relate to 'Asians', and to Australian policy makers and governments as to how they may relate to Asian governments. He gave grounds for this admiration in areas of continuing importance. For example, he spoke passionately for a humane approach to refugees in the Indochinese refugee crisis of the 1970s, promoting settlement schemes that could use the refugees' agricultural skills. He observed that 'I am one of those who owes his life to the fact that Australia was willing to open its doors to [a] sizeable number of European Jewish refugees in 1938–9' (Feith 1979: 25). Feith's self-perception as an educator was based on the need for all to fashion their own understanding of how to live in an interdependent world as one humanity. His personal example was too daunting and daring for most to be able to follow. In the area of cross-cultural understanding and empathy, he led a kind of exemplary life that began as an overseas volunteer and developed into an immersion in two cultures, to become an unconventional, yet striking and influential figure in both.

For all his cosmopolitanism, Feith was keenly aware of the policy settings of states in the international system, and acted and argued as though Australian policy makers and Indonesian policy makers could make a difference. They had choices on fundamental matters of human wellbeing; they could make different and better ones under the pressure of social movements and civil society activism. Feith certainly made a difference by opening up people-to-people exchanges between Australia and Indonesia, and by arguing persistently for the importance of a just world order. His voice, urging practical action towards such an order, was heard by many, as witnessed by the overflowing attendance at memorial ceremonies in three countries – Australia, Indonesia and East Timor – after his accidental death.

Long before the idea of an emerging global civil society that would influence and moderate the behaviour of states had become a familiar one, Feith was active in civil society networks across the two societies. He pursued complementary agendas, which could advance greater understanding between communities and shape inter-governmental relations towards directions that would advance peace and justice in the region. In this engagement with state power, Feith was always in some way 'arguing with the militia on the veranda'.

Note

1 I would like to thank Betty Feith, who kindly provided me with access to the Herb Feith archives at Monash University and the National Library of Australia, and also Roderic Pitty for his invaluable comments and suggestions for improvement.

References

Andrews, E. M. 2001. *The Australian Centenary History of Defence*. Melbourne: Oxford University Press.

Anheier, H. K., M. H. Kaldor and M. Glasius 2006. *Global Civil Society 2005/6*. London: Sage Publications.

Benda, H. J. 1964. 'Review article: Democracy in Indonesia.' *Journal of Asian Studies* 23(3):449–56.

Birmingham, J. 2005. 'Australia as a military power.' *Quarterly Essay* 20. Melbourne: Black Inc.

Bretherton, D., R. Burns and G. Davey (eds) 1989. *Peace Studies in Australia and New Zealand*. Melbourne: Victorian Association for Peace Studies.

Cheeseman, G. 2006. 'A time for war: Correspondence.' *Quarterly Essay* 21:76–81.

Diprose, R. 2002. 'The first volunteer.' *Inside Indonesia* (70):17.

Encounter 2003. 'In memory of Herb Feith.' ABC Radio National, 9 March 2003, viewed 14 January 2008, http://www.abc.net.au/rn/relig/enc/stories/s796902.htm

Feith, H. 1962. *The Decline of Constitutional Democracy in Indonesia*. Ithaca: Cornell University Press.

——1965. 'History, theory and Indonesian politics: A reply to Harry J. Benda.' *Journal of Asian Studies* 24(2):305–12.

——1967. 'The dynamics of guided democracy.' In R. T. McVey (ed.) *Indonesia*. New Haven, CT: Southeast Asia Studies, Yale University by arrangement with HRAF Press.

——1968a. 'A blot on the "New Order's" record: The fate of 80 000 political prisoners in Indonesia.' Unpublished longer draft of article for *The New Republic*.

——1968b. 'Suharto's search for a political format.' *Indonesia* (6):88–105.

——1971. *Asia's Flashpoint, 1971: Bangla Desh*. Bedford Park, SA: Flinders University of South Australia.

——1972. 'Growth and development in Asia: Some criticisms of conventional approaches.' Lecture to the Asia Leadership Development Centre. Tosanzo Japan: October.

——1979. 'Australian immigration policy and Asia.' In R. Birrell (ed.) *Refugees, Resources, Reunion: Australia's Immigration Dilemmas*. Fitzroy, VIC: VCTA Publishing, pp. 21–6.

——1980. Letter addressed 'Dear Fellow Nonians', 21 Feb. Feith correspondence with Dan Lev, National Library of Australia.

——1982a. 'The study of Indonesian politics: A survey and an apologia.' In B. R. O. G. Anderson and A. Kahin (eds) *Interpreting Indonesian Politics: Thirteen Contributions to the Debate*. Ithaca, NY: Cornell Modern Indonesia Project, Southeast Asia Program, Cornell University.

——1982b. 'Australia and the struggle for peace and justice in its region.' *Social Alternatives* 2(3):53–64.

——1982c. 'Repressive developmentalist regimes in Asia.' *Alternatives* 7(4):491–506.

——1992a. 'East Timor: The opening up, the crackdown and the possibility of a durable settlement.' In H. Crouch and H. Hill (eds) *Indonesia Assessment 1992: Political Perspectives on the 1990s*. Canberra, ACT: Australian National University, pp. 63–82.

——1992b. 'New moves for peace in East Timor – Jose Ramos Horta's proposals.' *Inside Indonesia* (31):12–14.

——1992c. 'East Timor: After the Dili massacre.' *Pacific Research* 5(1):3–5.

——1993. 'The East Timor issue since the capture of Xanana Gusmao.' Fitzroy, VIC: East Timor Talks Campaign.

——1994. 'Constitutional democracy: How well did it function?' In D. Bourchier and J. Legge (eds) *Democracy in Indonesia: 1950s and 1990s*. Clayton, VIC: Centre for Southeast Asian Studies, Monash University, pp. 16–25.

——2002. 'A syncretistic Jew.' *Inside Indonesia* (70):21–2.

Feith, H., I. Bell and R. Hatley 1986. 'The West Papuan challenge to Indonesian authority in Irian Jaya: Old problems, new possibilities.' *Asian Survey* (5):539–56.

Feith, H. and A. Smith 1994. 'Self determination in the 1990s: Equipping the UN to resolve ethno-nationalist conflict.' In K. Rupesinghe (ed.) *Conflict Transformation.* New York: St Martin's Press, pp. 143–61.

King, P. 2004. *West Papua and Indonesia Since Suharto: Independence, Autonomy or Chaos?* Sydney: UNSW Press.

Jakarata Post, 18 January 2001, as viewed 14 January 2008, http://www.1worldcommunication.org/policiesontroubledaceh.htm

Mackie, J. 2002. 'Ideas man: Herb Feith's search for better mental road maps to a complex Indonesia.' *Inside Indonesia* 70 (April–June):19–21.

Jack Mundey

Jack Mundey is a trade unionist and environmentalist. He was secretary of the New South Wales Builders Labourers Federation (NSW BLF) in the early 1970s during the 'green ban' movement, leading the protests against the destruction of inner-city heritage sites such as The Rocks and Kelly's Bush. Mundey was instrumental in creating alliances between local community groups and the trade unions to protect the urban environment. He continues to campaign on environmental issues, arguing the need for unions and communities to band together to create a better quality of life for all citizens. In 1997 he was named an Australian Living Treasure. In 2000 he was made an Officer of the Order of Australia. He joined the Australian Greens in 2003. The University of Sydney has created a Master of Environment degree to honour Mundey's work.

Trade unionist and green bans leader Jack Mundey continuing his work to protect urban heritage in later life. (Courtesy of NSW Historic Houses Trust Members.)

4

Jack Mundey: The Global Responsibilities of Labour

Michael Leach[1]

Jack Mundey is well known as a trade unionist, environmentalist and urban campaigner. As he has always maintained strong notions of the moral obligations of citizens belonging to a global community, and argued that political action should foster recognition of a common humanity, he may also be called a global citizen. While this is not the only way to understand Mundey's lifetime as an activist and radical thinker,[2] this chapter offers a complementary perspective on Mundey as a cosmopolitan activist, whose political ideas were expressions of a universalist civic and ecological concern. In particular, Mundey and the leadership group[3] of the New South Wales Builders Labourers Federation (NSW BLF) in the early 1970s spoke of the 'social responsibility of labour'. By this they meant that industrial struggles should be linked to ecological sustainability, and to broader social and moral obligations of solidarity with progressive international political movements (see e.g. Mundey 1980: 280–3). The most well known of these actions were the innovative 'green bans' on socially and ecologically damaging development, which had dramatic impacts both nationally and overseas. It is argued here that Jack Mundey's long life of activism has been characterised by an appeal to universal values and responsibilities, which he sees as a means for citizens to address political problems within and beyond Australia. This chapter first examines the political and historical context of the green bans, and then suggests five key themes of Mundey's political thought and activism which identify him as a global citizen. These themes cover Mundey's public commitments to the preservation of the urban environment, the 'social responsibility of labour', a critique of 'growthmania', solidarity within and beyond national borders and to re-enfranchising forms of direct, participatory democracy.

The green bans in context

In the early 1970s, urban planning and heritage protection controls were virtually non-existent. In the midst of an unprecedented building boom, many areas of Sydney came under threat of development, including Kelly's Bush, Woolloomooloo, Centennial Park, the Rocks area and Victoria Street in Kings Cross. An important context to the rise of the green bans was the failure of local and state governments in New South Wales to address widespread concerns over the social consequences of unfettered development. It was an era of unprecedented building expansion, and the then Askin Liberal government of New South Wales was notorious for its close personal and political ties with developers. At the time, planning regulations gave residents affected by development proposals no genuine avenues for appeal (Burgmann and Burgmann 1998: 46–9).

In this context of 'state failure' to address mounting public concerns over unfettered development, the BLF's coverage of over 90 per cent of builders' labourers gave it considerable influence. Equally, as Mundey put it at the time, builders' labourers had a unique influence by virtue of being the 'first on and last off site'. By the early 1970s, the NSW BLF had already established itself as a radical union, having taken an active stance on Aboriginal land rights, opposition to the Vietnam War, and other social issues. At this time, the NSW BLF leadership began to express the view that unions should be involved in wider ranging social and environmental issues.

In this sense, the actions of the NSW BLF may be understood within the context of New Left politics, which ventured beyond the traditional 'Old Left' focus on class to question other forms of social oppression and disenfranchisement. This generational shift included a wider questioning of the future of the cities (see e.g. Stretton 1970), and a renewed interest in urban politics with the rise of the Whitlam government in 1972. As a trade union, the NSW BLF had particular significance as a bridge between these 'old' and 'new' social movements. With distinctive ideological influences, it was a union particularly suited to this task. Part of the context to the green bans lies in the wider history of trade union political action.

As a member of the then non-aligned[4] Communist Party of Australia (CPA), Mundey came from a union tradition which saw broader social and political action as core aspects of union activity. Under the leadership of the Communist Party, important precursors of this tradition included Waterside Workers Federation bans to prevent pig-iron exports to Japan in 1938 (Mallory 1992: 44) and to support the Indonesian independence struggle in the late 1940s.

As this chapter seeks to demonstrate, Mundey and the leadership group of the NSW BLF transformed this existing CPA tradition of 'political action' into a broader form of global citizenship, in the universal interest of people from all classes. Notably, the popularity of these new forms of urban environmentalism saw Mundey's political influence survive the dissolution of the Australian CPA in 1991. Several important universalist themes emerge from Mundey's long history of political and environmental activism. The following point distinctively to Jack Mundey as a cosmopolitan political thinker and activist.[5]

Preservation of the urban environment

Responding to requests from local residents to stop an A. V. Jennings housing development in Kelly's Bush – one of inner Sydney's few remaining green spaces – the NSW BLF leadership sensed the opportunity to 'turn theory in practice' (Mundey 2004). Within a short time of the initial Sydney ban in June 1971, the concept of the 'green ban' was articulated. These were union work bans to prevent destruction of urban green space, historic and heritage buildings, and the corporate redevelopment of inner-city working-class neighbourhoods (see e.g. Burgmann and Burgmann 1998; 1999; Mundey 1980). It has been estimated that these innovative actions prevented around $5 billion of ecologically destructive development (Burgmann and Burgmann 1999: 44), most famously in the cases of Kelly's Bush and the Rocks in inner Sydney. Over the next three years, forty-two separate bans were imposed and some sixty heritage buildings were saved. These interventions added a new strength and focus to the conservation movement, by highlighting the universal problem of quality of life and socially and ecologically responsible planning in the cities (Mundey 1976b).

This innovative focus on the built environment as a conservation issue occurred at a time when inner cities were ceasing to be the exclusive domain of the working class. The green bans had a unique capacity to unite middle class concerns for 'quality of life' issues, with working class concerns over loss of housing and community in the inner city. This twin focus on preventing the destruction of older working class areas, and maintaining urban green space, gave the green bans a broad appeal. Ultimately, these actions had the effect of encouraging greater citizen participation in urban planning, and would be credited with the renovation of planning processes in Australia and the 'democratisation' of heritage protection (Freestone 1993). Importantly, the green ban movement was explicitly articulated in the context of 'state failure' at all levels of government, necessitating a new urban politics involving the coordination of trade union and resident action groups. More broadly, the emerging focus on 'socially useful' development (Mundey 1980: 285) prompted calls from the BLF for a building industry commission 'to determine which and what kind of buildings were to be constructed and to do this in a planned, and not in an anarchic manner' (Mundey 1980: 284). The green ban movement encouraged more socially responsible development and ultimately transformed the culture of urban planning. Crucial to these actions was Mundey's conception of the 'social responsibility of labour'.

Social responsibility of labour

> . . . [the green bans] were different because we weren't fighting to increase wages and conditions, but we were responding to a request to use our strength in a new way in the interests of the environment . . . it was a more noble, honourable action than just looking after the hip-pocket nerve (Mundey 2004).

Mundey and the NSW BLF in the 1970s spoke of the 'social responsibility of labour': the idea that industrial struggles should be linked to broader issues of ecological sustainability, and solidarity with international political movements. Most distinctively, the NSW BLF leadership boldly envisaged a new role for the union movement as a 'social conscience' in the protection of the natural and built environment (Mundey 1980: 280). Fundamental to this core philosophy was Mundey's view that all economic classes and social strata share interests in an ecologically sustainable future, particularly in the context of rapid global urbanisation (Mundey 1980: 280). This focus placed the NSW BLF in a cosmopolitan tradition of recognising moral affiliations and obligations beyond the local and immediate needs of members. The green bans were explicitly articulated as a form of moral political action, to distinguish them from the 'black bans' designed specifically to sustain members' wages and conditions. As Mundey (1980: 283) put it:

> . . . in 'green ban' actions, workers were making conscious decisions to withhold their labour. *It was a moral action, and it took into account other people's wishes, feelings and aspirations.* (emphasis in original)

The NSW BLF saw itself as developing a 'new concept of unionism', founded in the core concept of a wider responsibility to intervene on behalf of universal social and ecological interests. This 'new concept' offered a critique of traditional union and labourite 'economism', and outlined innovative concerns for socially responsible production and employment (Mundey 1973: 17–19; 1976a: 30). If necessary, these obligations could extend to refusing work, and, at times, sacrificing the immediate 'interests' of members, for wider social goods in the common interests of the community (Mundey 1976a: 34). While the concrete political actions of the NSW BLF inevitably took place in local contexts, they were motivated by wider concerns and conceived as universal issues. Primary among these were the protection of urban environments and a focus on 'quality of life', rather than 'standard of living' (Mundey 1988: 19).

Mundey extended the CPA concept of political action – itself a critique of a narrow trade union 'economism' which evinced concern for wages and conditions alone – to focus on the ends rather than the means of production, and particularly on the ecological impact of socially destructive work, arguing that workers should be concerned with the products of their labour (see Mallory 1992; 2000; Mundey 1981: 145). As Mundey put it (1976a: 30):

[a]ll strands of revolutionary thinking have been essentially economist in character, with a concentration on aiming to win control of the means of production, with insufficient consideration as to the ends of production, the social nature of labour, and almost total neglect of ecological consequences of the use of workers' labour and of industrial development.

Mundey thereby extended a more traditional CPA conception of internationalism by emphasising 'the importance of the more enlightened middle class and the more enlightened working class coming together' (Burgmann and Burgmann 1998: 286) in the universal interests of humanity in a sustainable future. Mundey and the BLF demonstrated these principles through their willingness to respond to appeals from different community groups, and by developing political alliances which transcended traditional class associations (Mundey 1980: 285). Here, Mundey's political activism entered a more distinctively cosmopolitan tradition (Mundey 1976a: 34).

If industrial workers and their organisations can break with economism, and commence to question which commodities, goods and services should be made *in the interests of society in general* – yes, there is a future – but only if the progressive section of the populations of the advanced industrialised countries . . . can give assistance to the third world countries. (emphasis in original).

This focus allowed the NSW BLF to present trade union activity in the form of work bans as representative of universal interests (Burgmann and Burgmann 1999: 45). Mundey was thereby able to express 'the way in which working class interests coincide with those of a constituency as large as the world itself' (Burgmann and Burgmann 1999: 46). Articulating a new ethic of the global responsibility of labour, with some roots in older utopian socialist traditions of class action in the interest of society as a whole, this stance allowed the green ban movement to position workers as global citizens, possessing the right and responsibility to 'insist that their labour was not used in harmful ways' (Burgmann and Burgmann 1998: 3). This was combined with a strong commitment to a democratising tradition of direct citizen participation in global issues. The green bans were thus a prototype of 'social movement unionism' and 'an entirely homegrown contribution to international environmental politics and radical practice' (Burgmann and Burgmann 1998: 4). Mundey responded to the criticism among some on the traditional left who labelled the BLF the 'darling of the trendies, engaging in middle class issues', by arguing that environmental issues transcended any one class. Equally, though, the NSW BLF and some urban activists of the time were quick to note that the working class had the most to lose from unregulated urban redevelopment (see Mundey 1973; Stretton 1970: 1, 5; Thomas 1973). For Jack Mundey, this core critique of unregulated urbanisation and quality of life in the cities led to a wider focus on sustainability.

Critique of 'growthmania'

Expanding his critique of urbanisation, Mundey criticised 'growthmania' in both East and West, rejecting the blind adherence in both systems to economic growth models. Both continued to 'worship the holy cow of GNP', and growth for growth's sake (Mundey 1976b: 346), failing to take account of the social and environmental costs. Trade union power, he argued, in league with sections of the progressive middle class, should be used to moderate the economic ideal of progress to ensure better social and environmental outcomes. As he noted in 1976, 'what is the good of winning higher wages if we are living in cities that are polluted; if we are living in cities without parks and bare of trees; if we live in a city without a soul' (Mundey 1976b: 346).

Here, Mundey explicitly articulated concerns for quality of life, socially useful production, and socially useful employment (Mundey 1976a: 33; 1988: 19) embodied in the 'Three Es': employment, energy use and environment. In the early 1970s, Mundey established and convened Environmentalists for Full Employment, dedicating himself to the central problem of 'the carefully orchestrated myth' that environmental protection would lead to increased unemployment (Burgmann and Burgmann 1999: 59).

The theme of 'socially useful production' (Mundey 1980: 297) comprised a critique of overdevelopment and consumer culture, and a commitment to moderating an exclusively economic notion of progress to ensure a better quality of life. Mundey (1988: 20) specifically advocated socially responsible job creation schemes to repair environmental damage. In a comment which continues to resonate in contemporary Australia, he noted that such jobs would be necessary to combat the short-sighted 'jobs versus the environment' argument (Mundey 1988: 19). Mundey saw these issues distinctively as local expressions of a global problem, which afflicted socialist command economies and capitalist countries alike. For the Burgmanns (1999: 60), Mundey and the NSW BLF offered inspiration to those 'who seek to use working class power to express the universal interests in environmental action'.

Solidarity politics

Not all bans were 'green'. The NSW BLF actively supported a range of other progressive causes, both within and beyond Australia. These included anti-apartheid activism, land rights, anti-war actions, women's and gay rights (see Mundey 1980: 280; Burgmann and Burgmann 1999: 52–3) and even prison reform (Mundey 1973: 18). As Mulligan and Hill (2002: 267) note, Mundey was heavily involved in the Gurindji land rights campaign as president of the Sydney district branch of the CPA.

For Mundey, workers had responsibilities as global citizens which could be expressed through union action. Mundey's explicit views on these questions accord strongly with the cosmopolitan notion of 'concentric circles' of moral and political commitment (Vertovec and Cohen 2002: 12): first, to improve wages and conditions of members; then to social action with other citizens; and finally, to solidarity with Third World movements (Mundey and Polites 1975: 60).[6] In debate with the then director of the Australian Council of Employers' Federations, George Polites, Mundey linked quality of life in urban environments and the social responsibility of labour to arguments about the importance of global solidarity. In so doing, he made some prescient comments, foreshadowing anti-globalisation protest positions of the 1990s and beyond. We are in a 'shrinking world', he argued, in which the 'grip of the multinational corporations can be felt in every part of the globe'. Unions must link together in international solidarity, with the aim of 'a more global response to [workers'] claims, with environmental considerations taken into account' (Mundey 1975: 14). Through the focus on a universal ecological interest, common to all humanity, the political actions of the NSW BLF moved well beyond a more traditional left conception of internationalism, towards a cosmopolitan conception of global citizenship.

The growing influence of these ideas within the Australian trade union movement was evident in the establishment of Union Aid Abroad in 1984. Also known as Australian People for Health, Education and Development Abroad (APHEDA),[7] Union Aid Abroad is strongly supported through subscriptions from trade union members, and emphasises direct aid to workers in developing countries, bypassing official state aid agencies. By fostering direct networks of global social responsibility, Union Aid Abroad highlights the distinction between the participatory forms of global citizenship that Mundey advocated, and the state-based forms of international citizenship embodied by official agencies such as AusAID. Tellingly, the rise of this particular expression of the global responsibility of labour contrasted markedly with the decline in official Australian aid levels since the 1980s. More broadly, Mundey's concern for democratic renewal within the union movement, along with the grassroots approach of the green bans, signalled a wider concern with a revitalised citizen politics.

Participatory democracy

> The Green bans had a heartening effect, and allowed people to feel their own strength (Mundey 2004).

Mundey and the NSW BLF were committed to developing both internal and wider social mechanisms for a more participatory democracy. Central to this project was the development of 'citizen/worker coalitions', to broaden community participation in political decision making. As Mundey put it (1975: 20), 'unions are beginning to link up with conservation, environment, ecology and resident action groups, in exciting alliances which have given a tangible new dimension to citizen activity on many "quality of life" issues'. This conception of the citizen–worker coalition was a response to the perceived failure of government to meet the needs of citizens (Mundey 1976b: 347), and opened the space for a new type of politics in which individuals have a greater voice in deciding issues affecting their communities. This notion of a new citizen politics, in which coalitions of individuals take direct action to address collective problems, accords strongly with the values of cosmopolitan democracy (Carter 1997: 71). Taken together, these actions encouraged the development of an alternative arena of direct citizen politics.

For Mundey, the green bans movement was explicitly conceived as a strategy to maximise political participation (Mundey 1976b: 351):

> I see Green Bans not as an end in themselves – [but] a tactic to bring about people's participation and not just allow the engineers, architects, town planners, developers and their friends in high places in government to determine how the community should develop.

Green ban actions were only ever initiated in response to requests by Resident Action Groups (RAGs) (Mundey 1973: 17).[8] In these actions, Mundey and the leadership group of the NSW BLF sought to work towards inclusive, participatory forms of democracy capable of connecting local actions with global problems. 'Community action,' he wrote, 'even though it can be in the interest of your particular house, your particular community can, in fact, lead to wider social understanding' (Mundey 1976b: 352). These forms of civic engagement represented a revitalisation of the public sphere (Mundey, 1976b: 352–3):

> I believe that action by people – extra-parliamentary action – has a vital role to play in bringing greater degrees of democracy into being . . . I believe in every-day democracy. Surely democracy doesn't mean going to a ballot box once every 3 years and casting a ballot paper. To me, democracy is acting on one's conscience every day and facing up to responsibilities.

Importantly, in a tradition of 'self-exemplification' more common to new social movements than to trade unions, Mundey and the NSW BLF focused strongly on radical democracy within the union, including limited tenure for office holders (Mundey 1973: 18–19). This position alienated many other union leaders and ultimately contributed to the downfall of the NSW BLF after the federal intervention in its affairs, led by Norm Gallagher (see Burgmann and Burgmann 1998: 267–74).

While many critics and political opponents protested that the green bans usurped or supplanted the role of government, defenders supported the NSW BLF precisely because they filled the vacuum created by the failure of mainstream political leadership; and did the 'State's job' for them (Burgmann and Burgmann 1998: 293). For supporters, the bans broadened public space and sought to realise more participatory models of democratic governance. Indeed, governments of the time had difficulty responding to the green ban movement, precisely because they were grassroots campaigns involving broad coalitions of citizen residents and unionists (Mundey 1973: 17). Effectively, the green bans operated as 'holding operations' (Mundey 1976b: 351) which opened the way for forms of participatory democracy, and delayed the impacts of unfettered development while politics 'caught up'. This emphasis on the moral responsibilities of citizens to see beyond local and national commitments and work towards a democratic, participatory and sustainable future signals Mundey and the NSW BLF as exemplars of cosmopolitan democracy in action.

Impacts: local and global

The innovative green ban movement had dramatic impacts – both nationally and internationally. The election of the Wran Labor government in 1976 was followed by the creation of official state environmental and planning mechanisms in New South Wales. These included the Land and Environment Court, legal aid for resident action groups' planning objections, and heritage protection legislation, including demolition controls over heritage buildings. In this way, the green bans contributed to establishing a legal and institutional framework that extended and gave substance to citizen rights and duties. Though some of these planning and heritage controls were watered down in the 1990s, these results of extra-parliamentary direct action, with their genesis in the green ban movement, set in train new community consultation, objection and approval procedures that continue to regulate urban planning regimes.

At a national level, the green bans were an integral element of wider concerns over urban politics. With Tom Uren as Minister for Urban and Regional Development, the Whitlam Labor government raised the profile of urban planning issues in the cities. In April 1973, Uren introduced legislation leading to the creation of the Australian Cities Commission.[9] The green bans movement also influenced the Whitlam government in setting up the Committee of Inquiry into the National Estate in 1973, and the *Environmental Protection Act* of 1974. The former led ultimately to the establishment of the Australian Heritage Commission.

More broadly, environmental groups around the world expressed interest in the green bans movement, and the possibility of involving broader coalitions of citizens in environmental actions (Roddewig 1978). Pitt (cited in Mulligan and Hill 2002: 269) uses the term 'green Guevara', noting that outside Australia, Jack Mundey is regarded a 'virtual Messiah' to environment movements. Mundey was one of twenty-four 'world thinkers' invited to address the first UN conference on the built environment in Vancouver in 1976 (Mulligan and Hill 2002: 264), and toured the UK at the invitation of the Centre for Environmental Studies in London. At this time, he was instrumental in instigating a ban to prevent the demolition of the Birmingham post office, a significant Victorian-era building with considerable heritage value in the eyes of local residents.

For Mulligan and Hill (2002: 264), the concept of citizen-worker alliances greatly impressed European political movements. Indeed, Bob Brown credits Mundey as the originator of the term 'green politics' internationally. German Greens leader Petra Kelly also regarded him as a 'major inspiration for the formation of green parties in Europe' (Mulligan and Hill 2002: 244, 264). Internationally renowned ecologist Paul Ehrlich said the green bans movement 'heralded the international birth of urban environmentalism as distinct from nature conservation' (Mulligan and Hill 2002: 269). Mundey has clearly been a major influence on Bob Brown, and the previously 'eco-centric' green movement – influencing the rise of policies relevant to those living in cities (Mulligan and Hill 2002: 244). As Mulligan and Hill (2002: 273) note, 'starting from different directions, Mundey and Brown have helped to build a bridge between the environmentalism of the city and the bush'.

Looking forward

Jack Mundey is still directly involved in environmental campaigns in Sydney, including the more recent – and successful – CFMEU green ban on the construction of a McDonald's outlet in Centennial Park in 2000. At the time of our interview in mid-2004, the Greens had recently enjoyed major victories in inner city council elections in Sydney, securing near majorities in the Leichhardt and Marrickville Councils, and doubling their representation across the state of New South Wales. For Mundey (2004), these developments hold out promise of a new coalition for a sustainable future:

> A left of the future must come together with a green agenda and win the hearts
> and minds of people . . . The union movement has a responsibility to move
> to the left, those who consider themselves left have to become more militant
> and link up with better grouping within the Greens, as has happened in local
> governments in many parts of the country.

When asked how trade unions can act with social responsibility in an era of higher unemployment and lower industry coverage, Jack Mundey refers back to the core themes of union militancy, direct democracy, and ecological action in the interest of workers and a wider public. In his view, the first task for unions is to become more militant in establishing greater control over the growing casualisation of work, to give more permanency to the workforce. The second and wider issue is one of direction. Mundey argues that the union movement has not taken up the issue of the environment at the grassroots level, with a 'vigorous leadership' going onto building sites and tapping the 'enormous potential' of rank and file workers. For Mundey, the key to the rejuvenation of unions, and the left more broadly, is an alliance with environmental and ecological movements, the new 'third force' in Australian politics. Mundey stood as the fourth Green candidate for the Senate in New South Wales in the 2007 federal election. Although a Green senator from that state was not re-elected, the Greens received nearly 460 000 votes and Mundey secured an unusually high 'below-the-line' personal vote.

Reflecting upon recent events, Mundey commented on the values and responsibilities of a 'globalist' in a new century. While he acknowledges that globalisation has concentrated unprecedented power in transnational corporations, the core issue of corporate power over the decisions affecting the daily lives of a majority remains the same. The main responsibilities of a globalist continue to be those of breaking the power of transnational corporations in the interests of a livable and sustainable future for humanity. For Mundey, the significance of globalisation lies in the reality that global action against corporate power is 'more pressing' than ever. Equally, given the rise of neo-conservatism in the United States, Mundey believes the UN must reassert itself after the 'devastating and dangerous' episodes of unilateralism. He is quick to note, however, that any progressive multilateralism is more likely to be driven by non-state actors and the massive 'global opposition' created in recent years, particularly in Europe. In these views, Mundey reflects a long held commitment to participatory democracy, and to the moral obligations of citizens to transcend local and national interests to address global problems of social and ecological sustainability. As for the green bans, Mundey (2004) remains optimistic, despite concerns over the relative decline in union influence.

> The idea of the green bans is still alive – nothing like they were – but even in these circumstances it is possible to bring environmentalists and unionists together in common action. That potential is there and will be in the future. It is there to be won, and the union movement must become more radical. It will wither on the vine if it takes the conservative path it is taking now. Unless the union movement becomes more involved in the environment and in ecological issues, you cannot see it making a comeback.

Conclusion

For recent cosmopolitan thinkers, economic globalisation poses new risks of citizen disenfranchisement at a national level, and increased possibilities for social and ecological harm (Elliot and Cheeseman 2002: 12; Heater 2001: 182). By the same token, these developments have created new possibilities for transnational political action, and added considerable urgency to ideas and practices of global citizenship. If, indeed, there are universal moral obligations on global citizens, a key question for modern cosmopolitan thinkers is that of identifying these particular responsibilities. This chapter has argued that one of the achievements of Jack Mundey was his role in articulating and popularising core aspects of these universal obligations in an Australian context. Specifically, it has been argued that Mundey and the NSW BLF made groundbreaking contributions to urban environmentalism and conservation, to a now influential critique of unregulated growth, and to broader notions of global citizenship embodied in the ideas and practices of socially responsible labour, participatory democracy, and global solidarity politics.

These political ideas, actions and alliances advocated by Jack Mundey stand as an important local expression of universal civic and ecological concerns. In an age of growing concern over climate change, they continue to inspire the types of radical thinking critical to an ecologically sustainable future. Mundey (1977: 11) explicitly put these political problems and actions in a cosmopolitan framework, stressing the need for local action to meet the universal responsibilities implicit in global ecological problems:

> self-help . . . actions in each country must be the main struggle . . . [but] this must not be posed against an increasing need for more global consider-ations of human problems, and the need to see these international problems as *our* problems, which we can do something about by increasing aware-ness, improving communications . . . and by coordinated actions of people concerned with retaining a habitable planet. (emphasis in original)

In light of the resurgence of exclusionist nationalism in Australia in the past decade, Jack Mundey may be celebrated as one of the forebears of an alter-native tradition of imagining a transnational 'moral community' to which Australians belong, in the universal interest of ecological sustainability.

Notes

1 I would like to thank Geoff Stokes and Roderic Pitty for their valuable comments on this chapter.
2 Burgmann and Burgmann (1999: 50), for example, see Mundey, quite properly, as a 'leading' intellectual figure within the working class who sought to give it a 'conscious-ness of its function not only in the economic field but in the social and political field as well'.

3 Key members of the NSW BLF leadership group of the period included Joe Owens and Bob Pringle. As I rely on his writings and interviews, I refer primarily to Mundey throughout.

4 The CPA declared itself independent of 'Moscow-line' politics following an internal split in 1971 over the invasion of Czechoslovakia in 1968.

5 As many commentators note, one obstacle to the renovation of cosmopolitan political thought is the predominance of a 'non-philosophical' (Kleingeld and Brown 2002) or everyday meaning of the cosmopolitan as an urbane traveller, at home every-where, enjoying a 'comfortable familiarity with a variety of geographical and cultural environments' (Heater 2001: 179). This conception of cosmopolitanism as the 'class consciousness of frequent travellers' (Calhoun cited in Vertovec and Cohen, 2002: 6) has informed much popular, and even intellectual suspicion of the term. It presents an 'elite' image of rootless cosmopolites – separated from and unsympathetic to the dominant sources of modern political identity and community. If one of the tasks of renovating cosmopolitan political thought is to displace this 'aloof, globetrotting bourgeois image of cosmopolitanism' (Vertovec and Cohen 2002: 21), and reclaim its political content, then the example of trade union leader and working class activist Jack Mundey may offer a useful corrective.

6 This example illustrates Kleingeld and Brown's (2002: 8) distinction between 'strict cosmopolitans' and 'moderate cosmopolitans' like Mundey, who would see 'special duties to compatriots' as legitimate provided a wider universal interest is not compromised. This distinction has roots in the Cynic and Stoic positions.

7 See http://www.apheda.org.au

8 Mundey noted in 1976 that there were over 500 RAGs in Australia – 'precisely because of the breakdown of government, particularly at state and municipal levels'.

9 Mundey resigned from the Cities Commission in 1974 as a result of what he saw as the low level of citizen participation is its processes (Mundey 1981: 128).

References

Burgmann, V. and M. Burgmann 1998. *Green Bans, Red Union: Environmentalism and the New South Wales Builders Labourers' Federation.* Sydney: University of New South Wales Press.

——1999. '"A rare shift in public thinking": Jack Mundey and the New South Wales Builders Labourers' Federation.' *Labour History* 77:44–63.

Carter, A. 1997. 'Nationalism and global citizenship.' *Australian Journal of Politics and History* 43(1):67–81.

Elliot, L. and G. Cheeseman 2002. 'Cosmopolitan theory, militaries and the deployment of force.' Department of International Relations Working Paper 2002/8. Canberra: ANU.

Freestone, R. 1993. 'Heritage, urban planning, and the postmodern city.' *Australian Geographer* 24(1):17–24.

Heater, D. 2001. 'Does cosmopolitan thinking have a future?' In Booth, K., T. Dunne and M. Cox (eds) *How Might We Live?* Cambridge: Cambridge University Press, pp. 179–97.

Kleingeld, P. and E. Brown 2002. 'Cosmopolitanism.' In E. N. Zalta (ed.) *The Stanford Encyclopedia of Philosophy.* (Fall 2002 Edition) The Metaphysics

Research Lab, Stanford University: Stanford, viewed 16 September 2003, at http://plato.stanford.edu/archives/fall2002/entries/cosmopolitanism/

Mallory, G. 1992. 'The social responsibility of labour: (1) The Waterside Workers Federation (2) The New South Wales Builders Labourers Federation.' Paper delivered to Oral History Association of Australia Conference (1991: University of Queensland). *Oral History Association of Australia Journal* 14:44–50.

——2000. 'Australia's red-green pioneers.' *Workers Liberty* 64, viewed 15 August 2003, http://archive.workersliberty.org/wlmags/wl64/greg.htm

Mulligan, M. and S. Hill 2002. *Ecological Pioneers: A Social History of Australian Ecological Thought and Action*. Melbourne: Cambridge University Press.

Mundey, J. 1973. 'Interview with Jack Mundey.' *Australian Left Review* 42:15–24.

——1976a. 'Ecology, capitalism, communism.' *Australian Left Review* 51:30–4.

——1976b. 'The common man.' In G. Seddon and M. Davis (eds) *Man and Landscape in Australia: Towards an Ecological Vision*. Canberra: AGPS, pp. 346–53.

——1977. 'Urbanisation: A challenge to socialism.' *Australian Left Review* 54:7–11.

——1980. 'A wider vision for trade unions.' In G. Crough, T. Wheelwright and T. Wilshire (eds) *Australia and World Capitalism*. Ringwood: Penguin Books, pp. 280–8.

——1981. *Green Bans and Beyond*. Sydney: Angus & Robertson.

——1988. 'From grey to green: Urban environmental issues.' *Australian Left Review* 108:17–20.

——2004. Interview with Michael Leach. 3 June.

Mundey, J. and G. Polites 1975. *Union Power: Jack Mundey Versus George Polites*. Edited by Ann Turner. South Yarra: Heinemann Educational Australia.

Roddewig, R. 1978. *Green Bans: The Birth of Australian Environmental Politics*. Sydney: Hale & Iremonger.

Stretton, H. 1970. *Ideas for Australian Cities*. Adelaide: Griffin Press.

Thomas, P. 1973. *Taming the Concrete Jungle: The Builders Labourers' Story*. Sydney: New South Wales Branch of the Australia Building Construction Employees and Builders Labourers' Federation.

Vertovec, S. and R. Cohen 2002. 'Introduction: Conceiving cosmopolitanism.' In S. Vertovec and R. Cohen (eds) *Conceiving Cosmopolitanism: Theory, Context, Practice*. Oxford: Oxford University Press, pp. 1–24.

Nancy Shelley

Nancy Shelley is a Quaker peace activist. She represented the Australian peace movement at the UN in 1982. She was a prominent speaker at the women's peace camp at Pine Gap in 1983, and at many conferences on peace and disarmament in Australia, New Zealand, Britain and Canada in the 1980s and early 1990s. She has been actively involved in formulating non-violent approaches to peace activism, and her writings about the conflict in Sri Lanka and about Australian militarism have been circulated widely among the churches and elsewhere. Since the mid-1990s she has been involved in consultations between government and various non-governmental human rights organisations. In her writing and public activity, she has advanced an active and positive concept of peace as the overcoming of all forms of violence instead of merely the absence of war. She received an Order of Australia Medal in 1989 for her dedicated work in peace making.

Nancy Shelley speaking to a peace rally outside the Australian War Memorial in late 1990. (Courtesy Norman Ainsworth.)

5

Nancy Shelley: Empowerment through Peace Education

Roderic Pitty[1]

> Peace involves love and care of the earth, its waters, its atmosphere. Peacemak–
> ers stand in the authority of the Spirit and dare to think with one another in
> terms of the whole planet.
>
> (Shelley 1986: 184)

In the early 1980s, there arose in Australia a mass movement committed to achieving nuclear disarmament. The movement was large and diverse. Hundreds of thousands of demonstrators marched at peace rallies on Palm Sunday for several years from 1982. The peace movement had many leaders and gave expression to many voices. Some belonged to well-known Australians, such as the Nobel laureate Patrick White. At a symposium in Canberra in May 1983, White called on Australian citizens to 'acquire identities of their own' by combining global concerns with courage and confidence in their ability to help others. He said that 'contemporary Australian women could play a leading part in preparing us to face and avert nuclear warfare, where all is uncertain, and where the masculine mind may be too orthodox in its approach' (White 1983: 253, 261). The speaker after White that day was Nancy Shelley, a Quaker peace worker and educator. She voiced the concerns of many citizens about the need to challenge militarism and violence in all its forms in order to avert the nuclear threat. She told her audience about inspiring examples of women's peace camps created at Greenham Common, in southern England, and at military bases elsewhere. She urged Australians to understand that peace requires action, not passivity (Shelley 1983b: 243–9).

Later that year, in November, 700 women assembled in the dry bed of a river near Alice Springs. They were there to begin the Women's Peace Camp at Pine Gap, a secret base collecting satellite information for the US military.

81

On Armistice Day, 11 November, buses transported the women from Alice Springs to a place one kilometre away from Pine Gap, enabling them to assemble and walk with their banners towards their destination. They had been given permission to camp by Aboriginal owners of the land. Shelley was the oldest speaker at the camp's opening. She led the women into the silence of remembrance. After defining the challenge they had embarked on, Shelley (2003) said:

> This installation is a symbol of global violence. It stands for war strategies. It stands for the arms escalation. And it stands for violence, violence against women, and violence against the spirit.

Those stirring words expressed Shelley's analysis of the nuclear threat, and her call for a global response.

The camp received favourable publicity both overseas and in Australia, but not from the Alice Springs media. This described the women in stereotypes, both inaccurate and unpleasant. The aim of the women in highlighting Australian involvement with a global system of violence was ignored. The diversity of the women acting for peace was seen as a problem, not as part of a solution to the nuclear threat. Yet for many Australians, this camp was a living example of global citizenship in action. It showed the crucial role that women's efforts of non-violent empowerment have in preventing nuclear war.

Throughout the peace camp, all actions by the women were peaceful. Shelley (2003) recalls the feelings of 'trust and fearlessness' that she experienced at the peace camp, which was done so peacefully. Near the end of the camp, she went to Alice Springs and rang the Australian head of Pine Gap. He immediately used stereotypes to describe her. Her reply was: 'How do you know I'm like that? We have never met. Perhaps we could meet and talk'. He agreed and suggested a time and a place. When the time came, Shelley was surprised at the length of time he was prepared to spend talking. At the end, he suggested it had all been futile. He asked where the women would go now. Shelley told him how women across the world would be linking up, saying: 'You know women can talk to women whether or not they know the language of each other'. It was with dismay that he agreed that that was true, and they parted (Shelley 2005).

Nancy Shelley is a Quaker and feminist who has worked full-time as a voluntary peace educator since 1980. In 1982 she attended the second United Nations Special Session on Disarmament in New York on behalf of a Canberra peace group. She has spoken at many conferences and meetings as an advocate for empowering people to overcome militarism and violence. She is a determined community activist who has endeavoured to communicate her understanding of peace as an active and creative process through speaking to a wide range of organisations, in Australia and overseas. She has used imagery and poetry effectively to make her message clear, such as when addressing an international conference of mathematics educators in Canada in 1992 (Shelley 1995). She has been a member of an advisory panel that has lobbied the government to protect human rights, raising vital issues like the need to stop the increasing use of child soldiers throughout the world.

This chapter will show how Shelley's vision of creating a peaceful world expresses key principles of cosmopolitanism, such as moral equality and responsibility for others. The first section will situate Shelley's vision in relation to different views of the nuclear threat prevalent in Australia in the 1980s. Then Shelley's basic approach to 'the power of thinking for peace' (Shelley 1983a) will be considered by reviewing her values and her approach to peace education. Then her program for change will be examined with reference to four of the many particular projects that Shelley has helped to promote. One was her effort to ensure that Australians understand the danger of militarism in a country like Sri Lanka. Another was her attempt to halt the rise of Australian exports of military materiel in the late 1980s. A third was her effort in the 1990s to redress media misrepresentation of community protests against those exports. And a fourth was her analysis of how the dominant ideology of economic violence has distorted Australia's relations with the world. Finally, Shelley's activity as a citizen of humanity, which was recognised by the National Committee on Human Rights Education in 2003, will be assessed in terms of the importance of her grassroots community activism.

Nuclear disarmament and the problem of militarism

When Shelley became a full-time peace worker, she did so 'because of the urgency of the world situation' (Shelley 1988a: 87). This was a time of nuclear arms build-up, particularly, but not only, in Europe. Many Australians were worried by this, and responded with great activity, as with the Women's Peace Camp. Shelley's key response to what she saw as 'the nuclear obscenity' (1983b: 228) was to promote a new paradigm of *common security*. This vision had been expressed in 1982 by an independent commission chaired by the former Swedish Prime Minister Olaf Palme (1982), and earlier by the former Australian diplomat and originator of conflict resolution theory, John Burton (1979). For Shelley (1987: 47), this paradigm shift was linked to viewing peace and security not just as the absence of war, but as a process requiring 'greater participation' from people concerned to supplant

83

militarism with a focus on human needs. To appreciate her perspective, it is useful to review three Australian responses to the nuclear threat in the 1980s.

First, there was a widespread concern that the presence of US bases such as Pine Gap had made Australia a target for a possible Soviet attack using nuclear weapons in the event of a world war. This concern reflected a major focus in the peace movement on the technology of fear, symbolised by more dangerous nuclear weapons. In response to this fear, many called for closing those bases, in order, as Falk (1983: 153) put it, to take Australia *off the map* of nuclear war. While this demand was radical, focusing on the weapons was not. In the 1980s, pressed by the peace movement, the Hawke government called Pine Gap a 'Joint Facility' that was needed to verify any disarmament (Leaver 1991: 38). When fear of a nuclear attack on Australia dissipated after the Cold War, the key US base at Pine Gap remained. Shelley's analysis of militarism shows that disarmament requires more than technical monitoring. It requires a broader democratic focus on human needs, not a combination of technological solutions and continuing fear of foreigners. Shelley (1983b: 240) argued that 'effective action to prevent nuclear war . . . MUST include simultaneous action to deal with human needs, actions to protect the environment, and action to eliminate all forms of violence'. Her emphasis on the need for a paradigm shift is confirmed by the lack of disarmament since the Cold War (Shelley 1995: 258–9).

Second, there was a related concern in the peace movement about the implications for Australia of continued participation in a military alliance with the USA. The focus of this concern was on how Australia was threatened, not protected, by this alliance. One response to this danger was to advocate replacing the alliance with armed neutrality, in which Australia could isolate itself from external rivalry (Martin 1984). In some other contexts, neutralism has been expressed in internationalist forms, such as in the position of Sweden. Yet, in Australia, neutralism tended to be a nationalistic response, linked to ideas of fortress Australia. It did not address the underlying problem of militarism. This became clear at the end of the Cold War, when the Hawke government pursued both a self-reliant defence policy and a large expansion of the Australian military industry. That expansion was criticised by Shelley (1987: 46) and others (e.g. Cheeseman and Kettle 1990). They saw security not in terms of the worst-case paradigm of military security, but in terms of a new paradigm focusing on the satisfaction of human needs, in a world where poverty and hunger are suffered by more people than ever before (Shelley 1995: 248).

Third, there was a growing recognition of the need for this paradigm shift in thinking about war and peace. Shelley (1987: 47) defined this as 'moving from competitive hostility . . . to cooperative interdependence with a commitment to joint survival'. The essence of this shift was towards greater participation by movements of people linked by a common vision of global solutions to the basic problem of militarism. This was a cosmopolitan outlook which promoted solutions that value all humans equally. One key feature of this outlook is that pacifism does not imply passivity. Instead, it requires a wide range of action. This message was highlighted by a slogan that Shelley proposed for the 1986 Palm Sunday peace rally in Canberra: 'Peace is action. Act for peace'.

The third response to the nuclear threat was distinguished from the other two by its emphasis on the need for a new way of thinking, or a paradigm shift, opening the path towards the ideal of global citizenship. Those who saw weapons as the sole problem thought solutions could be reached simply by international agreements between states, without building universal respect for human rights. They accepted the strict limits of international citizenship or orderly relations between states, in the hope that leaders would soon see reason and negotiate nuclear disarmament. Their critics doubted that substantial change would occur unless violence was renounced in all its forms. They acted as global citizens by respecting the dignity of all human beings, such as by defending the protests of independent peace groups in the Soviet bloc (Hersey 1987).

The end of the Cold War has not produced a peace dividend, but instead a declining world order in which the nuclear threat remains and militarism has not been reduced. Yet it is increasingly challenged by a rising global civil society, comprising those who see global citizenship and transnational political advocacy as necessary to ensure that agreements between governments serve broader humane purposes (Falk 2004: 182). One writer who was involved in the peace movement, Mary Kaldor (2003: 111), views this emerging society as containing an answer to war. She says this answer is emerging through new global movements, which can function only 'in an atmosphere free of fear'. For this to be so, it is vital that global citizens clearly understand the purpose of peace activism. Clarifying this was one of Shelley's primary aims in the 1980s, when she expressed her Quaker view of peace education.

The Quaker practice of speaking truth to power

As a Quaker, Shelley belongs to a strong tradition known as The Religious Society of Friends. This is an international network, formed in seventeenth-century England, based on upholding values of pacifism, integrity, equality, simplicity and community service. Two core principles of Quakerism are non-violence and personal courage. Both are expressed in the Quaker practice of 'speaking truth to power'. This aims to change the nature of power in society, so it is not exercised and enforced violently (Clements and Jones in Encounter 2005). Most Quakers are not evangelicals, but people committed to living their values through action for social justice. They have been active in various organisations, such as Greenpeace (Mayo 2005: 66). According to the peace activist Sabina Erika (Encounter 2005: 2), one aspect of Quakerism is a belief 'in having a calling'. This means reflecting on the right path to take at the right time and responding with action, not just adopting fashionable causes. Shelley's commitment to full-time peace work, and particularly to educating for peace, is such a calling.

There are several aspects of Shelley's practice of peace education. Broadly, she aims to change 'the framework within which thinking people operate', by bringing into view new issues that narrow approaches to a problem ignore (Shelley 1987: 47). She begins from the Quaker 'belief in the equal worth of all people', whose 'common humanity transcends our differences' (Australia Yearly Meeting 1996: 147). This idea includes the basic cosmopolitan values of moral equality, personal responsibility and genuine participation in decisions by all the people most affected by them (Held 2004: 171). These values express a global vision of creating a peaceful world, through focusing on positive experiences of cooperation, empowerment and non-violence.

Within this vision, peace is a global endeavour of education and understanding, not a national attainment secured by military means. When calling for this paradigm shift, Shelley (1987: 47) has expressed her global outlook through a redefinition of peace and security as essentially an ongoing process of mutual empowerment, not as an objective product of state structures. The reframing of peace as a positive and ongoing social process has several key dimensions that Shelley has emphasised. These are the vital principle of non-violence, the important role of language in either obscuring or demystifying the nature of peace, and the need to affirm all forms of life by adopting a courageous and uncompromisingly critical stance towards forces of destruction.

The principle of non-violence is fundamental to Shelley's philosophy of peace. She has described non-violence as 'not simply a technique of struggle', but a core principle that 'arises from a belief that all life is worth love and respect'. For Shelley (1983b: 245), it is 'the evil of a system [that] has to be attacked, not the person who operates that system'. This belief motivated her meeting with the Australian head at Pine Gap. In that meeting, Shelley was guided by her Quaker philosophy of considering the dignity of every person, because there is a good side to all humans, called 'that of God in Everyone' (Encounter 2005). Her action was informed by her whole outlook on the process of creating positive peace. For Shelley (1983b: 228), it is vital to reject any attitude that is 'narrow, unimaginative and arrogant', and 'which carries with it a violence to alternatives'. She sees careful use of language and routine affirmations of life as crucial dimensions of the creation of peace.

Shelley has developed an acute sense of how the powerlessness of people in the face of nuclear weapons has been reinforced by misleading language. This replaces concern about those weapons with false complacency and fear of others. She points out that, if used positively, 'language enables us to bring under our control those things which are named, as can readily be seen in the growth of confidence in a young child as nouns and objects are connected' in a process of learning (Shelley 1983a: 49). Yet language can also disorientate. Shelley (1983a: 50) says that, when old metaphors like 'balance' and 'umbrella' and familiar concepts like 'deterrence' and 'security' are falsely applied to weapons of mass destruction, peace is obstructed. Such criticism of nuclear discourse has also been made by people who saw this occur in the British military, or amongst civilian strategists in the US (Cohn 1987; Green 2000; MccGwire 1985/6; 1994).

The most fundamental deformation of thinking that Shelley criticises is the use of fear to distort the meaning of peace itself. In prescient comments, given the growing use of violence by state and non-state actors, Shelley highlighted over two decades ago the insidious manipulation of fear by politicians in a democracy. She said (1983a: 51) clearly: 'Our cornerstone must be to cast fear out, not as a reaction to its crippling power and demonic drive, but because it is incompatible with life-affirming living'. Fear has been used by politicians to maintain the illusion that only military solutions are valid, and to restrict the meaning of peace to a negative idea, the absence of war. Instead, Shelley advocates 'an alternative concept of peace', which 'confronts the attendant evils of the build-ups of armaments', such as 'hunger, poverty, homelessness, disease, dirty water, malnutrition, unemployment [and] illiteracy for vast numbers of the world's people'. For Shelley (1983a: 50), peace involves 'the removal of the causes of war', not just its consequences. This positive view of peace requires a practice of global citizenship based on genuine concern for all humanity's welfare, and for the earth that sustains all life (Shelley 1995: 257).

A vital dimension of Shelley's approach to peace education is her feminist view of what is needed to achieve nuclear disarmament and stop militarism. Shelley's approach directs our attention away from facts that could make peacemakers despair, like the absurd numbers of nuclear weapons that have been built, towards the social changes that are needed to reduce that despair. Shelley (1983b: 240) declared that 'women are saying that unless we link our action for preventing war with the total scene of the violence done to the poor throughout the world, we are being hypocritical and will fail in our intent'. This is because 'it is totally absurd, and structurally impossible, to try to bring about world peace when aggression and conquest are considered synonymous with manliness and masculinity' (Shelley 1983b: 238). A feminist approach values inclusiveness and local democracy, as seen in women's actions for peace (Warren and Cady 1996). These values are particularly appealing to women, who, as Urry (2003: 98) has noted, may be 'more likely to be drawn to notions of global citizenship', because masculine symbols of national power make them insecure. This was reflected in the growth in the 1980s of a distinctively feminist practice of global citizenship, based on direct action against military bases (Hutchings 2002: 57). What Shelley provided for those involved in such positive action was a broader conception of peacemaking, based on the idea of peace as positive action, not as merely the absence of war.

An inclusive agenda is vital to unlocking the power of positive peace. Shelley (1983b: 248) argued that this can be 'generated if the will, the means and the end are each of them grounded in peace'. Her main aim has been to help people understand the need for a global and inclusive perspective about peace-making. Shelley (1983b: 248) said that:

> in order to overcome militarism, we require an equal portioning of our energies to changing fear, injustice and oppression into hope, equity and liberation. If we would prevent nuclear war, we must at all levels of our life be life-affirming. Our policies must arise from the *will* to enhance the well-being of all humans, they must work at the *means* to fulfil human needs, and they must have human welfare as their *goal*. (emphasis in original)

The idea of the interconnectedness of all humans is central to Shelley's view of peace. It is something that reflects her experience as an educator, devoted to the teaching of mathematics, for which she developed teaching programs that enhanced diversity (Shelley 1995: 253).

Empowerment through recognising diversity

Shelley taught mathematics for thirty years in secondary schools in Victoria and New South Wales, and also in England, where she performed for a time as a professional classical singer, having lessons with Eleanor Gerhardt. Later, in the 1970s, Shelley worked at La Trobe University educating mathematics teachers and postgraduates, and completing a thesis about how students understand mathematical concepts (Shelley 1995: 249). She was concerned to redress the 'mechanistic view' that some students are unable to learn mathematics, when the real obstacle to their learning is that their form of teaching has 'little room for experience' and treats student diversity as 'a ped-agogic nuisance' (Shelley 1988a: 91–2). Through three different programs of mathematics education, involving Aboriginal children in Adelaide, and senior students and adults in Melbourne, Shelley helped people who had been told they 'lacked ability' to become confident in using mathematics (Shelley 1995: 249, 252). Her basic approach was to get teachers to create 'an atmosphere of trust', so that students could affirm their own experience and see 'that therein lies their personal power' (Shelley 1988a: 94, 102). Such use of diversity in mathematics education has been adopted by teachers who are aware of the cultural context of learning (Meaney 2002: 174).

These programs were most significant for Shelley because their success was based on the idea of empowering people to value their own experience. That idea is central to her vision of a peaceful world involving greater coop-eration and participation to meet human needs (Shelley 1987: 47). Since access to knowledge is a basic need, one of Shelley's main concerns has been to increase women's access to mathematics, while asking questions about the social purposes of this knowledge, and challenging the link that has grown between western mathematicians and militarism (Shelley 1988a: 101). In 1976, together with other women, she helped form the International Organ-isation of Women in Mathematics Education (IOWME), in response to male dominance of the podium at a conference where the audience was mostly women (Shelley 1995: 255). She served as the first convenor of IOWME for eight years, encouraging women to use mathematics in ways that respect human needs and presume diversity, not uniformity (Shelley 1988a: 101).

Shelley's educational experience has involved celebrating diversity. That is central to her view of the urgency of peace work. Shelley (1988a: 103) says 'it is our diversity and skills that not only the planet is crying out for, but humankind needs desperately'. Diversity and courage were evident at the Women's Peace Camp at Pine Gap. This action was an affirmation of 'knowledge which cannot be owned, manipulated and governed by the powerful', and was therefore 'a threat to their position' (Shelley 1988a: 102). In promoting peace education, Shelley (1982: 10) has focused on valuing the diversity and the 'connectedness of all human life' as the key to overcoming the ideology of militarism. This respect for diversity reflects her experience as an educator, and is evident in her emphasis on the need for a global approach to peace-making (Shelley 1995: 253, 257).

In the 1980s, Shelley often spoke about the need for a universal approach to militarism. She stressed (1983b: 249) that action in Australia to stop nuclear war means 'working to prevent the mining and export of uranium, that base of the nuclear chain, that source of death by radiation, that destroyer of Aboriginal lands'. She emphasised the need to link the growing movement for a nuclear-free Pacific with a rejection of militarism. Shelley (1983b: 249) called for 'the removal of the US military installations on our soil and our military presence in Asia', and for an end to the violence done to women, to the poor, and to the spirit. Instead of seeing Australia as vulnerable, needing military protection from Asia, Shelley saw the need to protect all humanity together through support for the basic principles of what is now called global citizenship. This was reflected in her international peace work. In 1986 she was invited by GABRIELA, a feminist peace network in the Philippines, to address a conference that included Christians and Muslims, because of her expertise in conflict resolution. She stayed with the group of women who were most isolated at the conference, despite not speaking their language. This showed the importance of empowering others in her peace work. Within Australia, she has focused on developing a strong relationship of trust and empowerment when working with Indigenous people (Shelley 1995: 248, 250, 252).

This contrast between fearing vulnerability itself and being responsible for others is linked to the need for a paradigm change towards a positive and inclusive vision of peace. In calling for such a change, Shelley (1983b: 249) has often used the power of metaphor to impress upon her audience 'the size of the stand' which women globally are making for peace, with their actions arising 'not from absolutes, but from compassion'. She evokes the 'gentleness and fragility' of natural wonders, and human life, to show that change must be inclusive and attentive. Shelley (cited in Australia Yearly Meeting 2003: 195) has evoked the image of someone who takes a very young baby in their hands, experiencing 'the miracle and the vulnerability of human life', in order to show that vulnerability is a part of human nature that needs to be appreciated, not denied. Accepting vulnerability can be a basis for compassion and responsibility (see also Butler 2004).

This image is central to the universal view of transcending violence that Shelley has emphasised. For Shelley (1986: 184), a holistic perspective is vital to creating peace:

> Peacemakers use truth to overcome lies, and love to overcome hatred – even to the point of sacrifice and suffering. Peace involves love and care of the earth, its waters, its atmosphere. Peacemakers stand in the authority of the Spirit and dare to think with one another in terms of the whole planet. They know that each of us is diminished by another's death, and will risk their part of the world that another might live. They understand the difference between insecurity and vulnerability – the one with its roots in fear and distrust, the other a condition of life and growth.

This is a strong statement of global concern, a call to link planetary thinking with an appreciation of how much people acting together can achieve in digging up the roots of fear, and nurturing life through careful use of language and active peace-making. It is a perspective that Shelley has subsequently applied to a number of specific projects.

Resisting militarism in Australia and Sri Lanka

In the late 1980s, with the Cold War ending in Europe, the peace movement faced a new challenge in Australia because of the rise of a military export industry, linked to what people such as Herb Feith termed a new Australian militarism (see Chapter 3). Shelley contributed in two specific ways to such broader concern in Australia about militarism. One involved research and education, especially for the Australian Council of Churches' Commission on International Affairs. The other developed into a major community project to give voice to courageous citizens resisting militarism.

In the late 1980s, Shelley exposed changes to export regulations that made it easier for Australian companies to profit from overseas wars. She edited an influential book for the Australian Council of Churches, titled *Whither Australia? A Response to Australia's Current Defence Policy* (Shelley 1990). This was the second publication she wrote for the Council of Churches, after a background paper in 1988 on the history and international implications of the destructive conflict in Sri Lanka, which was then in an intractable war with many civilian casualties (Chadda 2004: 95; Shelley 1988b). In both publications, Shelley raised the need for action by Australians to reduce militarism in other countries. She wanted Australians to stop government policies that could make conflicts such as that in Sri Lanka worse. In 1988, Australia sold military equipment to Sri Lanka, and to many other repressive governments such as Indonesia, Pakistan, Fiji, Burma and South Africa, and to the Philippines and Bangladesh (Bolt 1991: 9–10).

Shelley's account of the conflict in Sri Lanka focused on the social context of the war. She noted how severe human rights abuses followed the building of 'military camps all over the island' (Shelley 1988b: 16). She analysed the deep social and political causes of the conflict, highlighting the extraordinary increase in the military budget. These problems were linked to rising unemployment and exploitation of women, the decline of judicial authority, and the end of Sri Lanka's non-aligned foreign policy as the government lifted a ban on US warship visits. All these conditions meant that selling weapons to Sri Lanka was the opposite of an appropriate Australian policy committed to ending the violence. Shelley (1988b: 32) said that it was vital

91

to promote the efforts of local Peace Committees to build the community trust needed for creating peace.

There is a revealing contrast between Shelley's focus on local cooperation within Sri Lanka and the Australian Government's response to human rights abuses there in the mid-1980s. While the government advocated human rights for the Tamil community, and an end to arbitrary arrest and torture, it ignored positive sources of social change in Sri Lanka. Instead, the government 'was keen to aver its own credentials in this area, frequently invoking as exemplars its policy of multiculturalism and its policies to redress the injustices and discrimination affecting Aboriginal people' (Dutton 2003: 100). Yet, the Royal Commission into Aboriginal Deaths in Custody soon revealed that systemic injustice and racial discrimination continued in Australia. Australia reduced its aid to Sri Lanka in the late 1980s because of human rights abuses there. But there was no official criticism of Sri Lanka's high military spending, since that would have led to critical questions about Australian military exports.

The themes of Shelley's analysis of Sri Lankan militarism and its external sources were expanded in the book challenging Australia's military exports. The aim of *Whither Australia?* was to encourage debate about what the defence minister, Kim Beazley, had called the largest military investment in Australia's peacetime history. The book documented a shift from what the foreign minister, Gareth Evans (1989), had called 'good international citizenship' towards a militarised foreign policy. This shift was acknowledged by Evans, who accepted that his view of regional security had focused too much on military matters (Pitty 2003: 62). Shelley (1990: 13) pointed out that 'the dominance of military priorities' over diplomacy creates 'a particular way of running the world' through force, helping governments maintain 'authoritarian and repressive rule'. She said (1990: 14, 19) that relying on 'order defined in military terms', instead of upholding human rights, is a 'perversion of every aspect of our lives, across the globe', which involves 'a desensitisation, even a brutalisation, of the human spirit'. She saw Australia's need to build trust in the region as being sacrificed by new regulations that subjected exports of military materiel to merely routine bureaucratic approval.

Shelley's second contribution to resisting Australian militarism after the Cold War was done in response to media misrepresentation of a protest against a weapons exhibition in Canberra in November 1991 (known as AIDEX). The Australian Quaker Peace Committee ran a conflict resolution stall at the exhibition, and organised a simultaneous conference in Canberra on the social costs of military exports. During the exhibition, on 26–28 November, over a thousand protesters came to Canberra. Many were brutalised by police and misrepresented in the media, so that friends often would not talk to them after they went home. Some Canberra people, including Shelley, felt a need to address the experiences of bewilderment, shock and 'hurt all round' that marked the way this democratic protest had been handled and reported (Friends of the Hearings 1995: 4). With three colleagues, Shelley organised hearings in Canberra, Newcastle, Sydney and Adelaide to enable protest participants to tell their stories. This led to a massive book titled *Piecing It Together: Hearing the Stories of AIDEX '91*, which recorded many experiences of the protestors. In this project, Shelley put into practice her belief, expressed a decade before (1983b: 242), that, in order to stop war, 'it is essential we work at preventing the polarisation of society – for that can only aid militarism'.

Piecing It Together achieved community healing by recording some of the diversity that characterised participants in that protest against militarism. Three themes are evident in that diversity. First, the global and regional context of the protest was vital. Growing public concern in Australia about militarism was linked to the Gulf War of 1991, the conflicts in Bougainville and East Timor, and the urgent need for conflict resolution in these places. Opponents of AIDEX expressed strong cosmopolitan views. They argued for the need to focus on 'conflict resolution by peaceful means' instead of selling weapons (Friends of the Hearings 1995: 69, 191–3, 209, 214, 341). Second, it is clear that many people involved in the earlier protests against nuclear war had adopted Shelley's view that militarism had to be challenged entirely. Finally, there was strong support for a new vision of global citizenship, seen as an ethical commitment to the process of creating conditions of peace for people everywhere. This reflected the influence of Shelley's basic moral perspective of human interconnectedness.

Challenging an ideology of economic violence

In early 1997, when Shelley was asked to speak to the Quaker Yearly Meeting about raising the minimum armed forces recruitment age to eighteen, she said there were other ideas about ending violence that she thought needed urgent discussion and reflection. She spoke about Australia's involvement with the World Trade Organization (WTO), expressing concern that decisions were already being taken by the government with 'long lasting implications', yet amid widespread lack of public knowledge (Shelley 1997: i). Whereas the issue of military exports had been exposed, international trade decisions usually got less critical attention, despite concern expressed by trade unions and community groups. A written version of Shelley's talk, titled *The Future: Where Are We Being Taken? Is It Where We Want to Go?*, is a remarkably prescient expression of cosmopolitan thought in Australia.

Shelley (1997: 2) highlighted two aspects of Australia's involvement with the WTO as signs of a trend that 'will permeate areas of our lives most would consider far removed from trade'. First, she pointed out that, whereas the Howard government had made the process of ratifying international treaties subject to public consultation, this did not apply to agreements reached with the WTO, which, although binding on Australia, are not scrutinised publicly. Second, she noted that consultation on trade policy with non-governmental organisations was restricted to industry groups. For a recent WTO confer-ence, the government had consulted the farm, food and mineral industries, but no other groups concerned about social issues (Shelley 1997: 4–5).

Shelley illustrated such trends in three main areas: labour conditions, environmental protection and quarantine and food safety. The WTO rejects action to protect children against child labour, and undermines environ-mental protection and strict quarantine standards, which it dismisses as 'protectionist' (Shelley 1997: 6–13). Shelley (1997: 15) said it is 'alarming' for government to insist 'that NOTHING should be permitted to interfere with trade liberalisation', not even 'violations of human rights, loss of jobs or any other deleterious social effects'. She argued that 'what we are witnessing – and, indeed, are caught up in – is an ideology of the most simplistic kind with no evidence to substantiate the claims being made for it and plenty of instances of injurious effects' (Shelley 1997: 15). A recent exposure of declining quarantine standards in Australia confirms her analysis (Date-line 2005). Others have noted the influence 'of an ideology that regards the pursuit of free trade as an intrinsic virtue and the protection of human rights as a matter at the discretion of governments' (Charlesworth et al. 2006: 149).

Because of the pervasiveness of this neoliberal ideology, Shelley (1997: 17) saw it as important to challenge the core aspects of this dogma and its 'potential for conflict and violence', and to promote alternative ideas. She criticised three key elements of this ideology (Shelley 1997: 17–23):

1. its adversarial approach to different opinions.
2. its competitive approach to the value of human life, which entrenches inequality.
3. its individualistic view of society, which 'debases cooperation' and 'elimi-nates responsibility toward others'.

She used the Quaker heritage to outline an alternative vision of the future, based on three Quaker beliefs that are essential to it. In Shelley's (1997:

19–23) perspective, these are: that 'wisdom is seldom disposed toward exclusion'; that listening to others is vital in adversity; and that group responsibility must be encouraged. Shelley was particularly concerned to resist the rise of violence in Australian society. She highlighted the violence done to young imaginations by the conformity of competition, the 'violence done to truth' to gain political or corporate advantage, violence against the vulnerable, and the 'violence done to the spirit of all living things' (Shelley 1997: 24–6). She used the example of the soon to be discredited Multilateral Agreement on Investment (MAI) to show disturbing trends in Australian politics, such as a 'disdain for dialogue and negotiation', and the claim that human rights belong to states and corporations, rather than to people (Shelley 1997: 30–1).

Shelley's vision for responding to current social trends involved a brilliant exposition of positive thinking, giving expression to the core principles of personal responsibility and accountability, consent, and inclusiveness, all vital elements of cosmopolitanism (Held 2004: 173–4). Shelley (1997: 33–45) said there is 'cause for alarm' about how globalisation leads to 'a loss of accountability' by eroding responsible government and respect for equality and the human rights of others. She saw democracy in Australia as threatened by policies that deny social responsibility and tolerate equality only 'for those who can pay' (Shelley 1997: 45). Four years before the 2001 'children overboard' scandal, in which senior government ministers falsely claimed in an election campaign that refugees had thrown their children into the ocean, Shelley highlighted a dangerous political phenomenon, and called for an active civic response. She warned (1997: 46): 'with any decrease in reliable information, the responsibility of citizens grows: to seek out, test for accuracy and truth, and make known to others what is happening'.

In such a context, Shelley said that community responsibility must expand, to overcome increased government deceit. This need for greater social responsibility to balance diminished governmental accountability characterises the rise of cosmopolitan social movements. For Shelley (1997: 47), social responsibility is linked to the task of ending global violence:

> What is hard to be aware of is the extent to which parts of our well-being in Australia either depend upon violence done, or violence implied. For example, violence done, in another country, in extracting, growth, or manufacture of commodities we enjoy. Or, violence implied when those standards we value, freedoms we prize, tolerance we appreciate are underwritten by the power that lies with our military.

In her analysis of the impact of trade liberalisation, Shelley has continued a key theme of her peace activism, which is to call for action to affirm 'a culture of relationship, of care, of communion', in opposition to the 'culture of violence' which currently diminishes 'the ever-renewing capacity of living beings' (Shelley 1995: 253, 261).

Conclusion

Shelley's booklet *The Future*, like her earlier works, included proposals for change as well as a critique of current social problems. This combination reflects her Quaker belief in always seeking positive approaches to life, and to people. As Manning Clark (1997: 223) once said of an old friend, the diplomat Patrick Shaw, Shelley is 'an encourager – never a heart dimmer or a head shrinker'. Her optimism is expressed in her call for a paradigm shift from militarism towards positive peace, viewed as a process of change. Those who create such change are communities of global citizens. In Shelley's view (1997: 36), they 'develop a respect for each other' and 'responsibility toward others' by taking joint actions to enlarge their lives beyond the bounds of self-interest. Another Quaker, Nigel Dower (2003: 8), has defined the typical global citizen as being not an 'isolated individual' but 'a cautious optimist', who is 'engaged in what she does because she feels that it is possible that the world could become a better place with less violence, poverty, environmental degradation and violation of human rights'. That definition applies to Shelley, but courageous is a better adjective, since it expresses her Quaker practice of speaking truth to power. The community aspect is vital for Shelley since courage grows when shared, as, for example, in her experience of the Women's Peace Camp at Pine Gap, and the GABRIELA feminist network in the Philippines.

Shelley's dedication to human rights was recognised in 2003 when the National Committee on Human Rights Education acknowledged her role as a 'citizen of humanity'. The certificate features the principles of the 1948 Universal Declaration of Human Rights, surrounded by the flags of all states. This reflects the identity Shelley has created, in which the role of an Australian citizen is to contribute to the global cause of non-violence. This cause is linked to Shelley's spiritual values of pacifism, integrity, equality, simplicity, responsibility for others, and acceptance of diversity. Her actions have been informed by these values, both as a professional mathematics educator and as a proponent of positive peace. Shelley's vision of positive peace remains relevant, and not just because the nuclear threat continues. The views of many varied participants in the AIDEX protest, collected in *Piecing It Together*, indicate the influence of Shelley's call to challenge militarism. Her central principle of non-violence has become more important in reducing threats of non-state terrorism, which rely on fear, and on the excuse that states use violence.

Shelley's key message (1983a: 51) today is to 'cast fear out', since it denies life. Her perspective of non-violence remains an empowering vision of an alternative framework for global peace-making. Her influence as a global citizen has extended beyond Quaker circles, and the peace movement. When Shelley was nominated and received an Order of Australia Medal in 1989, it was by someone who had watched her peace work from outside the movement. Shelley's core values are shared by many Australians, and by many other advocates of non-violence. Her vision of what peace activists must do was affirmed by the recipient of the 2004 Sydney Peace Prize, the Indian writer Arundhati Roy (2004: 10), who said radical change 'will not be negotiated by governments', but rather will occur when a powerful public starts to 'link hands *across* national borders'. Shelley has contributed substantially to encouraging such global linkages through her positive education about the need for global citizens to become active peacemakers. She has shown such citizens that their task is to replace insecurity and fear with the growth of responsibility, trust, fearlessness, and respect for the rights of all humanity.

Note

1 I would like to thank particularly Nancy Shelley, and also April Carter, Ian Chalmers, Hellen Cooke, Jo-Anne Pemberton, Barbara Meyer, and Geoff Stokes, for their comments on this chapter. Since the writing of this chapter, Nancy Shelley's many peace movement speeches and papers in the 1980s and 1990s (only some of which were published at the time) have been collated by her niece, Jill Montgomery.

References

Australia Yearly Meeting 1996. *Gay and Lesbian People in the Religious Society of Friends (Quakers)*. Leaflet, excerpted in Australia Yearly Meeting 2003.

——2003. *This We Can Say: Australian Quaker Life, Faith and Thought*. Armadale North, VIC: Australia Yearly Meeting of the Religious Society of Friends (Quakers).

Bolt, R. 1991. 'Australia's military exports: The controversy grows.' *Social Alternatives* 10(4):9–10.

Butler, J. 2004. *Precarious Life: The Powers of Mourning and Violence*. London: Verso.

Burton, J. 1979. *Deviance, Terrorism and War*. Canberra: Australian National University Press.

Chadda, M. 2004. 'Between consociationalism and control: Sri Lanka.' In U. Schneckener and S. Wolff (eds) *Managing and Settling Ethnic Conflicts.* London: Hurst, pp. 94–114.

Charlesworth, H., M. Chaim, D. Hovell and G. Williams 2006. *No Country Is an Island: Australia and International Law.* Sydney: UNSW Press.

Cheeseman, G. and St John Kettle (eds) 1990. *The New Australian Militarism: Undermining our Future Security.* Sydney: Pluto.

Clark, M. 1997. 'Patrick Shaw.' In M. Clark, *Speaking Out of Turn: Lectures and Speeches 1940–1991.* Melbourne: Melbourne University Press.

Cohn, C. 1987. 'Sex and death in the rational world of defense intellectuals.' *Signs: Journal of Women in Culture and Society* 12(4):687–718.

Dateline 2005. 'Foot in mouth.' Television program. SBS Television: 3 August.

Dower, N. 2003. *An Introduction to Global Citizenship.* Edinburgh: Edinburgh University Press.

Dutton, D. 2003. 'Human rights diplomacy.' In P. Edwards and D. Goldsworthy (eds) *Facing North: A Century of Australian Engagement with Asia, volume 2: 1970s to 2000.* Melbourne: Melbourne University Press, pp. 81–129.

Encounter 2005. 'That of God in everyone.' Radio program. ABC Radio National: 24 July, transcript viewed 30 January 2007, http://www.abc.net.au/rn/relig/enc/stories/s1420515.htm

Evans, G. 1989. 'Australian foreign policy: Priorities in a changing world.' *Australian Outlook* 43(2):1–15.

Falk, J. 1983. *Taking Australia Off the Map: Facing the Threat of Nuclear War.* Melbourne: Penguin.

Falk, R. 2004. *The Declining World Order: America's Imperial Geopolitics.* New York: Routledge.

Friends of the Hearings. 1995. *Piecing It Together: Hearing the Stories of AIDEX '91.* Canberra: Penniless Publications.

Green, R. 2000. *The Naked Nuclear Emperor: Debunking Nuclear Deterrence.* Christchurch: Disarmament and Security Centre.

Held, D. 2004. *Global Covenant.* Cambridge: Polity.

Hersey, J. 1987. 'Asymmetry.' *The New Yorker* 7 September, pp. 33–53

Hutchings, K. 2002. 'Feminism and global citizenship.' In N. Dower and J. Williams (eds) *Global Citizenship: A Critical Reader.* Edinburgh: Edinburgh University Press, pp. 53–62.

Kaldor, Mary. 2003. *Global Civil Society: An Answer to War.* Cambridge: Polity.

Leaver, R. 1991. '"The shock of the new" and the habits of the past.' In G. Fry (ed.) *Australia's Regional Security.* Sydney: Allen & Unwin, pp. 32–44.

Martin, D. 1984. *Armed Neutrality for Australia.* Melbourne: Dove.

Mayo, M. 2005. *Global Citizens: Social Movements and the Challenge of Globalization.* London: Zed.

MccGwire, M. 1985/6. 'Deterrence: The problem – not the solution.' *International Affairs* 62(1):55–70.

——1994. 'Is there a future for nuclear weapons?' *International Affairs* 70(2):211–28.

Meaney, T. 2002. 'Symbiosis or cultural clash? Indigenous students learning mathematics.' *Journal of Intercultural Studies* 23(2):167–88.

Palme, O. 1982. *Common Security: A Programme for Disarmament – The Report of the Independent Commission on Disarmament and Security Issues under the Chairmanship of Olaf Palme.* London: Pan.

Pitty, R. 2003. 'Strategic engagement.' In P. Edwards and D. Goldsworthy (eds) *Facing North: A Century of Australian Engagement with Asia, volume 2: 1970s to 2000.* Melbourne: Melbourne University Press, pp. 48–80.

Roy, A. 2004. 'Public power in the age of empire.' *Frontline* (New Delhi) October, no. 22: 4–16.

Shelley, N. 1982. 'Why educate for peace?' In *Peace Education: Report of a Seminar held in the ACT.* Canberra: Australian College of Education, pp. 6–11.

——1983a. 'The power of thinking for peace.' *Social Alternatives* 3(2):49–51.

——1983b. 'Women and the prevention of nuclear war.' In M. Denborough (ed.) *Australia and Nuclear War.* Canberra: Croom Helm, pp. 228–51.

——1986. 'Peace: Who are the peacemakers?' Address to the Australian Association for Religious Education Conference, Brisbane, 1986. Excerpted in Australia Yearly Meeting 2003, pp. 184–5.

——1987. 'Interdependence and common security: The new paradigm.' *Social Alternatives* 6(2):43–8.

——1988a. 'My journey through mathematics with peace.' In S. Sewell, A. Kelly and L. Daws (eds) *Professions in the Nuclear Age.* Brisbane: Boolarong Publications, pp. 87–103.

——1988b. *Sri Lanka Background.* Sydney: Australian Council of Churches' Commission on International Affairs.

——1990. *Whither Australia? A Response to Australia's Current Defence Policy.* Sydney: Australian Council of Churches' Commission on International Affairs.

——1995. 'Mathematics: Beyond good and evil?' In P. Rogers and G. Kaiser (eds) *Equity in Mathematics Education: Influences of Feminism and Culture.* London: The Falmer Press, pp. 247–64.

——1997. *The Future: Where Are We Being Taken? Is it Where We Want to Go?* Canberra: Penniless Publications.

——2003. Recording from 11 November 1983 and recent interview broadcast in 'All We Are Saying . . . The 1983 Pine Gap Women's Peace Camp', ABC Radio National, Hindsight, 9 November.

——2005. Interview with Roderic Pitty. Telephone, 23 July.

Urry, J. 2003. *Global Complexity.* Cambridge: Polity.

Warren, K. and D. Cady 1996. 'Feminism and peace: Seeing connections.' In K. Warren and D. Cady (eds) *Bringing Peace Home: Feminism, Violence and Nature.* Bloomington: Indiana University Press, pp. 1–15.

White, P. 1983. 'The role of the Australian citizen in a nuclear war.' In M. Denborough (ed.) *Australia and Nuclear War.* Canberra: Croom Helm, pp. 252–64.

Bob Brown

Bob Brown is a parliamentarian, environmentalist and activist. He first rose to national prominence in the early 1980s as one of the figureheads in the campaign to save the Franklin River in Tasmania. On being elected to parliament at the state level in 1983, and at the federal level in 1996, he has maintained a high profile. He is the leader of the Australian Greens and one of the better-known politicians in Australia, and is frequently called upon to comment on environmental and social issues. He has received many honours and recognition for his work, including being named Australian of the Year by *The Australian* newspaper in 1983, called the 'World's Most Inspiring Politician' in 1996 by BBC *Wildlife* magazine and voted a living Australian National Treasure by the National Trust in 1998.

Greens Senator for Tasmania and party leader Bob Brown. (Courtesy Peter Whyte.)

6

Bob Brown: Ecology, Economy, Equality and Eternity

Peter Haeusler

Dr Bob Brown is an environment, peace and social justice activist who today stands as the public face of the environmental movement in Australia. He balances his global ideals with grassroots activism and engagement through mainstream political institutions as senator in the Australian Parliament. Regarded by many as 'Australia's leading Green', Bob Brown has come to occupy 'a singular place in the Australian political landscape' (Lohrey 2002: 74). In Maxine McKew's assessment (2002: 47), 'Brown comprehensively "owns" the progressive left of Australian politics'. But his support comes not only from those in the community most interested in idealism, radical social change, issues of environmental protection, and social justice; it also draws on those who are Christian and conservative (Lohrey 2002).

The wellspring of Bob Brown's commitment and action is his holistic, global view of the relationship between 'ecology, economy, equality and eternity' (Brown 1996). Brown has sought to extend Australian perspectives beyond the local, by expanding the traditional boundaries of national community and civic identity. As a strongly committed participatory democrat, Brown's cosmopolitanism involves the promotion of universal values and principles. In terms of the fundamental principles of cosmopolitanism identified by Held (2003: 470), the primary unit of moral concern for Brown is the individual rather than the state. His views and actions also underscore the principle of 'reciprocal recognition', namely the ethical requirement 'that every person should accord equal respect to every other person' (see Chapter 1). Alongside these moral principles, we can see the two cosmopolitan political principles articulated by Held (2003: 470-1): the principle of 'consent' involving the importance of participation through non-coercive political processes, and the principle of 'inclusiveness and subsidiarity', which expresses the need for people to have a genuine say in the decisions that affect them.

As we will see, however, Brown extends and in some respects challenges the more circumscribed formulations of cosmopolitanism. This occurs through the notions of 'ecology' and 'eternity' that are so central in his thought and action. 'Ecology' is not simply another term for the environment, or a means of encapsulating Brown's so-called green credentials. It denotes for Brown an essential interrelationship between people and the planet. The term 'ecology' expresses the need for individuals to be 'at one' with the environment, and each other. Equality and ecology must therefore travel together. Whereas 'economy' is integral to human activity, Brown wants to counter the problems wrought by 'extreme capitalism' and its emphasis on material values. In opposition to the dominance of material values, he supports a cosmopolitan ethic, but also the need for ethics to figure far more strongly in the transformed politics he seeks. 'Eternity' is tightly interwoven with these ideas. It expresses the need, as Brown sees it, for maintaining long-term perspectives in our actions, particularly regarding the wellbeing of the planet, and ourselves. More concretely, one of the key values implied in 'eternity' is encapsulated in the notion of inter-generational equity. These aspects of ecology and eternity represent a significant elaboration of cosmopolitan ideals in an Australian context.

In addition to helping us think critically about cosmopolitanism, Brown presents an opportunity to examine the nexus between cosmopolitan sensibilities and local concerns, and between acting through conventional institutions of the nation-state and reinventing these. At the same time, however, he stands awkwardly both in terms of ideals and practice. Although Australians might support the protection of picturesque, environmentally sensitive regions, their reasons are generally different from the sort of longer-term holistic outlook Brown urges. In addition, while Brown has benefited from his independence, his parliamentary position and the increasing success of the Australian Greens party draws him further onto the slippery ground of mainstream politics. In these respects, Brown's experiences shed light on challenges and dilemmas facing those wanting to give effect to cosmopolitan outlooks.

Brown's political ascendancy

Bob Brown's 'radicalisation' as a peace activist during the Vietnam War and rise to prominence coincided with a period of upheaval, domestically and globally. Whereas the labour movement had long been regarded as the principal force of social transformation, from the late 1960s the industrialised democracies of the world experienced the dramatic emergence of new social movements (NSMs) and interest groups organised around issues of racial and sexual equality, peace, and environmental quality (Burgmann 2003; Marsh 1995; Torrow 1994). Their appearance has been attributed in part to a marked shift in prevailing societal values from 'materialist' to 'post-materialist' values (Dalton et al. 1990; Inglehart 1977; 1990). At the same time, these movements sought to extend political perspectives beyond the local, expanding the boundaries of community and enlarging notions of political identity. Concurrently, the language of internationalisation and, later, globalisation, increasingly predominated in political discourse. Bob Brown emerges, therefore, as a leader through a particular historical context characterised by a rapidly expanding, globally oriented constituency that expressed particular concern with environmental and social justice issues. It is this constituency that he has striven to cultivate and represent.

Accompanying the rise of these social protest movements, the practice and ideals of liberal democracy were also put under the spotlight, with the result that movements arose seeking more participatory, open forms of democracy. The aim was to rehabilitate and extend the idea of democratic citizenship, domestically and globally (Heater 2002; Pateman 1970). Those associated with new social movements often regarded the existing institutions and practices of government as responsible for many of the perceived problems with which they were concerned (Burgmann 1993; Pakulski 1991). Accordingly, such movements made first recourse to strategies of protest and direct action, often forsaking the conventional domain of politics, and pursuit of parliamentary power. Pakulski (1991: 36) comments:

> They [NSMs] see movement events as addressed to the public-at-large rather than to the elites, and as attempts to publicise, re-assert and vindicate some general social values and moral principles which are threatened through neglect or distortion.

Alongside the new social movements, there emerged quite a different set of ideas and a different political agenda. In Australia, this saw strong attacks upon and challenges to the pattern of state-economy relations that had prevailed for much of the twentieth century (Argy 1998; Emy and Hughes 1991). The foremost impetus came from the economic, technological and cultural processes of global change, namely globalisation. Neoliberal ideas served as the intellectual vehicle for justifying broad measures such as embracing the free market, downsizing government and getting it 'off the back of business', and attempting to reduce the size of the welfare state. The aim was to change

103

values and expectations, as well as institutions and processes (Emy 1993; Emy and Hughes 1991). Neoliberalism also countered the social democratic agenda and many of the values articulated by the new social movements (Burgmann 2003).

It was into this maelstrom of ideas, outlooks and agendas that Bob Brown stepped in the 1970s. Having arrived as a locum in Launceston in 1972, Brown embraced green politics in the wake of the controversy over the flooding of Tasmania's Lake Pedder (Thompson 1984). Bowman and Grattan (1989: 85) comment:

> Tasmania was to provide him with a home and a cause to match his idealism;
> it acted as a forcing house in which the conservation movement and Brown
> as its leading activist came together and have continued to grow in strength.

By 1976, Brown had emerged as leader of the Tasmanian environmental movement, giving up his medical practice to become director of the newly formed Tasmanian Wilderness Society. Like many other NSM groups, this organisation 'was radical in style and purpose, anti-hierarchical on principle, and intent on avoiding bureaucratic organisation' (Bowman and Grattan 1989: 88). Bob Brown's role in the successful campaign to stop the damming of the Franklin River, which stands as a watershed in the politicisation of the environment in Australia, saw him achieve a high and continuing level of national prominence.

In 1983, Brown was elected to the Tasmanian Parliament, marking an important yet challenging shift from being outsider-activist to being both an outsider-activist and insider-reformer. In 1986, he started using the term Green Independent (with Gerry Bates, the environmental lawyer elected alongside him in the 1986 state election), and in the wake of the 1989 election five Green Independents led by Brown held the balance of power in Tasmania. In return for Green support in the Tasmanian Parliament, the ALP minority government negotiated an innovative, but short-lived, Labor–Green Accord. This agreement represented something of a middle ground in terms of debates among Greens between 'Fundamentalists' and 'Realists' on such political alliances (Brown 1990: 255–6; 2004: 120–34).[1] In August 1992, Brown joined with others in forming the Australian Greens party and in 1996 he was elected to the Australian Parliament as a senator for Tasmania.

In the eyes of many of his supporters and detractors, Brown embodies quintessentially *Australian* issues and concerns. At one level, this is reinforced by Brown's position in the Australian Parliament. Media images of Brown underscore this Australianness and his environmental credentials with photographs of him standing before a towering *Eucalyptus regnans*, or at his house at Liffey – a weatherboard cottage built in 1904 – set before the majestic wilderness of Tasmania's Dry Bluff. Yet, ultimately, there is little that is uniquely Australian or narrowly environmental about Brown's political critique or his agenda for change. He seeks to address wider issues and processes, and although acting locally is important, so, too, is the need to think and act globally.

Bob Brown's outlook and concerns have shifted somewhat as he has moved further onto the national and, indeed, international stages. But those who at times criticise him for privileging social justice issues over environmental ones ignore the continuities in Brown's concerns, ideas and prescriptions. Although he may, for example, draw attention to the logging of native forests in Tasmania, he also emphasises that the issues are often 'the same elsewhere in Australia and indeed the rest of the world' (Brown 2004: 3). Today, however, when he expresses his ideas he will often move seamlessly between his own views and those of the Greens. The key elements have long been there for him, however, even when he was carving out his credentials as an environmental activist. These core values include equality and justice, as well as extending democracy at both the local and the global level.

At one level, Brown is very much a reformer working within existing structures, but he also continues to juggle – and cherish – the role of outsider-activist committed to fundamental change. Indeed, while Brown may seem quite conventional, his politics are ultimately revolutionary (Norman 2004: 2). He argues strongly that, for the wellbeing of humanity and the future of the planet, fundamental changes are called for in the ethics and morals that guide us.

Ethical and moral renewal

Bob Brown's critique of contemporary Australian society is, in his view, applicable to modern industrialised, capitalist societies generally. It rests heavily on claims about the corrosiveness of materialism (or consumerism), the 'dominant ethic' of our times, coupled with the effects of an exploitative, destructive attitude towards nature. The dominant ethic is too concerned with the 'here and now', and predicated on narrow conceptions of human wellbeing and (self) interest. There needs to be much greater regard for the longer term effects of our actions and lifestyles upon communities and the planet as a whole, and future generations. In opposition to the dominant ethic, our 'true interests' are collective rather than individual (Brown and Singer 1996: 43–4, 49–50).[2] Moreover, these interests are to be found in building relationships that lie in harmony with the planet as a whole. Brown

105

(1990: 250) writes: 'Materialism is an ethos which cannot be sustained; either in terms of ecology of the Earth, or the spirit of human beings, for it impoverishes and destroys both . . .'

As Brown conceives it, the relationship between humans and nature is fundamental. 'The Earth', he says (Brown 2004: 5), 'is the cradle of our existence . . . We are all born bonded to nature'. Elsewhere, he (Brown 1990: 249) writes:

> Everyone knows that the Earth is our all. It is vital for everyone's future that the bond with nature is restored, nurtured and made our guide in planetary affairs . . . The Earth is us, and as we diminish it, so we diminish ourselves.

The growth model and 'freewheeling materialism' which has predominated under industrialisation and capitalism wrenches apart our 'deep connection' with nature and is bringing about 'the greatest crisis in human history' (Brown 2004: 7; 1990: 252). Current patterns of human growth and consumption are not sustainable, and dramatic alterations to existing values, institutions and patterns of resource use are necessary to avoid not just ecological catastrophe — 'our impending extinction' — but also social decay (Brown 2004: 12). Notwithstanding greater material output, the world's people are in many ways poorer and more vulnerable today. The increasingly globalised nature of threats and crises requires critique, reflexivity, and political transformation by cultivating a new universal ethic. Nonetheless, such critiques maintain faith in reason and the role of science. We need to learn to live with the planet as its (long-sighted) guardians rather than (short-sighted) exploiters (Brown 2004: 5).

Brown seeks a new ethic that gives voice to the need to 'globalise our humanity'. At a time when neoliberal prescriptions surrounding economic globalisation have been employed to narrow the scope and nature of political debate and privilege economic values over political values (Emy 1993; Walter 1996), Brown's ideas represent an important counter-position, broadly consonant with new social movement ideals. Instead of economics, it is ethics which is central to life and political action. But this ethic needs to be globally constituted: (Brown and Singer 1996: 51).

> For Greens, ethics is central to our vision of the direction in which we need to go. We are concerned for the whole world, now and in the future. We want to leave the lightest possible footprints on our planet. We see it as a fundamental obligation on each generation to pass on to our descendants a world that is at least as rich and diverse, and as capable of supporting its human population and the other beings who live on it, as the world we inherited from our ancestors

In calling for a major change in our attitudes towards nature and the planet, Brown also raises the principle of 'inter-generational equity'. This principle, largely new to political debate, insists that it is the responsibility of any given generation not to leave an impoverished environment for the next (Burgmann 2003: 202).

Ethics can provide the necessary foundation for social and political life. They must be put back into politics and gain greater prominence in political decisions at all levels (Brown and Singer 1996: 58–9).

> An approach to ethics that is based on our ability to think rationally and critically about our values, combined with empathy and concern for others, could become the most powerful force for change that the world has yet seen . . . The revolutionary element in Green ethics is its challenge *to see ourselves in universal terms* . . . The kind of interests that these people or beings [across the world] have will vary, but not the ethical requirement to give the same weight to similar interests (Brown and Singer 1996: 55. Emphasis added).

The shift towards this universal, indeed global, sensibility embracing the long-term good of the planet, not just the interests of the human population at any given time, is a long-term process. It involves a huge change in our intellect, says Brown. In addition, no one, including the Greens, has 'the answer'. It is, rather, a matter of questioning what is being done at any point in time and moving on (*Late Night Live* 2002). We can see here, as Lohrey (2002: ix) observes, the notion of 'the moral life revising itself', which the Green movement speaks to and is so strongly identified with today.

While Brown does not set his ideas and arguments in 'national versus global' frameworks, the life he urges involves a holistic, global outlook. For this reason, Brown does not rail against 'globalisation', except what he sees as the excesses and costs of economic globalisation, dominated as he sees it by largely unaccountable multinational corporations and backed up by governments of the most powerful developed countries (*Late Night Live* 2002; Norman 2004: 180). Brown says that globalisation needs to be treated 'as an opportunity, not a threat' (cited in McKew 2002: 48). That opportunity lies with human globalisation and affirming the value of diversity. While there are and will be different and overlapping attachments or 'partial loyalties', these are situated within a (re)imagined global community (Brown and Singer 1996: 56–7). Ultimately, this new moral life arises 'from a location in the heart, not the map' (Brown and Singer 1996: 1).

107

Equality and social justice

Bob Brown has become well recognised for speaking out on issues beyond environmental concerns, including native title and reconciliation, human rights, the treatment of refugees and asylum seekers, inequality, Australian foreign policy, privacy, and the position of minorities. In part, this is due to his media appeal and success at mastering the sound bite. It also stems from Brown's profile in the Senate, where minor parties and independents have in recent decades usually held the 'balance of power'. A further factor here has been his role as leader of the Greens in the Australian Parliament, who themselves have been concerned to shake the 'single issue party' tag. Above all, however, the scope of Brown's concerns reflects the nexus for him, and indeed the Greens, between environmental protection, social justice, democracy and peace. Brown (1990: 249) has expressed this in terms of ecology, economy, equality, eternity: ecology concerns understanding ourselves in relation to the planet, the interdependence of life, and ensuring life on Earth; economy means managing the planet; equality is about sharing the planet with others 'so that all may enjoy hope' and pursue 'freedom, sustenance and fulfillment'; eternity, which is centrally important, is about promoting life, in all its diversity, its 'infinite unfolding of possibilities', forever (Brown 1990: 249–51).

Issues of environmental protection, social justice and democracy have long been regarded by Bob Brown as fundamental to one another. In the late 1980s, Bowman and Grattan (1989: 94) could observe of the Tasmanian Greens that they 'are the innovators and change-makers, their philosophies embracing social justice, peace and democracy as well as the environment'. Nonetheless, in the years following the Franklin campaign, we see a broadening of Brown's agenda, with arguably more pronounced attention to social justice politics alongside the environment. This occurs at the same time as Brown emphasises the interrelatedness of ecological, social and economic processes, together with the compelling local–global connectivities. The goal, then, is to establish 'a sustainable relationship between the world's peoples, as well as between people and the planet itself' (Brown and Singer 1996: 1). It involves a global consciousness with a strong regard for future generations (Brown 2001; Brown on *Late Night Live* 2002).

It is evident, however, that many Australians who may support Bob Brown on the environment do not share his holistic and cosmopolitan perspective. Today, Brown is likely to be criticised not for his 'single issue' focus – always a misrepresentation or misunderstanding – but rather his 'left-wing' social justice stance, or even for 'neglecting' the environment through his commitment to these other issues (White 2001: 76). This points to tensions within Australian society between social justice and deep ecology formulations of the issues, and divisions within the environmental movement. One area where this has been manifest is population policy, with concerns even among environmentalists over Brown linking domestic immigration and refugee issues to care of the planet. For Bob Brown, social activism comes together with environmental activism. Ultimately we cannot, or must not, protect the environment at the expense of social justice. This would amount to a 'fortress Australia' mentality (Brown 2001; *Late Night Live* 2002). Nonetheless, scratch the surface of Australian political culture and we see the paradox of Brown's prominent public profile alongside uncertainty over what he stands for and often narrow ideas as to what he 'should' stand for. In October 2003, when Bob Brown, along with Greens Senate colleague Kerry Nettle, interrupted US President George W. Bush's speech in parliament, howls of protest came quick and fast. The more sensationalist and ludicrous claims aside (see Cassin 2003), Brown was castigated for not adhering to what made his name in Australian political life: the environment. But Brown was adamant: 'The single-issue tag went when we took our stand over the *Tampa*. The Greens' core issues globally are social justice, democracy, peace and the environment' (Brown quoted in Wright 2003). Confronting President Bush in the manner he did, while ALP MPs floundered over whether and how they might 'protest', underscored Brown's determination to speak out on these larger issues and to encourage public debate over Australia's place in the world, and Australians' relationship with the wider international community.

Political empowerment

Authentic democratic governance is integral to Brown's cosmopolitan world view, his commitment to the political development and empowerment of citizens effectively linking shorter-term reformist goals and his more revolutionary longer-term goals. For Brown, responsibility for enduring change rests in the hands of all people rather than elites, even environmental elites. In the manner of those advocating more participatory forms of democracy, his larger 'transformative project' involves raising awareness and increasing understanding, also the recognition that political participation itself is constitutive in the development of individual potentialities and social change. We can see here that Bob Brown's personal journey, finding strength through struggle, offers important insights into his hopes and aspirations for his fellow citizens (Brown quoted in Bowman and Grattan 1989: 86):

Once you get past the hurdle of realising that you are finite, that you are mortal, you are then freed up to use life as active and exciting – to do things . . . We're held back by feeling that we mustn't threaten ourselves, socially or physically. It's important to break out of that.

It was the Franklin campaign that underscored for Brown (1981: 303) that a community can successfully fight for ideals and 'people can change things, not only for the better now but for the better for the long term'.

Around the time Bob Brown discovered green politics, the Australian environmental movement was marked by 'outsider politics', with groups struggling to influence the state, and indeed often highly critical of state power and how it was exercised (Doyle 2000: 109–10). While NSMs espoused value change and declared their commitment to more pluralistic developmental models of democratic politics, in the 1980s and 1990s substantial sections of the environmental movement were coopted by governments and had become quite elitist in their operation. Powerful professional activists working closely with government bodies, the major political parties and business corporations became more influential in determining the movement's political agendas. As Doyle (2000: 170) puts it, the environmental movement 'was now playing the political game as defined for them by the dominant power-brokers'.

In part at least, for such reasons Bob Brown has remained very wary of strategies incorporating interest groups into decision-making processes and has questioned the long-term efficacy of close corporate alliances (Burgmann 2003: 228). For Burgmann (2003: 236), Bob Brown 'knows from decades of experience that power to negotiate is enhanced by continuing protest'. This is undoubtedly so, but for Brown it is people themselves — whether as local communities, groups or movements — who must act and can succeed. It is not just a matter, then, of which may be the more effective means of exercising political clout. His concerns over close corporate-type alliances also relate to the importance as he sees it of people taking responsibility and, as citizens, *acting for themselves.* Parliament broadened Brown's scope, but not his philosophy, nor his views on protest as a tool for change (Bowman and Grattan 1989: 84–5). Today, he remains committed to the view that as citizens we do not merely ascribe power to someone else (*Late Night Live* 2002). We are all responsible. Moreover as the Franklin campaign exemplified, the process of protest empowers the wider community and population, raising consciousness and understanding. Basic to Brown's view of democracy is the notion of 'people being informed and believing they can do things' (Brown cited in Bowman and Grattan 1989: 91). Self-development, self-determination, civic competence and responsibility go together in a positive, developmental view of politics and political life.

Notwithstanding the value of protest and direct political action, as a member of parliament, Brown today directs much of his energy to working through established institutions to effect change. The role of parliament is pivotal to reform and longer term political transformation. But it is parliament, not the executive, shored up as it is by disciplined party politics, which is the keystone of representative democratic government. While parliament has strengthened Brown's capacity to act both locally and more globally (Bowman and Grattan 1989: 93; Norman 2004: 179), there are substantive impediments to effective parliamentary democracy that must be addressed. Ideological convergence in the dominant parties and the negative logic of parliamentary politics that emphasises personality and point scoring mean that politics is devalued. The electoral system and parliamentary procedures need reform (Brown and Singer 1996: 49, 99). In addition, while governments must maintain the approval of the voters, in practice this often leads to a short-term electoral focus to the detriment of long-term decisions that take account of future generations. Brown and Singer (1996: 95) write, 'The only possible solution that does not abandon either democracy or the future of our planet is for ordinary people to start to think – and vote – with a more distant time-horizon'.

Quite how the sort of reorientation in values and horizons Brown has in mind is to be achieved is not made clear. The immediacies of everyday life such as job security, health care, and family needs are powerful 'localising' influences, especially when reinforced by vested economic and political interests. It is conceivable that they may only be effectively countered by crises or catastrophes. And as we have seen, Brown readily employs precisely such notions when he talks about the state of the planet. The 'real question', he says (quoted in Norman 2004: 189), is whether 'the world is going to move on through intelligence or catastrophe'. 'Intelligence' here involves bringing together ethical standards and scientific knowledge (concerning the state of the environment for instance), coming to informed decisions through genuinely democratic processes.

Towards a global politics

The changes which Brown (like the Greens) envisages are part of a 'profound worldwide transformation of politics' and government (Brown and Singer 1996: 2). Ultimately, he seeks to break with the dominant ideology of western societies, working to help create new values and a new consciousness.

111

Institutional change, ranging from reinventing existing structures and processes to establishing new ones, is integral to this picture. Brown is, of course, very aware that this is a formidable task that he and fellow Greens around the world face, and he entertains no illusions about the possible time frames. But his concern is with the 'ongoing human experience' and any Green ascendancy in the world will be long-term, 'probably after my life time'. For Brown, it is a matter of building the 'paving stones to that gate' today, and putting 'a set of references into the system'. In this context, optimism, along with 'a bit of defiance', remain very important (*Late Night Live* 2002).

As Bob Brown conceives it, Green politics is at the same time world politics. The Franklin River campaign was run under the banner 'Think globally, act locally', aimed at fulfilling a larger role and symbolic value in the fight to save the global environment. Even then, argues Thompson (1984: 64), 'conservation was not of itself his primary concern'. Issues such as nuclear disarmament and world poverty were among those that weighed most heavily on Brown's mind. According to Thompson (1984: 64), Brown felt that with the Franklin, 'Tasmanians had an historic opportunity to make a small mark for humanity by choosing to save rather than destroy'.

While 'think globally, act locally' remains a powerful theme for Brown, his actions over the past decade reveal a commitment to concerted action at the global level. This is evident in his strong stance over the Kyoto Protocol, which he sees as very inadequate, his support for institutions involving, for example, environmental issues and international criminal justice, and his stance over the treatment of Tibetans and repression of their culture under Chinese rule. His work with the Global Greens and the development of an associated international network of Green parties and political movements exemplify Brown's global ideals. In 1991, Brown (*Charge of the Greens* 1991) said that such action 'is the only way for us to go forward'. In 2001, he hosted the Global Greens 2001 conference in Canberra, which adopted the Global Greens Charter and established the Global Greens Coordination Network. The Charter represents something of a blueprint for Brown, both personally and as a member of the Greens (see Brown 2004: Appendix II). It outlines the principles upon which the policies of the Global Greens are founded, which include 'ecological wisdom', social justice, participatory democracy, non-violence, sustainability and respect for diversity. Its aims include building democracy from local through to global levels, ending poverty, universal primary education, amending the United Nations' Declaration on Human Rights to include the right to a healthy environment, reform or abolition of the World Trade Organization and World Bank, and establishment of an international court to deal with environmental damage. The document commits the Global Greens to acting globally as well as locally, establishing policies and structures that extend political power and opportunity to all members based on a model of participatory democracy, and working to extend these democratic principles to the broader society. According to Norman (2004: 183), with the Charter the Global Green movement is now 'directly engaging with the technological mechanisms to bring a truly global green decision-making capacity into place'. But in terms of such developments, the Greens are at a very nascent stage. Brown (2001: 72) is optimistic yet realistic, remarking that these developments involving the Global Greens and the Charter are as yet 'a small move towards global democracy'.

While Brown's cosmopolitan ideals involve the development of international regimes (organisations, agreements, etc.), it is global democracy which represents both an essential means and end for him. According to Norman (2004: 180–1),

> Brown's globalisation vision begins with global democracy . . . He has frequently put his vision for global democratic governance, based on the model of 'one person, one vote, one value', and sets the environment as the key issue from which all economic considerations should spring forth . . . The Green Party in its many international guises, is one of the first internationally networked political parties that has aspirations for global political power and influence. Bob Brown has been one of its most vociferous advocates. As much as the environment is an issue that crosses international borders . . . Green parties have arisen globally to meet that calling . . . Bob Brown [has] been one of the key proponents of the concept of 'green' or 'positive' globalisation.

As Norman (2004: 181) observes, however, Brown's strong advocacy of 'positive' globalisation puts him at odds with elements of the Greens in Australia and elsewhere who emphasise the need for action at the local community level and building up local governance. A feature of Bob Brown's politics has been his strong commitment to local community building accompanied by grassroots activism. But his overarching commitment to a global perspective and working for global changes has been there from the earliest days of his political 'radicalisation'. And even as a Tasmanian MP, he became 'increasingly frustrated', says Norman (2004: 179), 'by the narrow scope of the parliamentary work he was able to engage with'. It is not a matter, then, of being mesmerised by the bright lights of the national and international stages. Rather, Brown's global frame of reference expresses both his holistic perspective on humanity's interrelationship with the planet and the fact,

113

for him, that many of the most pressing needs and issues we all face today involving the environment, equality and social justice, are truly global.

Political influence

For over two decades, Bob Brown has enjoyed a profile in Australian political life that is surpassed by few and certainly coveted by many of his parliamentary colleagues. A search of media citations shows that he is sought out for comment on a wide array of issues from the local to the global. He is if anything more likely now to be referred to in connection with equity and social justice concerns, human rights, and Australia's relationship with the international community than with environmental concerns. For many Australians, Brown speaks to the changing political agenda and societal values, articulating the increasing prominence afforded 'post-materialist' values and the desire shared by many to put ethics back into politics. Brown is seen as sincere and respectable, a person of integrity and principle, and to the public at large he conveys a simple friendliness, consistency and optimism. For Lohrey (2002: 76), Bob Brown 'somehow manages to suggest that the radical and the respectable can co-exist within one moral framework, and that what we have been educated to think of as contradictory may not be in fact so'. Such has been his perceived influence that in 2002, the *Australian Financial Review* identified Brown as one of the ten most 'culturally powerful' Australians.

In an electorate that is widely distrustful of its politicians and quite cynical when it comes to electoral politics, Bob Brown is seen as authentic and ethical. This is of undoubted importance in terms of concerns in Australia and many other established democracies over the need to rebuild social – and political – capital. His role in the Franklin campaign forged in the Australian political consciousness a particular perception of Brown which has changed little since. In the wake of that campaign, Bowman and Grattan (1989: 91) could remark that Brown is seen among activists as a 'principled and effective protester'. And still, after almost two decades in parliament, Lohrey (2002: 76) remarks that he is an 'authentically organic leader' which 'gives him a credibility and a moral authority difficult to impugn'. While, however, the agenda of political debate has and is changing under pressure from the environmental movement, along with other NSMs and pressure groups, other influences have been at play in Australian politics which have worked to push value and institutional change in at times quite different directions. For instance, Brennan and Castles (2002: 1) identify 'a kind of institutional repositioning, a move to a more "competitive" institutional order increasingly like that of the United States and increasingly unlike the Australian egalitarianism of the past'.

What, then, can be said of Bob Brown's influence? It would be easy to dismiss his media profile as indicative of little more than a great capacity to 'feed the chooks' — as former Queensland Premier Sir Joh Bjelke-Peterson was fond of saying about his relationship with the media. This would be unfair. Brown has maintained a strong media profile both during times when the Greens have (with others) held the balance of power in the Senate, and when the Howard government controlled the Senate in its last term. However, it would be naïve to equate coverage with success in challenging the political agenda. Much of the media coverage Brown receives takes the form of very brief grabs where 'newsworthiness' factors weigh heavily. It is noteworthy, for instance, that the media did not report a word of Brown's maiden speech to the Australian Parliament in which he outlined his ideas and aspirations for social change in relatively measured, considered terms (Norman 2004: 191). Instead, they feasted on Pauline Hanson's sensational and inflammatory maiden speech, which attracted front-page coverage across the nation.[3] But, when Brown heckled President Bush during his speech to the Australian Parliament on 22 October 2003, media attention was massive (see Norman 2004: 205–10).

In seeking to account for Brown's support and popularity, commentators readily point to his 'charisma' (see, for example, Bowman and Grattan 1989: 91; Doyle and Kellow 1995: 118; Economou in *Background Briefing* 2003). But as Diani (2003) reminds us, this approach, which relies on the 'leader equals charismatic figure' equation, diminishes the importance of ideas, along with such factors as network location, connecting actors, sub-sectors and issues. Of course, commentators have long underestimated the role of ideas in Australian political culture (Stokes 1994; Walter 1988). In the case of Bob Brown, it is ideas and the goal of fashioning wide-reaching 'organic' networks like the Global Greens which are centrally important. These networks are necessarily broadly based because of the value attributed to diversity and difference, and interconnecting the local and the global. It is a very different form of political mobilisation and consciousness-raising to what we have become accustomed to over the past 100 years in Australia under the exigencies of disciplined party politics where, moreover, narrow national interests have predominated. For these reasons alone, change is likely to come slowly.

While Brown's political targets are often quite proximate, his more substantive agenda and that which enables us to speak of him in terms of cosmopolitan ideals is by his own admission much more long-term. Getting these ideas into the public domain, fixing them in the political agenda and having them considered and debated is not easy. As Norman (2004: 211)

115

concedes, 'For the most part the Australian media are not willing to report, much less champion, Brown's optimistic, aspirational politics for the Greens. Not yet, anyway'. So judgments are difficult to make. Yet Brown has succeeded in helping to increase the Greens' representation in the Senate at successive elections, so that by July 2008 they had attained 'minor party' status, and effectively replaced the Democrats as the third force in Australian politics. After the 2007 election, Brown emphasised that the Rudd government was elected thanks to Green preferences, and he is likely to reiterate this point in order to make the most of the Greens' growing influence.

Conclusion

Bob Brown self-consciously practices now the future that he seeks, which helps give him the very authenticity that so many commentators speak of. 'Idealism' and 'spirituality' are terms commentators are likely to employ to encapsulate the appeal and influence of Bob Brown and the Greens. Social commentator Hugh Mackay (cited in Lohrey 2002: 71) remarks that the Greens appear to offer a new 'moral compass . . . they are the closest thing we have to a political party that proceeds from a clear sense of its own meaning and purpose'. For Christian social justice activist Tim Costello, the Greens offer a 'fusion of the personal and the sacred with a renewed public politics' (Reynolds 2003). In Reynolds's (2003) assessment,

> The green message goes to the heart of the age-old human endeavour to create personal and collective meaning ... The green world view, with its emphasis on the interconnection of the self, the world and the universe, answers that basic human need to believe in something larger, more enduring than ourselves ... [it] is a project and language larger than the self to make sense of the world.

As a cosmopolitan thinker and activist, Bob Brown challenges narrow or parochial attachments, seeking to extend our horizons to embrace simultaneously the local and the global. In vitally important respects, we are citizens of one world. This extension of horizons or frameworks is not just spatial. As illustrated by the important principle of inter-generational equity, it is also temporal. In contrast to other political formulations, Brown's cosmopolitanism does not rest with the universal rights, duties and such afforded to fellow human beings, as important and valued as they are. Brown's philosophy is above all an eco-centric rather than anthropocentric formulation that entails a very different sensibility and disposition. It involves recognising and cultivating our humanity and at the same time (inescapably) our relationship to nature and the planet.

The indications are that Bob Brown's larger cosmopolitan outlook resonates with sizeable sections of the polity in Australia. Clearly, however, people support or admire him for very different reasons, and many would be troubled by the holistic, eco-centric ideas and strategies Brown advocates. Even among Greens supporters, his commitment to 'positive' globalisation and acting globally is far from being equally shared. Beyond these constituencies, while Australia's political culture includes diverse, even conflicting political traditions, the 'mainstream' of ideas and values are quite removed from those advocated by Brown. Of course, he is well aware of this. Prevailing ideas and practices are entrenched, propped up by inertia, uncertainty, and powerful vested interests. Barring global catastrophe, radical social and political transformation is likely to be a long way off. In the meantime, Brown continues to lay the paving stones to the gates of the global society he envisages.

Notes

1 Whereas the 'Fundamentalists' tended to oppose any compromise with mainstream (pro-development) political parties such as the ALP, the 'Realists' saw compromise more as pragmatic adaptation, and the need to begin giving effect to environmental policies.
2 In this chapter I draw upon *The Greens*, co-authored by Brown and Peter Singer (1996). While the book is primarily an introduction to the Australian Greens, it is evident that, for Bob Brown at least, what the Greens represent and what he stands for are essentially the same.
3 Even Ben Oquist, Brown's longstanding personal assistant, expresses surprise at the lack of attention Brown's speech received: 'Normally a maiden speech would attract some interest, even just a line . . . But the whole press gallery was just transfixed by Hanson. They were utterly galvanised by it. Bob's speech didn't get a mention' (quoted in Norman 2004: 192).

References

Argy, F. 1998. *Australia at the Crossroads: Radical Free Market or a Progressive Liberalism?* Sydney: Allen & Unwin.

Background Briefing 2003. 'The Australian Greens: Getting Real.' Radio program. ABC Radio, 1 June.

Beck, U. 2002. 'The cosmopolitan perspective: Sociology in the second age of modernity.' In S. Vertovec and R. Cohen (eds) *Conceiving Cosmopolitanism: Theory, Context, and Practice.* Oxford: Oxford University Press, pp. 61–85.

Bowman, M. and M. Grattan 1989. *Reformers: Shaping Australian Society from the 60s to the 80s.* Melbourne: Collins Dove.

Brennan, G. and F. Castles 2002. 'Introduction.' In G. Brennan and F. Castles (eds) *Australia Reshaped: 200 Years of Institutional Transformation*. Melbourne: Cambridge University Press, pp. 1–24.

Brown, B. 1981. 'Wild rivers saved.' In R. Green (ed.) *Battle for the Franklin: Conversations with Combatants in the Struggle for South West Tasmania*. Sydney: Fontana, pp. 301–3.

——1990. 'Ecology, Economy, Equality, Eternity.' In C. Pybus and R. Flanagan (eds) *The Rest of the World is Watching: Tasmania and the Greens*. Sydney: Sun, pp. 245–57.

——1996. Bob's first speech in the Senate. (Transcript of maiden speech as Senator, Australian Parliament, 10 September.) In The Australian Greens *Senator Bob Brown*. Canberra: Australian Greens, viewed 24 March 2003, http://www.bobbrown.org.au

——2001. 'The Greens: A rock of security in the Senate.' *Australian Rationalist* 58/59:71–6.

——2004. *Memo for a Saner World*. Melbourne: Penguin.

Brown, B. and P. Singer 1996. *The Greens*. Melbourne: Text.

Burgmann, V. 1993. *Power and Protest: Movements for Change in Australian Society*. Sydney: Allen & Unwin.

——2003. *Power, Profit and Protest: Australian Social Movements and Globalisation*. Sydney: Allen & Unwin.

Cassin, R. 2003. 'Democracy needs its dissidents.' *The Age* 7 November: 13.

Craven, P. 2002. 'Introduction.' *Quarterly Essay* 8:iii–vii.

Charge of the Greens: Green Issues, Politics and Philosophy 1991. Video. Bendigo: Video Education Australia,.

Dalton, R. J., M. Kuechler and W. Bürklin 1990. 'The challenge of new movements.' In R. J. Dalton and M. Kuechler (eds) *Challenging the Political Order: New Social and Political Movements in Western Democracies*. Cambridge: Polity, pp. 3–20.

Diani, M. 2003. 'Direct democracy and leadership in social movement networks.' In P. Ibarra (ed.) *Social Movements and Democracy*. New York: Palgrave Macmillan, pp. 47–59.

Doyle, T. 2000. *Green Power: The Environment Movement in Australia*. Sydney: UNSW Press.

Doyle, T. and A. Kellow 1995. *Environmental Politics and Policy Making in Australia*. Melbourne: Macmillan.

Emy, H. V. 1993. *Remaking Australia: The State, the Market and Australia's Future*. St Leonards: Allen & Unwin.

Emy, H. V. and O. E. Hughes 1991. *Australian Politics: Realities in Conflict*. 2nd edn, Melbourne: Macmillan.

Hay, P. 2002. *Main Currents in Western Environmental Thought*. UNSW Press: Sydney.

Heater, D. 2002. *World Citizenship: Cosmopolitan Thinking and its Opponents*. London: Continuum.

Held, D. 2003. 'Cosmopolitanism: Globalisation tamed?' *Review of International Studies* 29(4):465–80.

Inglehart, R. 1977. *The Silent Revolution: Changing Values and Political Styles Amongst Western Republics*. Princeton: Princeton University Press.

——1990. *Culture Shift in Advanced Industrial Society*. Princeton: Princeton University Press.

Late Night Live 2002. Senator Bob Brown. Bob Brown interviewed by Phillip Adams. Radio program. ABC Radio National, 19 December.

Lohrey, A. 2002. 'Groundswell: The rise of the Greens.' *Quarterly Essay* 8:1–86.

Marsh, I. 1995. *Beyond the Two Party System: Political Representation, Economic Competitiveness and Australian Politics.* Melbourne: Cambridge University Press.

McKew, M. 2002. 'Bob Brown.' *The Bulletin* 1 October:46–8.

Mulligan, M. and S. Hill 2001. *Ecological Pioneers: A Social History of Australian Ecological Thought and Action.* Melbourne: Cambridge University Press.

Norman, J. 2004. *Bob Brown: Gentle Revolutionary.* Sydney: Allen & Unwin.

Pakulski, J. 1991. *Social Movements: The Politics of Moral Protest.* Melbourne: Longman.

Papadakis, E. 1993. *Politics and the Environment: The Australian Experience.* Sydney: Allen & Unwin.

Pateman, C. 1970. *Participation and Democratic Theory.* Cambridge: Cambridge University Press.

Peatling, S. 2002. 'Jail at his own pleasure.' *Sydney Morning Herald*, Spectrum 27 April:3.

Pybus, C. and R. Flanagan (eds) 1990. *The Rest of the World Is Watching: Tasmania and the Greens.* Sydney: Sun.

Reynolds, R. 2003. 'The earth's my shepherd.' *Sydney Morning Herald*, Spectrum 15 February:4.

Stokes, G. 1994. 'Conceptions of Australian political thought: A methodological critique.' *Australian Journal of Political Science* 29(2):240–58.

Tarrow, S. 1994. *Power in Movement: Social Movements, Collective Action and Politics.* Cambridge: Cambridge University Press.

The Age 2001. 'A true believer puts his faith in Brown.' News 7 November:9.

Thompson, P. 1984. *Bob Brown of the Franklin River.* Sydney: Allen & Unwin.

Walter, J. 1988. 'Intellectuals and the political culture.' In B. Head and J. Walter (eds) *Intellectual Movements and Australian Society.* Melbourne: Oxford University Press, pp. 237–73.

——1996. *Tunnel Vision: The Failure of Political Imagination.* Sydney: Allen & Unwin.

White, M. 2001. 'Nature boy.' *HQ* August/September, 84:72–8.

Wright, T. 2003. 'The green house effect.' *The Bulletin* 29 October, online edition, viewed 3 November 2003, http://bulletin.ninemsn.com.au

Keith Suter

Keith Suter is a social commentator, international relations expert, peace activist and prominent Christian. He is well known in New South Wales for his weekly radio commentary on Radio 2GB's Brian Wilshire program and regular feature columns in the *Daily Telegraph*. Suter first became well known in Australia through his activities for the peace movement in the early 1980s, when he was President of the United Nations Association of Australia. He was a founding director of the Trinity Peace Research Institute, and was awarded the Australian Government Peace Medal in 1986. He is a prolific writer and speaker, and has written many books, chapters and articles on the subjects of peace, disarmament and globalisation.

Keith Suter, publicist for peace and regular media commentator. (Courtesy Keith Suter.)

7

Keith Suter: Christian Activism for Peace and Global Change

Lucinda Horrocks[1]

Am I a cosmopolitan? When I first heard about this book I didn't know what 'cosmopolitanism' meant. Once I'd seen your definition of cosmopolitanism I suddenly realised I had been a cosmopolitan for half a century without realising it. I can now see what it is. It's world citizenship.

(Suter 2004a)

For most of his career, Keith Suter has worked to make world citizenship a reality. Whether he has been aware of it or not, Suter is a cosmopolitan. He belongs to a tradition of political thought that includes the ancient Stoics, St Augustine and Immanuel Kant, and that continues to the present day. Cosmopolitans argue that we should not just consider ourselves members of our family group, local community, state or nation, but that we should also recognise ourselves as citizens of a world community. We are, cosmopolitans argue, linked to others around the world. We should therefore take on the rights and responsibilities this global citizenship entails. Suter, in many forums, has encouraged us to think of ourselves as world citizens. Through his writing and activism, he has sought to change attitudes and create a space for us to rethink our political obligations. Much of his work is dedicated to encouraging us to consider the global context, and to act beyond local boundaries and parochial concerns.

Suter is also an exemplar of world citizenship in action. He (Suter 2004a) describes his core values as 'working for international cooperation, justice, equity, fairness, and the peaceful settlement of disputes', but his understanding of how these values may be applied to society is extraordinarily broad. Suter's campaigns have included working for peace, fighting for human

121

rights and equality of treatment for all peoples, dealing with conflict and terrorism, acting to save the environment, and explaining the problems (and benefits) of globalisation. In support of these causes, he has taken on the diverse roles of public commentator, government adviser, corporate consultant, teacher, motivational speaker, lay preacher, and agitator for social change.

Suter uses all means available to him to communicate his message. A prolific author, he has written thirty books and hundreds of articles and opinion pieces. He is also an accomplished public speaker. One of his great talents is being able to talk to people, raise awareness, build up networks, and inspire action. In his own words, Suter (2004a) is 'a crusader, a campaigner and a communicator'. In the last decade, he has boosted his presence in the public realm, appearing as a feature columnist for Sydney's *Daily Telegraph*, and making regular guest appearances on Channel Seven's *Sunrise* program. He also speaks weekly on the high-rating Brian Wilshire radio program on 2GB, where he often engages in heated debates with 'narrow nationalists'. He chooses to work in the most popular commercial media because they reach the largest audience. He (Suter 2004a) is unfazed by the possibility that much of that audience disagrees with what he says: 'If I go on the ABC I'm just broadcasting to my friends. You've got to broadcast to Australia. And you do that on commercial radio'.

Suter has a powerful capacity to distil political ideas, as well as communicate and disseminate them. Thus, although he has never been involved in party politics, Suter's work is highly political. This is because he is interested not only in changing attitudes, but also in mobilising Australians to take action. In the process, he has made a substantial contribution to the debate in Australia about the role of the individual in a globalising world. And in his pursuit of world citizenship, Suter has participated in some of the great social movements for change of the twentieth and twenty-first centuries.

Because of its breadth, it is impossible to canvass all of Suter's work. Instead, I will focus on four major themes. First, I explore two of the key influences on Suter's life, namely his experience in joining the UN Association as a teenager, and his Christian faith. Each demonstrates how Suter has adopted a distinctively cosmopolitan outlook. Then I will focus on two of Suter's campaigns: his peace activism in the 1980s, and his more recent work on globalisation. Although at first glance these campaigns seem quite different, both highlight Suter's particularly cosmopolitan approach to political action.

The UN Association

The United Nations (UN) has occupied a central position in Suter's life. Suter (2004a) says that for most of his life he has 'really been working for what the UN is working for'. That is, he has been working for the goals of eliminating war, fostering international cooperation, and creating the conditions for a peaceful world. Nonetheless, Suter is far from uncritical of the UN. One of the major shifts in Suter's thought over the last thirty years has been a growing disappointment in the UN, and a 'lessening of optimism' (Suter 2004a) in the possibility that the UN can, on its own, bring about the lasting conditions for peace. Although he still believes in a role for the UN, Suter now places far more faith in the potential of other global actors such as non-governmental organisations (NGOs), corporations, and individual world citizens to bring about change.

Suter's commitment to the UN is most evident in his work for the United Nations Associations (UNAs) in England and Australia. Born in London in 1948, Suter left school early at fifteen to start work for the Ministry of Defence (the War Office) in London. At sixteen, he joined the youth movement arm of the UNA of London. Joining the UNA had a significant impact on his life because it 'got me involved in international affairs' (Suter 2004a). The UNA was critical in helping Suter develop his interest in international events, and focus his mind on issues of peace and war. At the age of twenty-one, Suter left the War Office to study international law, international politics and international economics at the University of Sussex. In 1973, he moved to Australia to study at the University of Sydney, where he completed his first doctorate on the international law of guerilla warfare. More than simply providing an impetus to continue his education, membership of the UNA allowed Suter to pursue his interest in promoting international change.

The UNAs are a collection of voluntary, non-governmental associations aimed at fostering knowledge of and support for the United Nations. Distinct from the UN, the UNAs are non-profit organisations, organised largely by volunteers. UNAs worldwide are linked through the World Federation of United Nations Associations (WFUNA). The UNAs emphasise the fact that they are a peoples movement (Suter 1986b: 108). It is the emblematic opening to the UN Charter 'We the Peoples of the United Nations, determined to save succeeding generations from the scourge of war . . .', and the ideals contained within it that has inspired much of the UNAs' work.

When Suter joined the UNA in the early 1960s, there was an atmosphere of both optimism and doubt. Where some looked towards a future of justice and peace, governed at least in part by the human rights covenants that were still to be released,[2] others were anxious about whether the UN would become another failed experiment in international cooperation, like its predecessor the League of Nations. The UNAs worked on the assumption that the UN would be more likely to succeed if the citizens of the UN member nations supported its activities. From its inception, the rationale for the foundation of the UNAs had been, as WFUNA puts it, an 'awareness of the importance of public support as fundamental to the success of the United Nations' (*WFUNA* n.d. [c.2005]).

After moving to Australia, Suter continued his involvement with the UNA. From 1978 he occupied many positions in the New South Wales, Western Australian and national branches, including Human Rights Officer and National President. Suter endeavoured to publicise the work and ideals of the UN, and to educate Australians about international law. In two early articles, for example, Suter presented an argument for Australia to ratify the *International Covenant on Civil and Political Rights* (1978a), and set out Australia's international obligations regarding the Indonesian invasion of East Timor (1978b). Throughout the early 1980s, Suter was a prominent spokesperson and writer on peace, human rights, international treaties and other UN issues in Australia. The breadth of his concerns was wide. Human rights, the UN law of the sea, nuclear disarmament, Antarctica and the environment all jostle for attention.[3]

But Suter was also aware of the weaknesses of the UN. Limited by its structure, funding, historical and political factors, and the reluctance of member nations to undertake reform, the UN had not lived up to the high ideals set out in the preamble to the Charter. Most nation-states remained dominated by self-interest. UN mechanisms to avoid conflict have been disregarded or bypassed. War and genocide have occurred repeatedly. Yet Suter is quick to point out the great successes of the UN in fostering international cooperation, and in formulating an international legal framework of human rights. The responsibility for the failure of the UN, Suter argues, rests squarely with its members, the nation-states (Suter 2001b).

Suter has increasingly argued that, although the UN is important, we need to look outside it if we want to create a fair, just and peaceful world. Accordingly, he has also found himself looking elsewhere for the drivers of world change. Suter was one of the early commentators to talk of the potential of the new international community of non-governmental organisations (NGOs) to influence decision making on the world stage (Suter 1981b; 1986b: 84–6). He has made a case for world federalism, a form of democratic global governance based on federalist principles. World federalists argue for a more democratic UN structure, a powerful, independent international criminal court, and a greater voice for the global civil society of NGOs. Importantly, for Suter, world federalism also requires recognition that *individuals* should be the basic moral unit of a global society. In a world federation, 'all people should see themselves as world citizens' (Suter 1993b: 208).

Suter also now sees potential in the power of business, through an emerging corporate ethical philosophy, to promote international change. In part because of the success of NGOs and publicists like Suter in raising awareness, he believes business is becoming more responsive to global issues and more ethical in its approach. 'Business itself has changed, Suter (2004a) says, and 'they now want to hear about sustainable development, corporate ethics and corporate social responsibility'. For Suter, the need to connect and communicate with business is a question of who really has the power. In his view, national governments, hampered by bureaucracy and their own immobility, lack sufficient power to make any real difference in the global arena.

Although Suter remains a life member of the UNA, he realised that the UN on its own is unable to bring about the changes he seeks. The distinction between cosmopolitanism and internationalism (see Chapter 1) may help us understand Suter's ambivalent position towards the role and achievements of the UN. Cosmopolitan thinkers emphasise that we are all members of a wider global community; that, as individuals, we are all world citizens. The cosmopolitan ideal of global citizenship is not necessarily incompatible with national citizenship, but it does suggest that individual responsibilities extend beyond national boundaries. Internationalists, like cosmopolitans, recognise that there are problems in the world that extend beyond national boundaries. But they advocate cooperation between nation-states as a means to solving these problems.

On this account, the UN is primarily an internationalist institution. The UN structure and decision-making processes assume that nations are sovereign. Nation-states have a 'voice' in the General Assembly. Nation-states decide whether to cooperate with each other or not. The UN Charter framework sets up rules and codes of actions for nation-states based on these internationalist principles. Yet, the UN Charter advocates cosmopolitan principles and values. The notion of universal human rights is a cosmopolitan one. It emphasises equality and justice, not between nation-states, but between the peoples of the world. Such principles have the potential to cut across national boundaries and national jurisdictions. The work of the UNAs and other NGOs can also be seen as advocating cosmopolitan values within the UN structure. Thus, there is a 'paradox at the heart of the

UN' (Dower 2003: 112), between its internationalist structure and the cosmopolitan ideals of the Charter preamble.

Suter's involvement in the UNAs derives from his cosmopolitan sympathies. His work indicates not a wholehearted support of the UN itself, but a support of the universal *principles* that underlie the UN Charter. This stance enables a critical perspective on the activity and success of the UN, which sees it as one instrument in the achievement of global peace and global justice. Suter has not discarded internationalist solutions entirely; he has simply taken a more pragmatic approach. This is reflected in his belief in the power of business, and his recognition that you must look to where the power is if you wish to influence international change. Suter's cosmopolitanism extends his internationalism, allowing for other forms of politics to help achieve the goals of world peace and justice.

Christianity: working for social justice

The other major shaping force on Suter's life has been Christianity. Suter sees his mission as trying to expand the awareness of Christians in the developed world, to make them aware of broader global concerns. In particular, Suter has tried to encourage Christians to *act* to pursue the goals of global peace and justice. Getting Christians involved in international issues is simply 'part of the outworking of the faith' (Suter 2004a). This project has involved challenging certain perceptions of what is considered acceptable intervention by the church.

Suter has never been ordained as a minister of religion, claiming (2004a) that he lacks the necessary talents: 'You need certain gifts and graces to become ordained and I don't have them. One of them is patience'. He is, however, a lay preacher, who trained with the Anglican Church while a young man in England. During this period he joined the William Temple Association. Temple, who was Archbishop of Canterbury in the 1940s, outlined a set of Christian principles to guide, and justify, Christian political and social action. Temple (1942) linked issues of economics, working life, and international relations to the traditional spheres of Christian concern. Following Temple, Suter has tried to expand the horizons of Christian responsibility and motivate Christians to engage in political and economic debates.

Almost as soon as he arrived in Australia, Suter worked on articulating a rationale for Christian social action. He was influential in shaping the policy platform of the newly formed Uniting Church, which from its inception aimed to inform public policy on a range of social and political issues (*Uniting Church in Australia NSW Synod* 2004).[4] From 1982 to

1985, Suter was the General Secretary of the Uniting Church Commission on Social Responsibility. During this period, Suter raised the profile of the Commission's work, taking 'every opportunity to speak to the issues before the church at presbyteries, in parishes, to interested groups, on radio and in the news media', and, according to Stringer (2000: 7), being almost solely responsible for the 'flurry of publications' arising from the Commission during this period.

In 1983, Suter was a contributor to *Changing Australia* (Anglican Social Responsibilities Commission et al. 1983), a joint statement by the Protestant and Catholic churches on social justice. In part, it attempted to set a new framework for Christian action and responsibility based on the Gospel concept of the Kingdom of God (Suter 1991). *Changing Australia* was controversial, and was highly criticised because it commented on political and economic issues. Suter (2004a) reflects on the experience:

> What was interesting was the debate about whether or not Christians should be speaking out at all. And what has intrigued me, because I also chair the Temperance Movement in NSW, is that as long as I stick to alcohol, I'm fine. But as soon as we get into some of the bigger issues, people will say 'well we don't want to hear Christians talking about economics – what gives you the right to talk about economics?' My reply is that when it comes to economics, Christians have been writing about it for hundreds of years. We were here first – you've only been here for a hundred years!

To Suter, the injunction against the church being involved in worldly affairs ignores both history and current necessity (Suter 1987a). He (Suter 1980: 53) writes: 'Christians need to see their actions as having an essentially political nature ... politics is too powerful and pervasive to be kept out'. Christians, as an aspect of their faith, he argues, have a responsibility to become involved in political and economic affairs. This applies equally to domestic and global problems. Wherever there are problems of poverty, inequality, environmental degradation, violent conflict, injustice and human rights abuses, these belong to the sphere of Christian social responsibility.

In Suter's (1991: 101) view, Christians in modern, affluent societies have tended to narrow their horizons. Christians go to church to be 'comforted – not confronted'. Church leaders reinforce this attitude through their own limited awareness of broader issues. Sermons often fail to deal with contemporary issues, and if they do, it is to focus on personal morality, not the broader and difficult social issues of 'for example, reconciliation between the races, militarism, sexism, taxation rorts and immoral business practices' (Suter 1990: 88). To Suter, Christians need to look beyond their own 'narrow piety' (Suter 2004a) and live up to their responsibilities to their local and global communities.

Suter rests his idea of Christian social responsibility on the concept of the Kingdom of God. According to Suter (1990: 4), the Kingdom of God 'as announced by Jesus' is a 'rule of justice, truth, loving service, sharing, fellowship, peace and reconciliation'. As Suter presents it, all Christians are called to work for the Kingdom. He emphasises two aspects of the Kingdom: *justice* and *community*. For Suter (1990: 5), 'God is concerned with injustice', and Christians should be moved to work for justice by their sense of community, their connection with and responsibility to their neighbours. 'The cult of the rugged individual', stresses Suter (1991: 111), 'is not a Christian creed'.

Suter's conception of the Kingdom of God parallels certain strands of cosmopolitan thought. As in cosmopolitanism, Suter's Kingdom of God emphasises membership in a broader, global community. Similarly, the Kingdom of God emphasises individual obligation and responsibility towards others. The parallels are not surprising. The early Christians were heavily influenced by the cosmopolitanism of the ancient Stoics, and cosmopolitan principles can be found in many of the Christian founding texts. Ultimately, however, the church limited its cosmopolitanism. In St Augustine's conception of the City of God, citizenship is limited to 'those who love God. All others are relegated to the inferior – though still universal – earthly city by their love of self' (Kleingeld and Brown 2002). Augustine also differentiated the work of politics from the Christian mission of living for righteousness and justice, thus separating the earthly and temporal political authority from the spiritual authority of the universal church (Kleingeld and Brown 2002).

Part of what Suter is doing is engaging in the old theological debate over the bounds of church authority. In place of the restraint upon political action implicit in Jesus's plea to '[R]ender unto Caesar the things which are Caesar's, and unto God the things that are God's' (Matthew 22:21), Suter puts forward Jesus's vision of the Kingdom of God. In this way, Suter is reconfiguring Christian obligation to contend that the worldly realm is precisely the domain of Christian action and responsibility. To Suter, the Kingdom of God needs to be sought here, in this world, now. Suter's conception of the Kingdom of God does not restrict Christian activity to the spiritual realm. There is thus little sense of the Augustinian separation of the realms of believer and non-believer. Christians have an obligation to seek justice for all their fellow world citizens, irrespective of nation, religion or creed.

In arguing that Christians should engage with political issues, Suter is not breaking new ground. The churches in Australia have a strong tradition of intervening in political affairs, and have played a major part in shaping Australian political culture. But Suter has been innovative in articulating and justifying Christian social activism. Through such concepts as the Kingdom of God, Suter has encouraged Christians to see themselves as members of a larger world community with responsibilities towards others. In his emphasis on justice and community, Suter can also be seen as attempting to recapture some of the broader cosmopolitanism of early Christian thought.

The peace movement

Not long after arriving in Australia, Suter became involved in the peace movement. At its height in the early 1980s, the Australian peace movement was a coalition of different interest groups who had little in common except for their commitment to nuclear disarmament. This was the last decade of the Cold War, when the US and the USSR were locked in a military rivalry. Each country was stockpiling an increasingly deadly and accurate nuclear arsenal. The Soviet threat was considered extreme, and communism was still regarded as a danger to national security. Many Australians saw themselves as a target of Soviet hostility because of US military installations in Australia. By the early 1980s, the peace movement had gained such momentum that the Palm Sunday peace rallies attracted crowds in their hundreds of thousands. These were the biggest political demonstrations in Australia since the Vietnam War protests over a decade before.

Suter's involvement with the Uniting Church and the UNAs, combined with his talent for being 'always there, somewhere, giving a talk' (Smith 2004), made him a prominent figure in the Australian peace movement. He was at the very least 'the most visible Christian' (Gill 1985), and the involvement of the Christian community was critically important to the success of the peace movement. Smith recalls Suter as being distinctive because he was 'the only one in a suit'. This image of Suter, conservatively dressed amidst the colourful crowd, symbolises how the church was perceived when the peace movement started gathering pace. The church, usually the bastion of establishment thinking, was suddenly agitating for social change. The participation of the churches in political matters was controversial, and Suter, as one of the church's leading voices, was strongly criticised by conservative commentators.[5]

As is characteristic of his style, Suter campaigned for peace on many fronts. In addition to his UN advocacy and his Christian involvement, Suter formed political alliances with other groups, spoke in many public forums, acted as a government consultant and published a seemingly endless array of articles, books and flyers. All this contributed to the impression of his omnipresence in the peace movement. As early as 1973, Suter had become interested in the method of conflict resolution as an alternative to war, and had entered the public arena in an attempt to raise awareness of the value of this method. He also focused on the issue of disarmament, joining the Association for International Co-operation and Disarmament (AICD), becoming its president in the early 1980s. The AICD had a somewhat radical membership, earning Suter the tag of 'communist sympathiser'[6] (Campbell 1987: 46; Suter 1987b). It was Suter's ability to navigate between, and communicate to, disparate political groupings that made him such an effective campaigner. In 1985 he was made the UNA Representative on the Australian Government National Consultative Committee on Peace and Disarmament (he remains a committee member today). In 1986 he became the founding Director of the Trinity Peace Research Institute, the first non-governmental peace research institute in Australia, and was in the same year awarded the Australian Government Peace Medal (Suter 1990; *Who's Who in Australia* 2002).

Suter's writing for peace was significantly different in style to his other work. It is brutally direct, full of the impending apocalypse of World War III, and the potential destruction that will result from nuclear fallout (Suter 1982a: 1; 1984: 13–14). Suter's aim was to mobilise the public, particularly the Christian public, into civil protest. He was not afraid to use dramatic rhetoric to get attention. But his aim was also to educate. In such works, Suter identifies and explains broader international issues, connecting them to the realm of individual action. He discusses complex issues in an accessible way, using plain language, and making great use of historical examples. To Suter (2004a), it is important that his audience understand the context in which an issue should be understood. He also takes care to explain the point of view of the opposing side. Importantly, he emphasises practical solutions, such as his emphasis on conflict resolution as an alternative to war (Suter 1986a), or his appeal to Christians concerned about disarmament to take political action (Suter 1984: 13). This method, of clearly explaining global problems, and linking them to a set of discrete and practical steps for resolving them, is typical of Suter's style. Suter appealed to everyday Australians to become peace activists.

A common criticism of the cosmopolitan viewpoint is that it is 'rootless'. Cosmopolitans, the critics argue, emphasise a membership with an abstract, elitist 'world community', and to do this they must reject local affiliations and local concerns. Suter's involvement in the peace movement counters this criticism. The success of the peace movement in changing attitudes lay in the fact that the public made a strong connection between the local and the global. The possibility of nuclear war and the devastation that could ensue, while it had international causes, was also intimately local in its possible effects. Suter and the other peace activists emphasised the notion of world community, but connected this vision of global citizenship with the individual's responsibility to act to resolve local problems. In effect, Suter's message was, and remains: 'These world problems affect you, personally, here. And this is what you can do about it'. The peace movement was transformational, challenging notions of what 'belonging' meant, and what links us to others in our community, and in the world. The peace movement also expanded the acceptable ranges of political action.

Globalisation: the politics of anger

In the late 1980s, Suter began moving away from the negative description of peace as 'the absence of war', and focused more on formulating a positive prescription for peace. This redirection culminated in *The Triangle of Peace* (1990). The global issues of peace, conflict resolution, human rights and justice, however, remain central.[7] Of late, he is frequently asked to speak about terrorism, a topic he first addressed in the 1970s, when he was completing his doctorate on guerilla warfare.[8] Suter has increasingly become a public commentator on a wider range of domestic policy issues, such as the economy, environment, ageing Australia and the ethical responsibility of corporations.[9] To Suter, these concerns are not disparate; they are all connected. Sustainable development, for example, is also a question of economics, and corporate responsibility is an ethical, economic and political concern. Each has both global and local dimensions. Suter's broad perspective, his ability to see and predict social trends, his insight into the ways in which the global always relates to the local, all come to prominence in his understanding of globalisation.

In 1981 Suter wrote *A New International Order* (1981b). This was, he (Suter 2004a) says, his 'first book on globalisation, as I now know, although I didn't use the word globalisation then. It was an introduction to ideas like world citizenship and all the rest of it'. This was followed by two books in the 1990s: *Global Change* (1992a) and *Global Agenda* (1995b). Influenced by earlier works such as Alvin Toffler's *Future Shock* (1970) and Barry Jones' *Sleepers, Wake!* (1982), Suter was attempting to describe the 'new world order' he could see emerging.

As Suter sees it, globalisation is an inevitable economic and historical process, which is leading to an era of heightened worldwide interconnectivity. This new world order will result in reduced significance for nation-states, as other global actors become increasingly dominant (Suter 2004b). While alert to the dangers inherent in the processes of globalisation (for example, the problem of the changing nature of warfare, the effects of the worldwide spread of consumerism), Suter also sees the positive aspects. To Suter, increased connectivity means increased opportunities for cooperation. Globalisation can enhance the possibility of solving common global problems, such as environmental degradation and Third World poverty. To Suter, globalisation is neither right nor wrong; it simply is.

Suter was quick to recognise the significance of the rise of Pauline Hanson and the One Nation movement. Supporters of One Nation saw the increasing influence of international organisations such as the UN and the WTO, the number of international treaties and the increasing power of transnational corporations as a direct challenge to Australian sovereignty. Suter (1997c: 7) saw in Hanson a voice against globalisation: 'The Hanson factor is to be understood as a reaction against the pace of global change'. Suter pointed out that Australians had been unprepared for the radical changes globalisation had brought. Politicians had failed to educate the public and the result was anger and fear. This in turn had led to a resurgence of ultranationalism and xenophobia. One Nation's early success was due to its exploitation of the fears of Australians, a tactic Suter labelled the 'politics of anger' (1997c).

In 2000, partly as a response to the anti-globalisation push, Suter published *In Defence of Globalisation.*[10] The book is a direct attempt to counter the politics of anger. In it, Suter tries not only to explain the process of globalisation, but to explain how global change can also bring about positive effects. He explains that there are three types of globalisation. The first, 'economic globalisation', is the most commonly understood form of globalisation. Economic globalisation refers to the increasing spread and power of transnational corporations. The spreading global culture of consumerism, and increasing inequalities between the rich and the poor at both the local and global levels, are all aspects of economic globalisation (Suter 2000c: 9, 19–24). It is this form of globalisation that is most visible and the most feared. There are two other aspects of globalisation, however, which can have beneficial effects. 'Public order globalisation' is the process of international or inter-governmental collaboration to resolve global problems, 'a process which has been underway for almost two centuries' (Suter 2000c: 24). The UN is the most obvious example of such inter-governmental collaboration. The UN, in fostering collaboration between nation-states, has established a new governance framework that has helped resolve a variety of common social and economic problems. This type of public order globalisation shows the abundant positive potential of governments 'working together for a better world' (Suter 2000c: 24–34). As Suter sees it, 'popular globalisation' is the mobilisation of 'people power'. 'People power' is most evident in campaigns by international non-governmental organisations such as Amnesty International and Greenpeace, and represents a powerful, and potentially beneficial, force (Suter 2000c: 9, 35–41). This form of globalisation refers to the increasing capacity of citizens around the world to act together to redress global ills. Through people power, for example, even very marginalised and oppressed indigenous peoples such as those in West Papua can mobilise external support for their right of self-determination (Suter 2000c: 52). 'The challenge', Suter (2000c: 9) writes, 'is to make sure that globalisation as a whole works for the benefit of ordinary people and not just the wealthy few'.

Suter's stance on globalisation combines internationalist and cosmopolitan perspectives. In Suter's vision of public order globalisation, we can see his continued faith in the work and the role of the UN. But we also see that now, for Suter, the UN is not the only force for positive world change. His 'people power' network complements the work of the UN and provides an alternative approach that does not rely on the often arbitrary and self-interested decisions of nation-states. He contends we should not be afraid of the growth of inter-governmental and non-governmental organisations. Suter (2000c: 50–1) goes further to argue that, not only can we not expect national governments to solve problems in the globalised world, but also that we should think forward to a future in which national governments form only part of a network of global governance organisations. In the increasingly interconnected world brought about by the globalisation process, Suter sees opportunities for collaboration and decision making by the citizens of the world. Globalisation allows people to join together through networks that exist outside national boundaries and national jurisdictions. The apparent weakening of the power of the nation-state that was so distressing to One Nation is not, for Suter, a negative effect. It has the potential to create new opportunities and new forums for expressing a truly global people's voice.

Suter concludes his defence of globalisation by offering practical suggestions for individuals on how they can 'take on the corporations'. He (Suter 2000c: 54–60) suggests a range of actions, including making use of consumer power, such as 'buying goods to do good'; for example, by boycotting unethical products, buying shares (to gain a voice in the corporation), and investing in socially responsible investment funds. In these proposals, Suter links economics to broader social, political and ethical issues. Economic globalisation has brought great problems, but global corporations can, through the work of 'people power', be made to reform. Corporations are powerful, but they also have the potential both to change and to drive change. Indeed, corporations themselves can become a vehicle for world citizenship. To Suter, economics is an inescapable aspect of life that impinges on us locally and globally. He urges us not to ignore it, but to engage with it, all in the interest of working for justice.

Conclusion

For thirty years, Keith Suter has been articulating a way of thinking that emphasises political action for a world community based upon justice. Suter's advocacy for and criticism of the UN, his attempts to broaden the sphere of Christian social responsibility, his peace activism and his stance on globalisation all illustrate his cosmopolitan values. Suter's changing attitude towards the UN shows a shift in his ideas towards a more cosmopolitan perspective, away from the internationalist solutions traditionally offered by the UN system. The way Suter has incorporated both internationalist and cosmopolitan approaches into his politics tells us much about how he considers the goal of world citizenship may be achieved.

Suter's practical commitments are underpinned by his philosophy of Christian social action. His vision of the Kingdom of God is a cosmopolitan one. In the peace movement, Suter successfully linked the global to the local, and inspired local action based on the recognition of a common global problem. Twenty years later, Suter's globalisation campaign emphasised the potential positive effects of a world order that valued all people as global citizens. Keith Suter has endeavoured to show, throughout his publications and activism, how we have obligations towards all peoples of the world. He has explained global problems in terms of their impact and relevance to Australians. At the same time, he has encouraged Australians to view themselves as, and act as if they were, global citizens.

Notes

1 I would like to thank Keith Suter, Geoff Stokes, Holli Thomas, Gary Smith, Roderic Pitty, Heather Horrocks, Bill Horrocks and Jary Nemo, for their comments on this chapter.
2 These were the *International Covenant on Civil and Political Rights* and the *International Covenant on Economic, Social and Cultural Rights* endorsed by the UN Commission on Human Rights in 1966. Although the Universal Declaration of Human Rights was released in 1948, it took almost two decades for the UN to define the obligations of each nation wanting to ratify the covenants.
3 For examples of Suter's UN advocacy work during this period, see McKnight and Suter (1983) and Suter (1978c; 1981a; 1982b; 1982c; 1985; 1986b).

4 The Uniting Church was formed in 1977 from the Congregational Union, the Methodist Church and the Presbyterian Church (*Uniting Church in Australia NSW Synod* 2004). Each denomination already had a strong tradition of social activism in Australia. The new church represented a unique and radical break with more conservative religious elements, and this allowed it to pursue, with new freedom, a social justice agenda.

5 See, for example, Campbell (1987) and Sheridan (1982; 1983).

6 Suter was not alone here. Many peace activists at this time were accused of having communist sympathies.

7 For Suter's more recent work on peace, disarmament, conflict resolution and the United Nations, see Leeden (1999) and Suter (1992b; 1995a; 1995d; 1995e; 1997a; 1997b; 1999b; 2000d; 2001a; 2003b).

8 For Suter on terrorism, see Suter (2002c; 2003c; 2004c).

9 For his broader social commentary, see Suter (1993a; 1995c; 1998a; 1998b; 1998c; 1999a; 2000a; 2000b; 2002a; 2002b; 2002c); on scenario planning, see Walters (2003) and Suter (2000c).

10 The book is a reduced version of a much larger book on globalisation Suter had written over a decade before (Suter 2004a), eventually published in 2003 as *Global Order and Global Disorder*.

References

Anglican Social Responsibilities Commission, Australian Council of Churches, Catholic Commission for Justice and Peace et al. 1983. *Changing Australia*. Melbourne: Dove.

Campbell, A. A. 1987. 'The radical dilemma of the Uniting Church: Keith Suter's crusade.' *Quadrant* 31(8):65–70.

Dower, N. 2003. *An Introduction to Global Citizenship*. Edinburgh: Edinburgh University Press.

Gill, A. 1985. 'Churches fighting a war of peace.' *Sydney Morning Herald* 30 March.

Jones, B. O. 1982. *Sleepers, Wake!: Technology and the Future of Work*. Melbourne: Oxford University Press.

Kleingeld, P. and E. Brown 2002. 'Cosmopolitanism.' In E. N. Zalta (ed.) *The Stanford Encyclopedia of Philosophy*. (Fall 2002 Edition) The Metaphysics Research Lab, Stanford University: Stanford, viewed 28 September 2004, http://plato.stanford.edu/archives/fall2002/entries/cosmopolitanism/

Leeden, J. 1999. 'Disarming idea.' *The Australian* 20 January:10.

McKnight, A. D. and K. Suter 1983. *The Forgotten Treaties: A Practical Plan for World Disarmament*. Melbourne: Law Council of Australia.

Sheridan, G. 1982. 'Peace coalition gathers pace.' *The Bulletin* 8 June:41–2.

——1983. 'Marching for whose peace?' *The Bulletin* 19 April:59–61.

Smith, G. 2004. Gary Smith interviewed by Lucinda Horrocks. Deakin University, Melbourne, 28 September.

Stringer, R. G. 2000. 'Uniting faith and justice: A bibliographic essay. 21 years of the Uniting Church in Australia's social justice and human rights: 1977–1998.' Unpublished essay. *UnitingJustice Australia*. Sydney: Uniting Church in Australia, National Assembly, viewed 5 October 2004, http://nat.uca.org.au/unitingjustice/index.htm

Suter, K. 1978a. 'Australia and the covenant on civil and political rights.' *Dyason House Papers* 4(4):1–6.

——1978b. 'International law and East Timor.' *Dyason House Papers* 5(2):1–10.

——1978c. *Protecting Human Rights.* Sydney: United Nations Association of Australia.

——1980. 'Evangelism in affluent societies.' *Word in Life* 28:46–54.

——1981a. *Human Rights: Today and Tomorrow.* Sydney: United Nations Association of Australia.

——1981b. *A New International Order: Proposals for Making a Better World.* Sydney: World Association of World Federalists.

——1982a. *Christians and the Arms Race.* Sydney: Board of Social Responsibility NSW Synod Uniting Church in Australia.

——1982b. 'Implications of new UN Law of the Sea Treaty.' *Australian Fisheries* 41:46–9.

——1982c. 'The international protection of minorities and Australia's obligations.' *World Review* 21:6–23.

——1984. 'The Bible and World War III.' *St. Mark's Review* 118:13–22.

——1985. *Peaceworking: The United Nations and Disarmament.* Sydney: United Nations Association of Australia.

——1986a. *Alternative to War: Conflict Resolution and the Peaceful Settlement of International Disputes.* 2nd edn. Sydney: Women's International League for Peace and Freedom.

——1986b. *Reshaping the Global Agenda: The UN at 40.* Sydney: United Nations Association of Australia.

——1987a. 'The church and the politics of economics.' *Dayspring* December:10–11.

——1987b. 'The politics of peace education.' *Island Magazine* 31:42–7.

——1990. *The Triangle of Peace: Trinity Peace Research Institute, 1986–1990.* Perth, WA: Parish Council of Trinity Uniting Church for the Trinity Peace Research Institute.

——1991. 'The Assembly Commission on Social Responsibility, 1977/ 82.' *Church Heritage* 7(2):95–121.

——1992a. *Global Change: Armageddon and the New World Order.* Sutherland, NSW and Claremont, CA: Albatross Books.

——1992b. 'Reducing armaments and increasing security: The continuing issues in preserving peace.' In J. Davidson and M. Tidman (eds) *Cooperative Peace Strategies.* Ingleside, NSW: Baha'i Publications Australia, pp. 157–70.

——1993a. 'Good money after bad.' *National Outlook* 15(4):21–3.

——1993b. 'Towards a federal world state?' In M. Salla, W. Tonetto and E. Martinez (eds) *Essays on Peace.* Rockhampton: Central Queensland University Press, pp.196–212.

——1995a. *The East Timor Case and the International Court of Justice.* Fairfield, NSW: East Timor Relief Association.

——1995b. *Global Agenda: Economics, the Environment and the Nation-State.* Sutherland, NSW: Albatross Books.

——1995c. 'Protecting the environment: Old political borders and new legal concepts.' *Contemporary Review* 267(1559):286.

——1995d. 'Reforming the United Nations: An agenda for development.' *Development Bulletin* 35:40–4.

——1995e. 'War is not a dying business.' *Evatt Papers* 3(2):124–31.

——1997a. 'The backlash against the United Nations.' *Social Alternatives* 16(4):15–17.

——1997b. *East Timor, West Papua/Irian and Indonesia.* London: Minority Rights Group.

——1997c. 'Pauline Hanson and the process of globalisation.' *Ethos* 1(1):7–9.

——1998a. 'Ageing Australia. Keith Suter comments.' Transcript of 2GB Radio program, 17 April. *Wesley Mission Resources for the Growing Christian*. Sydney: Wesley Mission, viewed 9 October 2003, http://www.wesleymission.org.au/ministry/suter/17apr98.htm

——1998b. 'All politics is local. (Australian politics eclipses Asian economic crisis)' *The World Today* 54(11):282–4.

——1998c. 'GST and the taxation debate. Keith Suter comments.' Transcript of 2GB Radio program, 4 September. *Wesley Mission Resources for the Growing Christian*. Sydney: Wesley Mission, viewed 9 October 2003, http://www.wesleymission.org.au/ministry/suter/4sep98.htm

——1999a. 'Australia: Wealth and despair.' *Contemporary Review* 274(1598):137(6).

——1999b. 'Reforming the United Nations.' *Contemporary Review* 275(1605):170.

——2000a. 'Australia's deadlock over a republic.' *Contemporary Review* 276(1610):144.

——2000b. 'Golden oldies: Australians are getting older but employers still prefer to hire younger workers.' *CFO* (Sydney, NSW) 5(4):40–1.

——2000c. *In Defence of Globalisation*. Sydney: UNSW Press.

——2000d. 'Kosovo and postmodern warfare.' *Peace Research* 32(1):22–3.

——2001a. 'A culture of peace. Keith Suter comments.' Transcript of 2GB Radio program, 11 May. *Wesley Mission Resources for the Growing Christian*. Sydney: Wesley Mission, viewed 9 October 2003, http://www.wesleymission.org.au/ministry/suter/010511.htm

——2001b. 'Has the UN received a new lease of life?' Reprint of an article originally published in the *Canberra Times*, 13 December. *Global Policy Forum Website*. New York: Global Policy Forum, viewed 23 July 2004, http://www.globalpolicy.org/finance/unitedstates/2001/1213newlife.htm

——2002a. 'The baby boomers in old age. Keith Suter comments.' Transcript of 2GB Radio program, 23 August. *Wesley Mission Resources for the Growing Christian*. Sydney: Wesley Mission, viewed 9 October 2003, http://www.wesleymission.org.au/ministry/suter/020823.asp

——2002b. 'Corporate social responsibility. Keith Suter comments.' Transcript of 2GB Radio program, 13 September. *Wesley Mission Resources for the Growing Christian*. Sydney: Wesley Mission, viewed 9 October 2003, http://www.wesleymission.org.au/ministry/suter/020913.asp

——2002c. 'Does terrorism work? Keith Suter comments.' Transcript of 2GB Radio program, 25 October. *Wesley Mission Resources for the Growing Christian*. Sydney: Wesley Mission, viewed 9 October 2003, http://www.wesleymission.org.au/ministry/suter/021025.asp

——2003a. *Global Order and Global Disorder: Globalization and the Nation-State*. Westport, CT: Praeger.

——2003b. 'The health and environmental costs of war on Iraq. Keith Suter comments.' Transcript of 2GB Radio program, 3 January. *Wesley Mission Resources for the Growing Christian*. Sydney: Wesley Mission, viewed 9 October 2003, http://www.wesleymission.org.au/ministry/suter/030103.asp

——2003c. 'Terror in paradise: The Bali bombing. (Australian perspective)' *Contemporary Review* 282(1644):1–7.

——2004a. Keith Suter interviewed by Lucinda Horrocks. Melbourne, 13 August.

——2004b. 'Making sense of the new world order.' *The Newcastle Herald* 26 August, p. 9.

——2004c. 'Why has there been so little progress in outlawing terrorism under international law?' *Social Alternatives* 23(2):54–8.

Temple, W. 1942. *Christianity and Social Order.* Harmondsworth: Penguin.

Toffler, A. 1970. *Future Shock.* London: The Bodley Head.

Uniting Church in Australia NSW Synod. 2004. Sydney South: The Communications Unit, Uniting Church in Australia, NSW Synod, viewed 5 October 2004, http://www.nsw.uca.org.au

Walters, K. 2003. 'Ready for anything: Public-sector accountants are advised to use scenario planning to prepare for any eventuality.' *Business Review Weekly* 4–10 December: 70.

WFUNA n.d. [c.2005]. New York and Geneva: World Federation of United Nations Associations (WFUNA-FMANU), viewed 13 March 2005, http://www.wfuna.org/index.cfm

Who's Who in Australia 2002. 38th edn. Melbourne: Information Australia.

World Federalist Movement n.d. [c.2004]. New York: World Federalist Movement International Secretariat, viewed 14 March 2005, http://www.wfm.org/index.html

Margaret Reynolds

Margaret Reynolds is a human rights spokesperson, feminist activist and former parliamentarian. Elected to the Senate in 1983, Reynolds was on the front bench in the latter stages of the Hawke government, as Minister for Local Government from 1987 to 1990 and Minister Assisting the Prime Minister on the Status of Women from 1988 to 1990. A persistent advocate of equal opportunity for women and of the rights of Indigenous Australians, Reynolds has become increasingly involved in international human rights forums. She acted as Australian Parliamentary Representative to the United Nations General Assembly in 1997. On retiring from the Senate in 1999, she became President of the United Nations Association of Australia until 2005. She has been Adjunct Professor at the University of Queensland, teaching Human Rights and International Politics.

Senator Margaret Reynolds and delegates from India, South Africa and the UK at a meeting in New Delhi of the Commonwealth Human Rights Advisory Commission in 1994. (Courtesy Margaret Reynolds.)

139

8

Margaret Reynolds: Community Activism for Universal Values

Linda Hancock[1]

> . . . the agenda of the new millennium must be to set down the principles of
> global citizenship and the social obligations we have for each other.
>
> (Reynolds 1999c: 157)

For four decades since moving from Tasmania to Townsville in the mid-
1960s, Margaret Reynolds has championed human rights locally, nationally and internationally. She was a head teacher of a school for intellec-
tually disabled children in Tasmania. She did similar work in London in
1964, before moving to north Queensland with her husband, the historian
Henry Reynolds, in 1965. After being an activist for Indigenous education
in Townsville, Margaret began a long career as a federal politician. After
retiring from parliament in 1999, she returned to Launceston, but not to a
quiet life. Instead, she continued her global activism, focusing on holding
the Australian Government accountable for its mistreatment of Indigenous
peoples and refugees.

Reynolds's lifelong commitment to universal rights is linked to the search
for a humane world guided by feminist principles of power sharing and social
justice. She recalls that her childhood 'was profoundly affected by strong-
minded women and by circumstances that taught me to be independent'
(Reynolds 2007: 1). She grew up after World War II, when racism was being
discredited in international politics. She says 'there have always been local
advocates for cosmopolitanism' going back many generations, but much of
her life's work has focused on mainstreaming cosmopolitan ideals (Reynolds
2003b). Reynolds presents an image of a thoughtful politician always trying
to place local issues in a wider context. This is reinforced by her range of
concerns, which include women's rights, Indigenous rights, immigration,

uranium mining, defence policy, drug law reform, the peace movement, and, most recently, refugee issues.

Because of the way that she links local and global concerns, and her wide range of commitments, Reynolds is the quintessential cosmopolitan. She is a champion of universal rights in practice, having been involved in many political campaigns aimed at improving respect for human rights in Australia, and by Australians internationally. For many years, she has taken a keen interest in relating local and regional issues to broader human rights agendas (Reynolds 1981; 1987; 1988). Two examples from 1990, when she was a minister in the Hawke Labor government, show this. As Commonwealth Minister for Local Government, she rejected departmental advice that a regional office of the International Union of Local Government Associations should be in Australia. Instead, she recommended that it be located in Indonesia, since more people would benefit from having it there. This was a cosmopolitan gesture, albeit one influenced by the government's concern to foster engagement with East Asia (Reynolds 2000b).

On a visit to the Philippines as Minister for the Status of Women, Reynolds was asked by local feminists to help stop Australian men from abusing women and children while visiting as tourists. This plea, linked with what she had been told by a constituent in Queensland, led her to push for legislation to make child sex tourism perpetrated by Australians overseas punishable in Australia (Reynolds 2007: 176–8). When such a law was eventually enacted in 1994, it made a practical difference for oppressed women in Australia's region (Reynolds 2000b). While representing the Australian Government abroad, she tried to ensure that Australia supported human rights without discrimination.

Reynolds's commitment in these cases to global citizenship in action shows the shift from internationalism to cosmopolitanism outlined in Chapter 1. Reynolds was motivated by achieving human security for all people, not merely by ideas of local, national or state security. This reflected her involvement in community activism and her openness to transnational social movements. Reynolds's activity shows the strength of cosmopolitanism as a practice of redefining citizenship both from above and, in this case, from below. Her activity is part of what Vertovec and Cohen (2002: 11) note is 'an exponential growth in the number, size and range of activities of transnational social movements and networks concerned with issues including the environment, labour conditions, human rights, women and peace'. Such movements are part of an emerging global civil society.

After leaving parliament, Reynolds spent much time helping to direct criticism against regressive policies adopted by the Howard government, at times supported (such as over refugees) by the Labor Party. In doing so, she returned to particular human rights struggles that she thought were already hard-won, trying to open Australian politics to influences from transnational civil society. She has done this, not because of despair about Australians' capacity for initiating social change, but because she believes many Australians support the human rights agenda about which she is passionate. This belief is based upon her extensive community activity in difficult circumstances, and her commitment to 'provide a voice for vulnerable groups in our community' (Reynolds 2007: 202). In Townsville in 1967, Reynolds organised a conference on the implications of the Commonwealth constitutional referendum earlier that year, which affirmed Indigenous rights. Her flat was raided by the Queensland Police Special Branch, who seized the list of people who had registered (Reynolds 2007: 73). This action did not deter her and the conference was a huge success (Reynolds 1994a: 13). Some Aborigines were forced back to Palm Island so they could not attend, but a large Indigenous audience still heard prominent speakers such as Faith Bandler and Joe McGuiness (H. Reynolds 1999: 65, 75–6). Through this conference, the first that she had helped organise, Reynolds succeeded in bringing together local people and those at the forefront of vital social and political change.

This account of Reynolds's activity as a global citizen begins by assessing how her approach to human rights was shaped by her experience of community activism in north Queensland. It then focuses on her continuing activity in the areas of women's rights, Indigenous rights, and refugee rights. It also examines her involvement with the UN and the British Commonwealth, before considering the distinctive features of her feminist cosmopolitanism.

Community activism and global awareness

An enduring theme of Reynolds's activity is her base in local communities, her links with community-based non-governmental organisations (NGOs), and her use of formal institutions and positions of influence to promote social justice. Reynolds thinks that a cosmopolitan approach has to be holistic. It must recognise the connectedness of local and national struggles with global duties to the rest of humanity. Reynolds is concerned to emphasise that Australia's national identity should be seen as supported, not undermined, by a cosmopolitan vision. She says (Reynolds 2003b):

> People see you as if you are either Australian or cosmopolitan. They see a
> clear division between the two. What leadership is about is showing that the
> two are not mutually exclusive. The only way that Australians can continue

to enjoy the kind of lifestyle we expect and the kind of opportunities we have is if we become cosmopolitan in our agenda setting, because we can't hide away from the rest of the world. If we continue to isolate ourselves and put asylum seekers out to sea and only follow one country, the USA, it's going to risk our future security.

This concern for the impact of regressive domestic and foreign policies on Australia's image in its region partly reflects Reynolds's experience as a government minister in the late 1980s, when the Hawke government made engaging with Asia a national priority. Beyond that source of concern, there is a deeper belief about Australia's regional connections that derives from Reynolds's community activism in north Queensland.

Consistently looking beyond Australia dates back to Reynolds's involvement in the anti-conscription movement in the 1960s, and her early work with Indigenous people. Many of these ideas came about because she had lived overseas, in cosmopolitan London, at a time of increasing decolonisation. She brought back to Australia ideas such as Operation Headstart, which began in the US as a program of compensatory education for the children of minorities. This program was emulated in Townsville by Reynolds, who started a kindergarten for Aboriginal children (Reynolds 2007: 67). It soon attracted a large Indigenous enrolment, including the children of Eddie Mabo, long before he became famous as a native title claimant (H Reynolds 1999: 70–2). Reynolds was also politicised by the Vietnam War, and started a local branch in Townsville of Save Our Sons, an organisation of women protesting against the conscription of Australian men to fight in an unjustified war (Reynolds 2007: 53–5).

Reynolds became involved in social justice causes before they became popular. This was partly because she linked local causes directly to global concerns. She recalls not being very globally involved as a student, but came to adopt a more global perspective through her community activism. As a result, she became interested in global movements, such as feminism, anti-racism, pacifism and environmentalism. She says that 'all those issues led me to look more globally than I might have. The combination of seeing the outside world, and finding out more, and then ending up on the frontier probably influenced my cosmopolitanism' (Reynolds 2003b). It is significant that, while living in London was an important influence on her struggle for universal rights, Reynolds became a cosmopolitan grounded in the politics not of a big city, but 'the frontier' in north Queensland. The difficulties of challenging militarism and racism in a parochial environment seemed to demand both an active approach and a transnational outlook (Reynolds 2007: 59–60).

Women's rights as human rights

Reynolds's election as a senator for Queensland occurred together with the Hawke government's 1983 victory over the conservative Liberal–National Party Coalition, marking the beginning of thirteen years of Labor government. As Susan Ryan (2003: 202), Minister for Women in the first Hawke ministry, notes, it was the first time that an Australian government came to power 'with a set of detailed policy commitments to women', and 'that over 50 per cent of Australian women had voted Labor'. Hence, the government was mindful of the importance of women's issues for the advancement of women, and to maintaining a Labor mandate. Women were appointed to positions as speaker of the House of Representatives, as Secretary to the Department of Education, and as judges on the High Court and Federal Court. Barry Jones (2003: 418) says this was 'more than tokenism, but not much'. The Office of the Status of Women was given input into Cabinet submissions.

In terms of the broader issue of women's policy under the Hawke government, there were improvements to women's access to education and to jobs, family payments and the social wage and subsidised childcare. In 1984, the Hawke government passed the *Sex Discrimination Act*, giving legislative expression to CEDAW (The UN Convention on the Elimination of all Forms of Discrimination Against Women), which it had ratified in 1983 (Reynolds 1995a: 158). In 1986, the *Affirmative Action (Equal Opportunity) Act* made equal employment opportunity a core value of the Commonwealth Public Service (Ryan 2003: 203–4). Reynolds was a key participant in extending the human right to gender equality in Australia, and she strenuously defended the right of women in Queensland to privacy about their medical records and to control over their bodies (Reynolds 2007: 138–9).

There was less support, however, for gender equality in the structures of the Labor Party. In the years after Reynolds took over from Ryan as Minister for the Status of Women in 1988, she promoted the drive for a 35 per cent affirmative action rule to be implemented in all state and territory Labor branches by 2002 (Reynolds 1995b; 1996b). She also worked for the greater autonomy of the National Women's Consultative Council as a vehicle for community consultation with women (Reynolds 2003b). She initiated exchanges between Australian women and women from South-East Asia in an effort to facilitate gender equity in Australia's engagement with East Asia. Yet, change inside the Labor Party proceeded more slowly. In her book *The Last Bastion* (1995), Reynolds criticised the government for not seeing that, in accordance with CEDAW, special measures were still needed to increase the number of women in parliament (Reynolds 1995a: 159). She hoped that increased female representation would bring a new style of leadership that would be 'more consensual and less confrontational than their male colleagues', and play a role in 'reducing the gladiatorial, adversarial atmosphere' in Australian politics (Reynolds 1995a: 122).

Reynolds also hoped that the republican movement would spearhead feminist advocacy for a Bill of Rights that would enshrine equality for women in the Constitution. Accordingly, she supported Justice Elizabeth Evatt's call for Australia to follow a United States-style equal protection clause, or a Canadian-style Charter of Rights and Freedoms (Reynolds 1995a: 148). But she was not overly optimistic. She noted that in the Labor Party, 'mateship has prevailed to protect aspiring men from the challenges of women' (Reynolds 1995a: 173). She has criticised the poor performance of both political parties in failing to improve women's participation in politics, as well as the double standards used by the media in representing male and female politicians (Reynolds 2007: 223).

Looking back on the period when she was a federal politician advocating equal representation for women by 2000, Reynolds (2003b) expressed nostalgia, not for the trappings of office, but for a time when Australia was more influential on human rights:

> As a member of the Hawke–Keating government I would say that along with all the other women involved we did make a tremendous impact on recognition of women's rights as human rights internationally, but far too much of that has dissipated since 1996. On issues related to gender I am quite nostalgic for the days when we used to be at the forefront as a country, and other countries looked to us for leadership. Over a period of time, I have been one of the women, or one of the people, depending on the issue, articulating issues that regrettably, have not been part of the mainstream.

Global activism has been a strong driving force for her work, since she recognizes its effectiveness as a way to reassert the agenda of gender equity within Australia.

Reynolds's action can be seen as linking the women's rights agenda directly with a broader cosmopolitan project in a number of ways. She has connected women's rights to human rights, by drawing on and actively using the UN human rights reporting framework to elevate women's rights both domestically and internationally (Larmour 1995; Reynolds 1997a; 1997c; 1998a). She played a leadership role in the 1995 UN Fourth World Conference on Women in Beijing, reinforcing the importance of countries reporting their progress on raising women's status and the centrality of nation-state commitments to universal rights. Because of her global links, and her hopes for the potential of global rights to influence Australia, Reynolds was dismayed by Australia's declining commitment to human rights after the election of the Howard government. She highlighted a UN Committee report on Australia that expressed alarm about 'policy changes that apparently slowed down or reversed Australia's progress in achieving equality between women and men' (Reynolds 1997b: 27). She drew the attention of NGOs to the deficiencies in existing government priorities for women, when compared with the Beijing Plan of Action, to which Australia had agreed in 1995 (Reynolds 1999a). In 1999, she was instrumental in getting the Senate to call on the prime minister to honour Australia's obligations under CEDAW, and to implement the eleven recommendations specified by the UN CEDAW Committee in July 1997.

Reynolds laments Australia's reversal on women's policy in the past decade. Australia is one of the few developed countries that have not ratified the Optional Protocol on CEDAW, enabling women to take complaints of sexual discrimination to the UN. Reynolds (2003b) sees CEDAW as an important treaty that has to be made relevant:

> I have tried to get support for what are quite complex issues such as CEDAW. This was a complex, cosmopolitan idea, but you can't afford to just say that out there if you are trying to persuade women in the general community that what happens internationally has a bearing on their lives and on their daughters. It has always been one of my interests, and commitments, to translate what are essentially cosmopolitan ideas to the grassroots level, whether in government, local government, or in the international sphere.

Reynolds has been involved in the past decade in promoting human rights throughout the British Commonwealth. She says that when she started in this arena she was working almost entirely with lawyers and journalists, who were very masculine and legalistic, and concerned only with civil and political rights (Reynolds 2007: 192). She supported the promotion of such rights, but she says she 'was much more concerned about the rights of women, children and Indigenous people, and how that related to the inequities around the world, and in the Commonwealth' (Reynolds 2003b). She has contributed to a number of reports, and helped raise these issues publicly during meetings of Commonwealth leaders.

Reynolds is intrigued by the way that some Australians react defensively when it is suggested that we are part of the global community. She sees cosmopolitanism as not just about something 'out there', and not only about standards we ourselves can achieve, but also about what we can do to help the rest of the world to achieve human dignity. Reynolds (2003b) recounts a case showing how issues of international relevance are often triggered by local concerns:

> A woman walked into my office in 1985. She was a mail order bride from the Philippines, who lived in a coal mining community in Central Queensland, and was a victim of domestic violence and this was a revelation to me. It had never occurred to me that a person would be brought to Australia in that way.

Subsequently, in 1990, Reynolds as Minister for the Status of Women spoke with women in Manila who urged her to also protect young girls in the Philippines who were being forced into prostitution for Australian men. Her continued agitation against this abuse contributed to federal legislation prohibiting child sex tourism, which was passed when Duncan Kerr was Justice Minister (Reynolds 2007: 178).

This example highlights Reynolds's approach to political change, which has been to respond to cases at the local level by agitating for broader institutional change. This form of human rights activism has been called 'promoting change by reporting facts' (Keck and Sikkink 1998: 183). It aims to promote transcultural awareness, and 'boost the legitimacy of marginalized opinions within a domestic movement' (Keck and Sikkink 1998: 197). Reynolds has used this approach to promote human rights in Australia and globally, particularly concerning the right of Indigenous peoples to self-determination, and the rights of refugees to protection.

Racism, Indigenous rights and self-determination

From early in her career, a consistent theme in Reynolds's policy work, activism and personal life has been as a vocal advocate of Indigenous rights. She began such activism soon after she arrived in Townsville in 1965. One example of her activity shows the extent of her practical commitment to eliminating racism. In Townsville in late 1968, Woolworths opened a new store and advertised a large number of sales positions. Henry Reynolds (1999: 69) recalls that Margaret adopted a 'direct approach' in opposing racial discrimination in employment:

> On the morning that interviews were to take place Margaret stationed herself by Woolworths' door and I began collecting mainly Torres Strait Islander women from nearby South Townsville and driving successive carloads over the bridge to Flinders Street. The management was completely thrown by this sudden visitation of Islander women in bright print frocks and with flowers in their hair. Margaret insisted that every woman receive an interview and

147

helped them fill out their forms. The management went through the process, but not a single one . . . was offered a job.

Although she complained directly to the Woolworths regional manager, and sought to expose this racism in the local media, it was a long time before large Townsville stores employed Indigenous people (Reynolds 2007: 76). This episode shows how Reynolds developed a passion for challenging institutionalised discrimination, as well as racism entrenched by law. Within a few years of her arrival in Townsville, she became well known to Indigenous people as a strong source of social support when someone of courage was needed to make government officials accountable.

Later, as a senator and minister, Reynolds gave many speeches on Indigenous rights, in which she stressed the importance of self-determination (Reynolds 1994a). She had extensive correspondence with Indigenous Land Councils, communities and activists over many years. Together with Democrats' Senator John Woodley, she initiated the Parliamentary Code of Race Ethics in response to the publicity given to Pauline Hanson's views (Reynolds 2007: 215–7; Reynolds and Woodley 1998). It was later used as a model in developing a similar code in the United Kingdom. She was a strong critic of the Howard government's refusal both to apologise to the Stolen Generations, and to end mandatory sentencing (Reynolds 2001a: 17). On 26 May 1998, a year after the *Bringing Them Home* report about the forced removal of Aboriginal children from their families, she presented to the Indigenous peoples of Australia a collection of personal letters and extracts from parliamentary debates, through which thousands of Australians sent messages of sorrow and hope and demands for justice. Reynolds (1998c: foreword) pointed out that six of Australia's nine parliaments had passed motions of apology, but the federal parliament, 'the national voice of democracy was unable to speak unanimous words of apology regarding the actions of previous administrations'. She has also publicised UN criticisms of Australia for continued discrimination against Indigenous peoples (Reynolds 2001a: 16).

Although Reynolds became a federal senator during the Hawke and Keating era, her ideals remained closer to those first espoused by Gough Whitlam, particularly in his policy speech during the 1972 election campaign. Two themes of that speech resonated strongly with Reynolds. The first was the need to turn engagement with Asia from war to peace. The second was the international need for Australia to negotiate a just settlement with Indigenous peoples. Whitlam (cited in Clark 1973: 203) had defined the international dimensions of the latter task by saying that, 'in a very real sense, the Aborigines are our true link with our region', and observing that 'Australia's

148

treatment of her Aboriginal people will be the thing upon which the rest of the world will judge Australia and Australians'. Those statements reflected a broad wave of public concern about human rights within Australia, in which Reynolds was actively involved. Later, Reynolds (2003b) reflected on how a historic change in Australia away from racism seemed to have stalled:

> I don't know the damage to Australia that our White Australia Policy and our treatment of Indigenous people inflicted over a number of years. So many people used to ask about it, and ask what happened about the Aborigines. From the 1970s on, through the Whitlam, Fraser, Hawke and Keating years, we gradually started to put all that behind us. There was an appreciation that Australia had changed, that we no longer had a White Australia Policy, and we were starting to give the 'fair go' some real meaning, albeit not as successfully as many of us would have liked, that there were moves in terms of Indigenous rights and this was communicated around the world. This is one of the reasons why we were chosen to host the Olympic Games. Then, suddenly, with Hansonism and the Howard government there was this amazement internationally at just what is going on here, both with our treatment of vulnerable people, and our lack of independence from the American alliance, and our antipathy to people in the region.

Reynolds is concerned that Australia's diminished international reputation on human rights will compound problems in relations with neighbouring states. She has actively defended the rights of asylum seekers and refugees in Australia.

Defending the rights of refugees in Australia

As President of the United Nations Association of Australia (UNAA) from 1999 until 2005, Reynolds was a vocal critic of both the Howard government and the Labor Party on rights for refugees, human rights abuses, and on Australian foreign policy (Briggs 2002). She identified key areas in which Australia has contravened its international treaty obligations: mandatory detention of asylum seekers for the duration of the determination process; the use of temporary protection visas since October 1999; and the process of 'refoulement' (involuntary return to country of origin, directly or by forcing refugees back to a country, such as Indonesia, which has no legal obligation to protect refugees under the Refugee Convention). Reynolds has addressed meetings of activists, lobbied politicians, engaged in public debates with senior Labor women (such as Julia Gillard, when she was the Immigration spokesperson), and spoken to UN human rights committees. This was all part of a sustained effort to help change refugee policy.

Reynolds is troubled by the longer-term ramifications of current refugee policies. She is concerned not only about the denial of human rights to refugees, but also about the effect of Australian policies on other countries. Reynolds (2003b) says:

> If a spoilt, affluent Australia with its small population, its wealth, its democracy and peaceful society, with everything going for it, can't cope with a few asylum seekers, well why should any other country bother to take the UN protocol seriously? There is the immediate humanitarian issue: what they have been through, why they have come. Don't they deserve a hearing at least? We know that at least 90 percent of refugees who apply for asylum are genuine. So we should be hearing their stories. But after that, we should be concerned with what Australia is doing to undermine the global system. If Australia gets away with it, why would any other country, with their multiplicity of problems and poverty, why would they try?

Reynolds believes that, in the end, Australia will not get away with it, because too many Australians will use action abroad to challenge a denial of human rights.

Reynolds has actively lobbied UN human rights bodies, as part of a grass-roots campaign to present an alternative image abroad of Australia and Australians. Reynolds (2001a: 18) consistently challenged the Howard government's opposition to effective international monitoring of Australia's human rights performance:

> At an official level the Federal Government has used selfish domestic motives to undermine the basic structure of the international human rights monitoring bodies. It has challenged the right of human rights advocates to question government policy. It has misrepresented the processes which rely on government co-operation and transparency. It has encouraged negative perceptions of the United Nations as an outsider interfering in national decision making.

In 2002, Reynolds presented to Mary Robinson, the UN High Commissioner for Human Rights, a report containing letters from numerous asylum seekers detained in Australia and drawings by their children. This report convinced Robinson to instruct the former Chief Justice of India, P. N. Bhagwati, to visit detention camps such as Woomera. In 2003, when the new UN High Commissioner, Sergio Vieira de Mello, asked her 'why is the Australian Government so ruthless towards such vulnerable people?', Reynolds (2007: 219) told him that many Australians did not support that policy. In 2004, another opportunity arose to highlight the treatment of refugees, and show that many Australians are practically helping asylum seekers. Reynolds presented a report to the UN in Geneva titled *Australians Welcome Refugees: The Untold Story*. The report led many people there to respond: 'we didn't know so many Australians cared' (Reynolds 2004a; 2004b). Reynolds (2004a: 1) said that government deceit over the *Tampa* episode and the children overboard affair in 2001 had 'galvanised thousands of Australians into action to personally support individuals and to lobby for reform'. Such active public support for refugees shows that cosmopolitan concern can motivate effective political action, especially through publicising human rights abuses internationally.

Involvement with the United Nations and Commonwealth activism

Reynolds has had a long-standing involvement with the United Nations, including as a delegate to many UN meetings on behalf of both the government and NGOs. In 2000, she represented Australian NGOs at the review conference of the Nuclear Non-Proliferation Treaty at the UN in New York (Reynolds 2000a). Earlier, in 1997, as a Parliamentary Adviser to Australia's delegation to the General Assembly of the United Nations, she argued that Australia's role at the UN needed to be more independent, with a focus on priority areas where the Australian Government can take a leadership role and raise a positive profile internationally. This reflected her belief that a country like Australia should be at the forefront of protecting and extending the UN's capacity, not undermining it. Reynolds has been a fierce defender and a firm advocate of the UN system, but not an uncritical one. She is aware that NGOs often find many UN procedures and outcomes inadequate (Reynolds 2003a). Yet Reynolds (1997b: 13) is reluctant to criticise the UN, because she says 'its failings are always over-emphasised and its highly commendable achievements over-shadowed'.

As President of the UNAA, Reynolds often called for a better balance between Australia's military and development spending. She highlighted the steady decline in Australian overseas aid over the past twenty years. She says that overcoming poverty and inequality is 'in all our interests', because it is the only way to achieve genuine security. Australia's dismal level of overseas aid compares badly with that of a smaller affluent country such as Denmark, which spends US$337 per capita on aid, in contrast to Australia's US$54 (Reynolds 2004b; see Singer and Gregg 2004: 22–4). Reynolds wonders what has gone wrong in Australia since 1985, when Australian overseas aid was

151

much higher. Yet she has maintained a hope that the idealism of young people involved across Australia in the UN Youth Association may eventually reverse that downward trend (Reynolds 2004b).

As well as the UN, Reynolds has been involved with the British Commonwealth Human Rights Initiative, a London-based NGO which broadened its campaigning against human rights abuses after the end of apartheid (Reynolds 2007: 192). She hopes that, instead of remaining an old entity, the Commonwealth could become a force for reform, as a means of maintaining international interest in human rights. This would be particularly relevant where regressive political change occurs within a country, whether it is Australia or another Commonwealth member. In her activism around the Commonwealth Heads of Government summits, Reynolds has focused on Indigenous rights. She says (Reynolds 2003b) that other Commonwealth countries, such as New Zealand, have been 'prepared to speak out and to follow international standards and to try to lead'. Yet in Australia, while there have always been local advocates for cosmopolitanism going right back to the Anti-Slavery League, more people have avoided coming to terms with history. She wonders how many more generations justice for Indigenous peoples in Australia will take. Meanwhile, she sees the Commonwealth as a means that NGOs can use, along with UN human rights committees, to embarrass countries like Australia when they ignore their treaty obligations. She has taken this approach to the Commonwealth in response to what she sees as the decline in Australia's standing internationally. Before retiring from parliament, Reynolds (1998b: 127) wrote: 'When travelling I had always experienced warm enthusiasm as a welcome Australian visitor, yet now I found I was met with a certain reserve from people unsure about Australia's current reputation internationally'. For Reynolds, involvement with the Commonwealth is another way to protect human rights in Australia.

Is there a feminist cosmopolitanism?

Reflecting on who inspired her international rights work, Reynolds cites Mary Robinson, the former UN High Commissioner for Human Rights; Madeline Albright, the former US Secretary of State; and New Zealand Prime Minister Helen Clark. Reynolds says that when they had the opportunity to meet and talk formally and informally, parliamentary women like herself and Clark were struck by the privilege of their opportunities to create a better world and by the local agendas that they pursued in a global context. Reynolds believes women gain legitimacy for global social action from their local connections; and when no longer in political office, they have these roots and concerns to anchor their lives. She saw her role as a parliamentarian as similar to many other women working at a broader community level. She claims (Reynolds 2003b) that 'too many men have been conditioned to believe that power is all that matters, and that once you get it you hold onto it no matter what, and you don't necessarily share it or use it as creatively as you might'. By contrast, she was interested in joining official structures like parliament to try to share power with NGOs. She thinks women's lack of acceptance of power as their birthright gives them a better opportunity to transform power and to be much more egalitarian in their use of power. Reynolds does not see women as better human beings than men, but she says they can make a difference when they make important decisions, such as deciding to stop sexual abuse of women and children by Australians overseas.

The question of whether there is a distinctively feminist cosmopolitan practice arises in connection with Reynolds's approach, her forms of political engagement, and the core values of her activism. The time when Reynolds moved from local to federal politics, in the early 1980s, was one of extensive global networking amongst feminists worldwide, which generated 'trust, information sharing, and discovery of common concerns' (Keck and Sikkink 1998: 169). In many respects, the feminist rights project is transnational. It is based on a conception of citizenship as 'bounded, but by sex/gender role rather than by nationality' (Hutchings 1999: 138). The feminist approach is collaborative, and grounded in sharing the realities of women's lives through global networking (Evans 2002: 174). Reynolds has participated in many international NGO networks, building links between them and domestic NGOs. She says that leading parliamentary women of her generation, such as former Premier of Victoria Joan Kirner, and former Premier of Western Australia Carmen Lawrence, have often come from a grassroots community background, and have worked through issues at the local level; be it racism or sexism or disregard for the environment. Reynolds (2003b) says that, although 'many of my male advisors, and even the female ones, advised me to work within the factions and the party, it always seemed protracted, long-winded, petty and personal'.

One member of the Australian Women's Rights Action Network, Carolyn Lambert (2004), sees Reynolds as expressing a pragmatic cosmopolitanism, serving as 'a link in a long chain of people committed to making a change and committed to making the link between the global and the local, open, and transparent'. Retaining her links to community groups was crucial for Reynolds's ability to respond to pleas for practical support, such as from the Filipina wife abused by her Australian husband. Her action

153

in seeking an institutional change in response to an immediate human need reflected the transformative approach that she developed to help Indigenous women and men in Townsville who needed a kindergarten that respected their culture and heritage. This grassroots practice of reform is a familiar feminist activist tactic (Hutchings 1999: 140). More broadly, it is part of an attempt to transcend national and institutional limitations by acting beyond the state, to expand the transnational dimensions of feminist politics. Reynolds (2007: 173, 183) has consistently sought to develop informal networks uniting women committed to universal rights and gender equality, both when operating as a minister or government delegate and when involved with transnational groups such as the International Parliamentary Union.

Conclusion

One of the distinctive features of the cosmopolitan activism taken up by Reynolds is that it has been global in outlook and perspective, while anchored in provincial and local realities and impact. Reynolds has shown that cosmopolitanism in Australia is not an attitude or practice confined to national or state capitals, but a set of humane values which can be adopted, developed and deployed by activists anywhere in Australia. Reynolds has been a champion of global citizenship rights underpinned by social justice values, and has been involved in a wide range of international campaigns directed at improving respect for human rights in Australia, and by Australians internationally.

Reynolds's cosmopolitan outlook is something she began to articulate in north Queensland in the mid-1960s, many years before going to Canberra as a parliamentarian. Through her long involvement with community organisations, she has shown that living in a remote region in Australia is no obstacle to taking a cosmopolitan approach to activism. Several examples of such linkage have been mentioned. Another one concerns why Australians should take global warming seriously. Reynolds (2003b) says we must think 'in terms of our own future, particularly relating to drought', and take a broader, humane approach:

> It's not just a matter of looking at us and about how it affects us but how it affects our neighbours. Are we going to turn around the boatloads of Pacific Islanders when the water level rises?

Crucially, Reynolds sees no contradiction between looking after Australian interests and also being cosmopolitan. While she accepts that most

Australians do not yet identify as global citizens, Reynolds (1999c: 157) has called on us to recognise the 'Planetary Interest' that unites humanity, and to realise that 'the agenda of the new millennium must be to set down the principles of global citizenship and the social obligations we have for each other' as humans. She believes that young Australians are increasingly open to the ideals of global citizenship.

After a parliamentary career that included initiating legislative change to protect women from sexual violence committed by Australians over-seas, Reynolds became a strong critic of the nationalistic isolationism of the Howard government. She has linked global and local activism to help defend the rights of asylum seekers and refugees. She feels such activism has made a real difference, leading to the closure of the Woomera detention centre, despite the Labor Party's acceptance of the false rhetoric and policies of 'border protection' (Reynolds 2004b). Yet, reflecting on the state of Aus-tralia early in the new century, Reynolds (2003b) was concerned about what she called 'a reversal of the cultural cringe', saying that now 'we are almost rejecting outside influences in a way where back in the 50s and 60s we were embracing the need to go overseas and to take our skills, and take advantage of opportunities overseas'. She says that 'the best interests of the individ-ual and local society in Australia are really dependent on cosmopolitanism', which can help overcome 'the fear of outsiders' that nationalistic politi-cians create (Reynolds 2003b). Despite this new 'mood of conservatism', which Reynolds (2007: 226) sees as the main legacy of the Howard govern-ment, and her concern about the threat posed to human rights by neoliberal projects that entrench inequality, Reynolds remains optimistic about the future. One reason for her optimism is the idealism and commitment to improving humanity that she sees in many members of UN Youth Associa-tions throughout Australia (Reynolds 2004b). People such as Thao Nguyen, interviewed in Chapter 10, are continuing a tradition of action as global citizens, to which cosmopolitan advocates of social justice such as Margaret Reynolds have contributed substantially.

Note

1 I would like to thank Margaret Reynolds especially for her comments on this chapter and for the interview on which it is based, and Roderic Pitty for editorial work.

References

Briggs, J. 2002. 'Ex-Senator slams Labor on refugees.' *Hobart Mercury* 6 May. LexisNexis Academic database, viewed 11 September 2003, http://weblexis-nexis/universe.

Clark, C. (ed.) 1973. *Australian Foreign Policy: Towards a Reassessment.* Melbourne: Cassell.

Commonwealth Human Rights Initiative 2003. New Delhi: Commonwealth Human Rights Initiative, viewed 12 September 2003, http://www.humanrightsinitiative.org/default.htm

Cullen, J., S. Duncan and P. Flokis et al. 2001. 'The 10 most admired Australian women.' *Australian Women's Weekly* November:39–48.

Curthoys, A. and C. Moore 1995. 'Working for the white people: An historiographic essay on Aboriginal and Torres Strait Islander labour.' *Labour History* 69, November:1–29.

Evans, S. M. 2002. 'Women and global citizenship.' In R. Oshiba, E. Rhodes and C. Kitagawa Otsuru (eds) *"We the People" in the Global Age: Re-examination of Nationalism and Citizenship.* Osaka: Japan Center for Area Studies, Symposium series no. 18:167–80.

Gentle, N. 1999. 'Former MP links rights struggles.' *The Weekend Australian* 24 October:11.

Hutchings, K. 1999. 'Feminist politics and cosmopolitan citizenship.' In K. Hutchings and R. Dannreuther (eds) *Cosmopolitan Citizenship.* Houndmills: Macmillan, pp. 121–41.

Jones, B. 2003. 'The Hawke Government: An assessment from the inside.' In S. Ryan and T. Branston (eds) *The Hawke Government: A Critical Perspective.* North Melbourne: Pluto Press, pp. 408–25.

Keck, E. and K. Sikkink 1998. *Activists Beyond Borders: Advocacy Networks in International Politics.* Ithaca: Cornell University Press.

Kingston, M. 1993. 'A question of status – A push to restore power and influence to the Office of the Status of Women.' *Canberra Times* 24 July:C1.

Lambert, C. 2004. 'Interview.' December. Melbourne: WRANA, Women's Rights Action Network of Australia, 15 November.

Larmour, C. 1995. 'UN Fourth World Conference on Women: Planning, setbacks and achievements.' *Current Issues Briefs* (Social Policy Group) 5, 27 September.

Meade, K. 1998. 'Activist had black view of racist world.' *The Weekend Australian* 24 October:11.

Milliner, K. 1999. 'Still fighting for the underdogs.' *Courier Mail* 29 July:13.

National Archives of Australia: M Reynolds. Correspondence files and other documents relating to Ministerial activities. 1975–1999. CP 362.

National Archives of Australia nd [c 2001]. Person notes for person CP 362. Biographical entry on Margaret Reynolds. Canberra: National Archives of Australia, viewed 10 September 2003, http://www.naa.gov.au/

Parliamentary Library 2000. 'Reynolds, the Hon Margaret. Biography.' *Parlinfo Web.* Canberra: Parliament of Australia, 7 June, viewed 4 September 2003, http://parlinfoweb.aph.gov.au/piweb/

Reynolds, H. 1999. *Why Weren't We Told?* Ringwood: Penguin.

Reynolds, M. 1981. 'The black community school in Townsville.' *Social Alternatives* 2:64–8.

——1987. 'The needs of North-West Queensland: Do governments really care?' In G. N. F. Gregory (ed.) *Isolated Communities: A Major Report on the Needs of Inland Australia: Proceedings of the Needs of the West Conference.* TRDC Publication no. 149. Armidale: Rural Development Centre, pp. 15–26.

——1988. Hon Senator Margaret Reynolds. Federal Minister for Local Government. Address to the 2nd Combined Northern Territory Local Government Conference, Darwin.

——1989. Address. *1988 FECCA Congress Report: Multiculturalism: a Commitment for Australia*. Canberra: Federation of Ethnic Communities' Councils of Australia.

——1991. 'Urban sprawl: The need for reform.' *Social Alternatives* 10(2):23–4.

——1993. '"Half by 2000" say Australian women.' *Socialist Affairs* 2:41–3.

——1994a. 'Self determination: Dispelling some of the public myths.' In C. Fletcher (ed.) *Aboriginal Self-Determination in Australia*. Canberra: Aboriginal Studies Press, pp. 13–17.

——1994b. 'Censorship: Whose freedom?' *Wiser* 1(3):30–2.

——1995a. *The Last Bastion: Labor Women Working towards Equality in the Parliaments of Australia*. Chatswood, NSW: Business & Professional Publishing.

——1995b. 'The last say: The Australian Labor Party has adopted a policy of achieving a quota of 35% of winnable seats for women by 2001.' *Wiser* 2(2):29–30.

——1996a. 'Towards a republic and women's equal participation in parliament.' *Journal of Australian Studies* 47:87–94.

——1996b. 'Women, pre-selection and merit: Who decides?' *Papers on Parliament* 27, March:31–47.

——1997a. 'Women and decision making.' In S. Mitchell and R. Das Pradham (eds) *Back to Basics from Beijing: United Nations Fourth World Conference on Women: An Australian Guide to the International Platform for Action*. Development Dossier 39. Australian Council for Overseas Aid, pp. 37–40.

——1997b. Report of Senator Margaret Reynolds. Parliamentary Adviser to the Australian Delegation 52nd General Assembly of the United Nations. Townsville.

——1997c. 'One step forward. Two steps back: Australian Government criticised by the United Nations for downgrading women's policy initiatives.' Address to the Women and the Law Society. Brisbane, 11 September.

——1998a. 'Global issues: Local action. Women's role in implementing a human rights agenda.' Speech given at the Association of Women Educators inaugural National Conference, Brisbane. *Redress* 7(3): 2–4.

——1998b. 'Australia's ailing reputation in human rights.' In *Bringing Australia Together: the Structure and Experience of Racism in Australia*. Woolloongabba: The Foundation for Aboriginal and Islander Research Action, pp. 127–9.

——1998c. *On the occasion of National Sorry Day 26 May 1998: A Collection of Personal Letters and Extracts from Parliamentary Debates Presented to the Indigenous Peoples of Australia*. Canberra: Senate Printing Unit.

——1999a. 'Government's CEDAW obligations.' AusfemPolnet, 2 May, viewed November 2003, ausfem-polnet@postofficeutaseduau

——1999b. 'Racism and Australia's human rights policy.' *Socialist Affairs and Women & Politics* 4(47):57–60.

——1999c. 'Australia.' In Kennedy Graham (ed.) *The Planetary Interest: A New Concept for the Global Age*. London: UCL Press, pp. 151–8.

——2000a. 'Year 2000 signals focus on indigenous justice.' *Land Rights Queensland* February:5.

——2000b. Interview with Roderic Pitty. Canberra, 24 October.

——2001a. 'Testing the friendship: Australia's relationship with the United Nations 1996–2001.' *Polemic* (Sydney) 12(1):9–19.

——2001b. *Human Rights and Poverty Eradication.* New Delhi: Commonwealth Human Rights Initiative.

——2001c. 'A woman in politics.' *Inkwel* January, online edition, viewed 4 April 2004, http://www.wel.org.au/inkwel/index.htm

——2002. 'Why is Australia so paranoid about refugees?' Public Lecture presented by the Hawke Institute and the Freilich Foundation as part of the 'Fear of Strangers' conference, 6 December 2002. Adelaide: Elder Hall, Adelaide University.

——2003a. 'Protecting the UN in the national interest.' *Australian Mosaic* 3, June: 9–11.

——2003b. Interview with Linda Hancock. Melbourne, 11 November.

——2004a. *Australians Welcome Refugees: The Untold Story.* A Report to the 60th Session of The United Nations Commission on Human rights. President's Report, United Nations Association of Australia.

——2004b. 'Australia and the United Nations: Why multilateralism is in our national interest.' Address to the UNAA, ACT Branch AGM, Canberra: 8 July.

——2007. *Living Politics.* St Lucia: University of Queensland Press.

Reynolds, M. and D. Flint 2003. 'Security Council membership poses a permanent debate: Margaret Reynolds, The National President of the United Nations Association of Australia vs David Flint, Emeritus Professor of Law.' *Australian Financial Review* 22 March:50.

Reynolds, M. and J. Gillard 2002. 'Human rights and border protection are in the balance: Opposition Spokeswoman for population and immigration Julia Gillard v former Labor Minister and National President of the United Nations Association of Australia Margaret Reynolds.' *Australian Financial Review* 7 December:50.

Reynolds, M. and J. Woodley 1998. 'Federal Parliamentarian's Code of Ethics – a contribution towards a more tolerant Australia.' December. Townsville.

Ryan, S. 2003. 'Women's policy.' In S. Ryan and T. Branston (eds) *The Hawke Government: A Critical Perspective.* North Melbourne: Pluto Press, pp. 202–14.

Singer, P. and T. Gregg 2004. *How Ethical Is Australia? An Examination of Australia's Record as a Global Citizen.* Melbourne: Black Inc.

Vertovec, S. and R. Cohen 2002. 'Introduction.' In S. Vertovec and R. Cohen (eds) *Conceiving Cosmopolitanism: Theory, Context and Practice.* Oxford: Oxford University Press, pp. 1–22.

Who's Who in Australia 2002. 38th edn. Adelaide: F. Johns.

Michael Kirby

Michael Kirby is a High Court judge and a proponent of international human rights. After serving on the Australian Law Reform Commission, the Federal Court of Australia, and the New South Wales Court of Appeal, he became a Justice of the High Court in 1996. He is well known for his work in promoting and advocating human rights. While on the High Court, he has applied international principles wherever possible in his reasoning. Between 1993 and 1996, he served as Special Representative of the UN Secretary-General monitoring human rights in Cambodia. He has worked extensively for United Nations agencies, particularly for UNESCO, as well as for other international organisations. In 1983 he was made a Companion of the Order of St Michael and St George, and in 1991 he received an Order of Australia Medal, and was awarded the Australian Human Rights Medal. He was Laureate of the UNESCO Prize for Human Rights Education in 1998 and he has received several other international awards.

The Honourable Justice Michael Kirby AC CMG, Justice of the High Court of Australia, as photographed by Ian Provest. (Courtesy Justice Kirby and Ian Provest.)

9

Michael Kirby: Speaking for Human Rights

Roderic Pitty[1]

... all Australians must be citizens of the world. They must lift their sights from their own society. They must be engaged in the struggle for constitutionalism, the rule of law and basic human rights throughout the world.

(Kirby 2003a: 4)

Michael Kirby is a High Court judge, and a fervent advocate of international human rights law. This has been the core area of his public commitment in Australia and overseas, for which he was honoured in 1998 with the prize for human rights education awarded by the United Nations Educational, Scientific and Cultural Organisation (UNESCO). He is an able communicator who has been unusually prolific for a judge in contributing to public debate about a range of social and legal issues. He is committed to helping Australians overcome parochialism and provincialism, and to sharing his compassion for humanity (Kirby 2000a). Among lawyers, Kirby has done most to widen the horizons of Australian law, both through his role as the first head of the Australian Law Reform Commission, from 1975 until 1984, and particularly through his development of cosmopolitan judicial reasoning since 1988.

Kirby has acted on his belief (1988a: 530) that, 'in the world after Hiroshima, all educated people have a responsibility to think and act as citizens of a wider world'. What makes Kirby a cosmopolitan is his ethical commitment to all of humanity. He was originally sceptical, when interviewed in 2003, of the label *cosmopolitan*, because of its popular usage to mean what is in vogue or trendy, stylish and fashionable (Pitty 2003: 1). On reflection, he accepts the term cosmopolitan as meaning a world citizen, who supports international human rights law (Heater 2002: 103–5). In his international activity, such as the UN Secretary-General's Special Representative for Cambodia from 1993–96, Kirby has been part of what has been called a 'cosmopolitan movement' in law. As explained by Koskenniemi (2003: 473), cosmopolitans are not internationalists, since they have 'little faith in States'. Instead, they place 'much hope in increasing contacts between peoples'. They firmly believe in judging the laws of their countries 'from the perspective of the requirements of humanity', and so are 'always ready to take account of reforms carried out elsewhere' to improve justice (Koskenniemi 2003: 473).

While he is one of Australia's major public intellectuals, Kirby is not a party political figure. Indeed, he is opposed to the politics of 'exclusive teams', seeing that as 'really pathetic' (Kirby 2003f: 7). He is also emphatically opposed to discrimination and prejudice. Because of his outspokenness on social issues, he says he has 'irritated a lot of people in my own profession, and . . . had that effect on a lot of political leaders' (Kirby 1991: 531). Some prejudiced people have been irritated by Kirby's openness about his homosexuality and his thirty-nine-year relationship with his partner, Johan van Vloten. It was van Vloten who encouraged Kirby to travel overland through Asia to Europe twice, in 1970 and 1974, in a Kombi van. On these journeys, Kirby came to appreciate both the unity and the individuality of humanity. Later, in the 1980s, a senior Labor politician was so prejudiced against Kirby's homosexuality that he opposed Kirby's possible appointment to the highest court in the land (Kirby 2004d: 3). Later still, an influential Liberal politician, Senator Heffernan, conducted a vendetta of innuendo against Kirby in 2002, only to be met with gracious forgiveness when his malicious gossip fizzled. Kirby's parents and religious teachers taught him never to hate people, even when they hurt you. It is one of his 'very core' beliefs, and one reason why he has been outspoken in opposing the death penalty throughout the world (Kirby 2004a: 9; 2003e). Personal experience of discrimination has led Kirby (2000b: 13) to believe that: 'To be human is to feel the pain of brothers and sisters everywhere. Feeling that pain we must each do whatever we can to build a better world'.

This chapter presents an overview of the ways in which Kirby has brought a qualitatively new perspective to bear on Australian law and society since the 1970s. The focus is on explaining the general features of his philosophy, not on examining the details of his legal reasoning. The period covered is largely that since 1988, when he embraced the idea of applying international human rights norms in Australian law. Kirby has been the High Court's most prolific recent dissenter, expressing another view of the law in about a third of its cases (Kirby 2006c: 21). He says this is a reflection of what has become a 'more conservative' bench since 1996 (Kirby 2003f: 4). Yet, in 1974, when at age thirty-five he became the youngest Australian appointed to judicial office, he was a fairly orthodox lawyer, albeit with a strong social conscience (Kirby 2004d: 2).

The making of a cosmopolitan optimist

Kirby's openness to viewing Australia in a global context arose from three factors: his family background and commitment to social justice, his exploration of different legal traditions, and his involvement in international organisations. Kirby grew up in Sydney in the late 1940s and 1950s, in a loving family that was affected by 'the anticommunist hysteria in Australia' being promoted by the government (Kirby 2002: 56). His grandmother, whom he greatly admired, had married a communist. Kirby (2003d: 194) is proud of the fact that the Australian people, and the Australian High Court (unlike the US Supreme Court), resisted Menzies's efforts to expel communists from Australian democracy. He says that Dr H. V. Evatt's stand against the 1951 referendum that sought to ban the Communist Party was more important than winning a few elections. He calls on 'politicians of all parties' to pursue *inclusion not exclusion* (Kirby, quoted in Oldaker 2003: 30). Kirby learnt about inclusion by getting involved in the NSW Council for Civil Liberties when it was established in the mid-1960s. He became active defending 'the human dignity of minorities' (Kirby 1996c: 47). In the winter of 1965, he was one of the Council's young lawyers who went to Walgett in NSW to investigate discrimination, six months after the Freedom Ride had challenged racism in NSW country towns (Horner 2004: 107).

Kirby developed an interest in exploring the different legal traditions that emerged after decolonisation throughout the British Commonwealth. He grew up during the twilight of the British Empire, not during the heat of its conquests. In his working life, he has enjoyed the fruits of that empire's end, as decolonisation created new and vibrant common law traditions in places like India. Kirby recalls that while he was growing up there was a widespread 'international awareness', which was 'partly due to the British connection'. He says this was later overshadowed by the growth of a 'local nationalism in Australia' (Pitty 2003: 3). That awareness has helped him, both at the Law Reform Commission and as a judge, to use the illumination provided by knowledge of other common law jurisdictions. Thus, in 1984, after becoming the President of the New South Wales Court of Appeal, Kirby's mind was broadened by a talk with P. N. Bhagwati, soon to be India's Chief Justice. Kirby adopted a principle from a recent Indian case to help clarify an old obscurity in New South Wales administrative law. He was overruled by the High Court, but, undaunted, he soon became a strong proponent of comparative judicial reasoning (Kirby 1998b). Recently, he seized on an important shift by the US Supreme Court towards accepting that international human rights norms do influence domestic law. He argues that, since that court is now finally escaping the 'intellectual prison' of an isolated jurisdiction, Australian law must surely follow that precedent (Kirby 2003d: 184).

The need for a broad outlook was outlined by Kirby in his 1983 book *Reform the Law*. He propounded a vision of the common law as a creative and adaptive tradition, which keeps pace with social change. A belief in the possibility of progressive reform is central to his optimism about the future, especially in the context of scientific and technological change (Kirby 1983a: 236–8; 1988c). He thinks the common law must be continually adjusted to cope with a changing society. In 1980, Kirby (1983a: 37–9) criticised 'the general retreat in judicial lawmaking' evident then 'in recent decisions of the highest courts of Australia'. His view of the need to develop the common law was influenced by the Law Reform Commission's major inquiry into Aboriginal customary laws. Although it was not completed until after Kirby left the Commission, this inquiry raised basic legal questions about the need for the white majority to institutionalise 'tolerance of legal pluralism' (Kirby 1983a: 21). Kirby rejected the despairing view of the influential anthropologist T. G. H. Strehlow, who died in his arms in 1978, still thinking that Aboriginal customary law had less of a future than the British Empire. Kirby (1983a: 125–6) argued that 'we should expect Aboriginal laws to change and adapt', just as the common law must do. His view is that an evolving Aboriginal traditional law can still help 'restore acceptable social control to at least some Aboriginal communities', and provide 'answers to some of our own legal and social problems'. This view of a dynamic and evolving Aboriginal law has not been adopted by the High Court in most native title cases. Nonetheless, other reports from the Law Reform Commission helped to initiate new laws, such as those to protect privacy, or to focus on new issues requiring attention, like the legal implications of genetic technology.

Kirby has had a long involvement with many international organisations, particularly with UNESCO. He heard about UNESCO at school in the late 1940s, soon after it was created. In the 1980s, he participated in UNESCO's Committee on Human Rights, becoming the chair of its Expert Group on the Rights of Peoples in 1989, which investigated the controversial topic of self-determination. His capacity for synthesising ideas has given him a key role in various bodies, such as with the Organisation for Economic Cooperation and Development (OECD) on privacy. Kirby has been active in the International Commission of Jurists, becoming its President from 1995–98, when he tried to get it to address all issues of discrimination. He was involved in the World Health Organization's Global Commission on AIDS, and in an inquiry into South Africa in the early 1990s for the International Labour Organisation (ILO), a body he respects because of his commitment to an equitable industrial relations system. He has been a member of UNESCO's International Bioethics Committee, helping to formulate the 1997 Universal Declaration on the Human Genome and Human Rights (Kirby 2003b; 2005k: 67, 71).

Kirby sees no conflict between his extensive international civic activities and his judicial office. He regards his occupation as 'inescapably bound up in the promotion and application of human rights' (Kirby 1999a). He believes that it 'is the obligation of each of us to rid our minds of the notion that human rights is a confined and limited topic, restricted to civil and political rights' (Kirby 2000g: 147). From working with the UN in Cambodia, Kirby (2000g: 146) learnt directly from Cambodian peasants 'that for the ordinary citizen, economic, social and cultural rights (as well as group rights and peoples' rights) are just as important as civil and political rights'. This broadened his awareness of the core value of human equality, and developed his commitment to the vision of creating what a Maori judge, Justice Eddie Durie (2000: 54), has called an emerging 'world common law' of human rights.

A proponent of the global context of law

In 1988, Kirby attended a judicial meeting, convened by Bhagwati in Bangalore, comprising ten senior judges from Commonwealth countries and one from the USA. Kirby was the only justice from Australia. This meeting changed Kirby's approach to the use of international law by judges to protect human rights. Before this meeting, Kirby (1987: 8) had accepted the orthodox view that 'international law was not part of the domestic law unless specifically incorporated as such by a valid statute'. But this meeting suggested an alternative framework. A key principle arising from the meeting was that judges do have a legitimate role in using relevant international human rights norms to remove 'ambiguity or uncertainty from national constitutions, legislation or common law'. Another principle called for the education, not only of students, but also of practising judges, about international human rights norms (Kirby 1988a: 531–2). The meeting inspired Kirby to engage fervently in such education back in Australia. Initially, he was a lone voice in this endeavour. Yet he says that 'by about 1991 the tide of judicial opinion in Australia began to change' (Kirby 1993a: 384–5). To understand the significance of this shift, it is useful to note what Kirby learnt in his time with the Law Reform Commission about relations between law and politics.

While head of the Law Reform Commission, Kirby observed that changing the law about controversial social issues can be difficult, because 'unless Parliaments are given help, they are likely to put these issues to one side' (Kirby 1983b: 16). If that occurs, the law will be increasingly inadequate in a changing society, and many forms of social discrimination will persist. For Kirby (2000f: 61), the need to end discrimination 'goes to the very essence of what it should be to be an Australian'. Experiencing discrimination personally taught him resilience and empathy for those excluded from society for other reasons. It challenged him to ensure that nobody is wronged by the law. Yet Kirby is aware of huge political obstacles to overcoming discrimination. He sees an institutional flaw in what he has called 'the slow pace of change in the Australian democracy' (Kirby 2002: 55). In his view, political agendas are shaped, not by a careful consideration of rational proposals for reform, but by personality and party differences, which he sees as shallow and short-sighted. Kirby (2005h: 445) says this 'logjam in our institutions' endangers the effectiveness of government, and so its legitimacy. This poses a philosophical challenge for Kirby, given his anti-elitist view of democracy, and his belief in rationality based on science (Kirby 2004b). Often sensible solutions to urgent problems are discarded, and for Kirby, such obstruction of social change is hard to accept.

Kirby's response to these frustrations of Australian democracy has been to seek an external means of overcoming the effects on individuals of the logjam, if not the basic problem itself. This is a cosmopolitan response. It comes from Kirby's experience of discrimination and his commitment to assisting others whose dignity is denied. It reflects how he was taught, by Professor Julius Stone, an international jurist of high repute, to recognise that public policy choices are inherent in judicial decisions and should not be hidden by a pretence of value-free neutrality (Kirby 2005h: 443). At the Law Reform Commission, Kirby pushed an extensive agenda of fundamental reform and renewal. He came to believe very strongly in being open about the political aspects, or public policy choices, of a judge's role. Kirby (1988b: 369) said 'there is an obligation on the judges who, after all, are sworn to do justice according to law, to face up to the responsibility to develop the legal system'. He has been a strong critic of what he calls the 'discredited mythology' which asserts that judges merely *apply*, but must never *make* law (Kirby 2005g: 2). He has compared this view with the nonsense of official propaganda in the old Soviet Union before Gorbachev admitted that diverse opinions really existed in that society (Kirby 2005a: 1).

In Australia, the *Mabo* case, decided in 1992, stands out as the high point of judicial acceptance that legal decisions involve policy choices, including those about the relevance of global human rights norms, adopted in comparable countries, and in treaties ratified by Australia. Although not then on the High Court, Kirby (1993b: 73, 75–6) defended its 'modest' recognition of native title as being 'appropriately' inspired by the creative and adaptive spirit of the common law, and as showing the influence of international human rights principles on Australian law. He defended not just the *Mabo* decision itself, but also its implications for bringing about a harmonious relationship between Australian law and international law.

Kirby saw this decision as a good example of breaking the institutional logjam. He disputed the view of those critics who said the court usurped a legislative function. Kirby (1993b: 77) asked, given the failure of legislatures to recognise prior Aboriginal ownership of Australia, 'how long must the courts wait before discharging their own constitutional duty to ensure justice under the law?' He believes his efforts to articulate the Bangalore Principles in the three years before the final hearing of that case in 1991 (including a polite questioning of Chief Justice Mason's earlier view) played a small part in helping Justice Brennan (with the Chief Justice and Justice McHugh) declare that international human rights norms are now a legitimate influence on Australian law (Kirby 1988a: 522; Pitty 2003: 4). In adopting international law in the *Mabo* case, the High Court was influenced by Australia's acceptance of the First Optional Protocol to the International Covenant on Civil and Political Rights. This enables people in Australia to petition the UN Human Rights Committee about persistent human rights abuses. Kirby's key contribution was to provide a conceptual framework for judges to see their role in helping to resolve a shameful logjam, by seeing that case in terms of international human rights norms (Kirby 1995: 35).

Kirby sees the influence of international human rights law on Australia as part of a broader, irreversible globalising trend (Kirby 2005k: 67, 71). He thinks believers in human progress are obliged 'in every proper way' to hasten the arrival of a dignified world, especially in an insular place like Australia (Kirby 2006a: 283). He is not surprised by the resurgence of Australian judicial conservatism after 1996, nor by the political promotion of what he then called the 'barren philosophy' of 'narrow nationalism' (Kirby 1996a: 1102). Ironically, this resurgence has helped Kirby become a great judicial dissenter, similar to Lionel Murphy in the period 1975–86 (Kirby 1987). Murphy and Kirby share a premise, which is that the contemporary world is interconnected, and so any aspect of law must be considered in a changing global context (Jones 2003; Kirby 2007e: 8). Both seek guidance not from 'disputable antiquarian research' into ancient English decisions, but from international law that Australia is obliged to uphold (Kirby 1993a: 380).

Yet Kirby has distinguished his view of Australian law in important respects from Murphy's (see Kirby 1997b: 403–5). He has a different approach to social change from Murphy, who once (1986: 134) celebrated the role of an agitator, or a stirrer, as 'absolutely necessary' in Australia. Kirby fits Murphy's definition of an agitator, since he finds it 'hard to tolerate lawyers' complacency or indifference to injustice and inequality in the law' (Kirby 2003c: 4). Yet Kirby does not present himself as a radical at all, but rather as the authentic voice of a very old common law tradition. He is a cosmopolitan stirrer without appearing to be an agitator. This is evident in two key aspects of his judicial reasoning: first, his emphasis on getting the basic principles of constitutional interpretation correct; and second, his commitment to defending human rights primarily as a global citizen, not as an elitist judge with a special role.

Kirby's cosmopolitan judicial reasoning

The need for a dynamic approach to law is something Kirby shares not only with Murphy but also with Anthony Mason (2001: 9), who in the 1990s led the High Court towards understanding the Australian Constitution in terms of its changing social context. Kirby has followed and extended Mason's reasoning. For Kirby (2000c: 14), the Constitution should be read in new and imaginative ways in a 'world of globalism and regionalism' that is becoming increasingly interconnected. The Constitution must not be seen as an old and stagnant text, locked within the values that predominated in the British Empire in 1900. Rather, it must be questioned anew for what it can say to the world today. This is a dialogical and essentially cosmopolitan approach to constitutional interpretation. It has been the hallmark of Kirby's thought during his period on the High Court. As a judge, Kirby engages in a dialogue not merely with his current colleagues, but also with his successors. He is well aware that, as a British Law Lord said in 1998, 'a dissenting judgment anchored in the circumstances of today sometimes appeals to the judges of tomorrow' (Kirby 1999c: 9). When addressing younger lawyers, Kirby (2005f: 160–1) even dreams, like Martin Luther King, of big tasks that will be fulfilled by those who follow him. He hopes they will be bolder than him (Kirby 2007e: 10).

Kirby's dynamic understanding of the Constitution lacks majority endorsement on the current High Court, although he has used international law consistently to clarify ambiguity both in statutes and in the

Constitution (Johns 2001: 311–17). His view does have strong support from one of the Constitution's founders, Andrew Inglis Clark, and from Sir William Deane, the judge whom Kirby replaced on the High Court (Kirby 2000d: 79–80). Kirby (2000e: 520) rejects the idea that the Constitution's words should be 'shackled' to legal understandings that prevailed in 1900. Releasing the chains of what he labels 'an *originalist* approach' to the Constitution, he argues for the alternative, which is a '*contemporary* approach' (Kirby 2000d: 81; Kirby 1999b: 124). This approach to the Constitution facilitates cosmopolitan solutions to Australian problems. His judicial responses to three controversial questions lend support to this view. The first concerns the beneficial nature of the so-called race power in section 51(xxvi), which arose in the 1998 *Kartinyeri* case. The second is the issue of whether an innocent, stateless person can be lawfully detained forever in Australia. The third concerns the role of judges in issuing 'control orders' that deprive people (such as David Hicks) of liberty based merely on a suspicion that this might stop others from terrorist acts in future.

The *Kartinyeri* case resulted from the Hindmarsh Island bridge controversy in the mid-1990s. Aboriginal opposition on spiritual grounds failed to stop a punt being replaced with a bridge at Goolwa, near the mouth of the Murray River. This was because the High Court ruled that the government could use the *Aboriginal and Torres Strait Islander Heritage Protection Act* not to protect Indigenous culture, but to threaten or disregard it. A basic issue that the case did not resolve is whether section 51(xxvi) of the Constitution can support legislation only *benefiting* Aborigines, not legislation taking away rights only from them. The *Kartinyeri* case potentially had great historical importance. It raised the possibility that the massive *Yes* vote in the 1967 referendum, which amended section 51(xxvi), could be disregarded, to permit discrimination against Aboriginal people. Kirby stated, well before the case (1980a: 177), that 'the declared aim of the *Constitution Alteration (Aboriginals) Act 1967* was to remove any ground for the belief that the Constitution of Australia discriminated against people of the Aboriginal race, and at the same time to make it possible for the Commonwealth Parliament to enact special laws for these people'. In the *Kartinyeri* case, he restated this point without equivocation. His key argument was cosmopolitan, based on the premise that the Constitution 'does not operate in a vacuum' of national isolation. Instead, he said it 'speaks to the international community as the basic law of the Australian nation which is a member of that community' (Kirby 1998a: 418). He argued that the racist laws of Nazi Germany and apartheid South Africa are part of the global context in which the Australian Constitution is now understood by Australians. Consequently, Kirby (1998a: 416–19) said there is no place 'in late twentieth century Australia' for a view of the Constitution which 'supports detrimental and adversely discriminatory laws when the provision is read against the history of racism' in the twentieth century, and 'the 1967 referendum in Australia intended to address that history'. Because the meaning of section 51(xxvi) of the Constitution is now ambiguous, Kirby argued that its meaning must be read in accordance with, not in opposition to, Australia's international obligations. Since the clearest principle of international human rights law, ratified by Australia in 1975, is the prohibition of detrimental distinctions based on race, Kirby said that section 51(xxvi) must now be only a beneficial power.

Kirby has applied this cosmopolitan reading of the Constitution in several other cases. Most other High Court judges have barely responded to his reasoning, except for an exchange with Justice McHugh in a 2004 refugee detention case, *Al-Kateb*. This case highlights the contrast between Kirby's cosmopolitan approach and an alternative reading of international law given by McHugh (who had joined Mason and Brennan in accepting the Bangalore Principles in the *Mabo* decision). While both Kirby and McHugh have been attacked in the press for having a liberal view on same-gender marriage, their approaches to international law are very different (Kirby 2004c: 2). The background to the *Al-Kateb* case is the punitive form of administrative detention in Australia directed since 1992 against refugees, exacerbated at the turn of the century by the lead up to, and the results of, the *Tampa* episode. Kirby is strongly opposed to any unnecessary deprivation of liberty. Mr Al-Kateb's case reached the High Court in 2004 when Australia could not deport him, because no other country would accept him (Head 2005). But the case raises broader issues than refugee rights. It concerns whether a state can determine the limits of its own power, without regard for justice (Marr 2005). Kirby once defined himself (1991: 531), along with a few others, as being 'among the last of the true liberals' in Australia. His debate with McHugh over the *Al-Kateb* case is animated by his concern about the 'grave implications for the liberty of the individual' in Australia if unlimited detention without trial is accepted as a legal norm (Kirby 2004e: 162). Such detention is inconsistent with basic civil rights, as declared in international law, and with English precedent since the Magna Carta of 1215. Its acceptance in Australia would be a dangerous reversion to nationalist isolationism.

The dispute between Kirby and McHugh concerned whether the Constitution should be read, as far as possible, as consistent with Australia's obligations under international law. McHugh denied this, viewing the executive powers established under the Constitution as paramount, unlimited by any rules of international law that are mostly 'of recent origin' (McHugh 2004: 142). The image of international law underlying this approach is of a conventional inter-state order, where states are absolutely sovereign. As a

169

previous High Court judge, Justice Starke (quoted in Hovell and Williams 2005: 111), once claimed in 1945, 'the law of nations is a law for the inter-course of States with one another and not a law for individuals' (see also Charlesworth et al. 2003: 449). There is no place in such an image for cos-mopolitan concern, either for refugees or other victims of executive tyranny. Kirby responded by emphasising how much the world has changed since 1945. He argued that now 'the complete isolation of constitutional law from the dynamic impact of international law is neither possible nor desirable'. He cited the acceptance of the interdependence of domestic and interna-tional law in countries like Canada, Germany, India, New Zealand, the UK and the US as a sign of a 'paradigm shift'. This means that those who seek 'to cut off contemporary Australian law (including constitutional law) from the persuasive force of international law are doomed to fail' (Kirby 2004e: 169, 171, 173). Kirby is optimistic in the long term about the influence of his perspective, despite a lack of support from High Court colleagues, because he is convinced that 'a transnational law is emerging, especially on common issues concerning human rights' (Kirby 2005d: 6).

Kirby's concern for individual liberty was very evident in his reasoning in the first case concerning a 'control order'. This involved Jack Thomas, who was suspected by federal police of susceptibility to supporting terrorism but not convicted of any offence. Whereas in the *Al-Kateb* case Kirby had agreed with Justice Gummow and Chief Justice Gleeson, in the case of *Thomas v Mowbray* he forcefully disagreed with the acceptance of control orders by those judges and others in the majority (Kirby 2007d: 4; 2007e: 4). Kirby thought it abhorrent for judges to be used to 'deprive individuals of their liberty on the chance that such restrictions will prevent *others* from commit-ting certain acts in the future' (Kirby 2007b: 292). The extent of his concern is clear from his historical comparison of this case with the *Communist Party Case*. He said it went 'far beyond' that case in restricting civil liberties, and he lamented the 'unfortunate surrender' that many of his colleagues had made 'to demands for more and more governmental powers', which in his view contradicted the 'abiding values' of the Constitution (Kirby 2007b: 293, 301–2). He warned that the control order 'seriously alters the balance between the state and the individual', and has transformed federal courts in this respect into mere 'rubber stamps for the assertions of officers of the Executive Government' (Kirby 2007b: 296–7). While Kirby's arguments were based on careful analysis of the constitutional authorities, he supported his conclusions by reaffirming his basic interpretative principle. This states that the Constitution 'should be read, as far as the text allows, in a way that is harmonious with the universal principles of the international law of human rights and not destructive of them' (Kirby 2007b: 301). Not doing this, in Kirby's view, risks profoundly diminishing the value of liberty, and 'would deliver to terrorists successes that their own acts could never secure in Australia' (Kirby 2007b: 302). Kirby has described a dissenting opinion as 'an appeal to the future', and he hopes to see his rejection of control orders vindicated in future, just as he looks forward to the eventual creation of an Australian bill of rights, sometime following his retirement from the High Court in early 2009 (Kirby 2007c: 9–10, 16).

When he joined the High Court, Kirby (1996b: 275) said Australia is 'no longer a historical anachronism or settler or purely European society', but one which must come 'to terms with the challenges and opportunities of our geography and our regional destiny'. One of these challenges is treating refugees with dignity and respect. In a lecture in 1995 about refugees, Kirby (2000b: 22–3) said about his country:

> Australians share one continent. But we do not only share it among ourselves, selfishly and nationalistically. Australia is part of a wider region and a larger world. We must therefore consider how, in the future, we can do better. Doing better means more help to refugees here and abroad. But it also means urgent attention to the underlying causes of their terrible plight. And the journey to these truths will be helped by seeing refugees as we see ourselves – as people aspiring to life, dignity and hope.

The image underlying Kirby's approach to refugees, and to human rights law, is of a new world order which is global rather than merely international. Kirby (2005c: 2) believes that 'to survive, humanity must globalise and diversify'. He sees inclusive societies as worth struggling for, and acceptance of diversity as vital for defending freedom. He says learning 'from legal cultures different from our own' is crucial if Australians are to become 'less insular' and be able, optimistically and inclusively, 'to interpret the future to the present' (Kirby 2004g: 17; 2001b: 2).

A democratic defender of fundamental rights

While Kirby is often called a judicial activist, he has shown that all judges engage in judicial law-making, either creatively and openly, or otherwise. He regards the label as a compliment, since 'the common law itself is the product of judicial activists' over the long term (Kirby 2000b: 109). Yet Kirby does not see judges having a special role as elite guardians of human rights. This is clear from a long debate with his New Zealand colleague, Robin Cooke, about how far judges can go to stop fundamental rights from being annulled by a parliament facing no political constraints. During the 1980s,

Cooke raised the possibility that some rights, such as protection against torture, 'presumably lie so deep that even Parliament could not override them' (quoted in Kirby 1997a: 336). When asked to accept this idea in a 1986 case, while he was President of the NSW Court of Appeal, Kirby rejected it clearly. He said that, 'even in a hard case' involving the most oppressive legislation, judges have no authority to substitute their humanism for draconian laws, if the purpose of the law is clear (Kirby 1997a: 343–4). His reasoning was pragmatic. He said for judges to claim sovereignty themselves is politically unsustainable (Kirby 1997a: 344–5). Kirby did not view this institutional weakness of judges compared to politicians as a reason for despair, despite his sceptical view of what motivates most politicians. He thinks judges are usually able to protect fundamental rights by other means, such as interpreting legislation if at all possible in conformity with human rights, and using international law to resolve legal ambiguities in favour of protecting human dignity.

Kirby rejected Cooke's proposition about an ultimate judicial role in protecting people against tyrannical political authority. He called this 'heresy' (Kirby 1997a: 354). Ironically, this is just what McHugh later accused him of, by opening Australia to the influence of international law (McHugh 2004: 140). Yet there is a big difference between judges using international law to overcome ambiguity, which Kirby supports, and invalidating oppressive laws without reference to any other authority, such as a bill of rights, but merely because of their own reading of the common law. Kirby (1997a: 353) rejected Cooke's idea that deep rights should be protected finally by judges, saying that it 'challenges the democratic character of the system of which the judiciary is a part', and thus its legitimacy. For Kirby, it is vital to realise that a judge is a citizen too. He thinks that fundamental rights are best defended not by judges acting as a superior elite, but through their community engagement with fellow citizens. It is Kirby's egalitarianism that underlies his rejection of Cooke's view. The result of relying on an elite group of judges to salvage human rights from any attacks by oppressive politicians would be to diminish the role of the public political process, and to encourage apathy and complacency. Yet, despite firmly rejecting Cooke's view in 1997, Kirby recently (2004f: 13) said that it may be persuasive in New Zealand, where a political logjam over the status of the Treaty of Waitangi might be resolved partly through judicial creativity to entrench the rights of Maori. He argues that judges can protect 'especially the rights of minorities' if they take a longer view, and use 'a different time-frame' to politicians (Kirby 2004f: 13–14; 2006b: 11).

Kirby's commitment to a common, not an elitist, defence of human rights is why he opposed the minimalist project for an Australian republic in the

172

1990s. It would have replaced the Queen with a resident president elected by parliament, but ignored all of the constitutional 'tidying up' that Kirby (like many others) considers necessary (Kirby 2005i: 4). Kirby joined the conservative former High Court Chief Justice Sir Harry Gibbs and others to establish Australians for a Constitutional Monarchy. This was not a club of imperial fogies. Kirby had a central role in ensuring that this group was 'open to people of every race, creed, political persuasion and manner of life' (Kirby 2005e: 9). Popular sentiment in favour of a republic challenged monarchists to overcome their prejudices against homosexuals and intellectual free spirits like Kirby. They may not have realised that he opposed the republic proposal mainly because of what he calls his 'slightly anarchistic view about the Crown'. Kirby (2004b: 4) says he has a conservative view of the Queen, but this is because she is *not* an Australian, and rarely here, so 'we are spared the stretch limo from the president and the first lady and all of that sort of stuff'. His view is similar to those who argue that Australia is already a 'federal republic' in terms of government (Galligan 1995). Indeed, Kirby's belief in the core value of federalism, together with his commitment to an arbitration system giving workers industrial protection, is why he strongly disputed the legality of the Howard government's concentration of unlimited power in the *Workplace Relations Act*. In that case, Kirby sought to protect federalism and diversity. He argued that 'the common experience of humanity' warns against concentrated power, which now threatens 'an important part of the nation's institutional history and the egalitarian and idealistic values that such history has reinforced in the field of industrial disputes and employment standards' (Kirby 2006d: 144, 150, 164).

After his role opposing a shift to a republic, Kirby was surprised that the republican Keating appointed him to the High Court, whereupon he ceased his public monarchist agitation. He shares with Keating a big picture vision of Australia's changing role in the wider world, but he warns republicans to avoid 'the dangers of crude nationalism' (Kirby 2000h: 16). Kirby's experience on the High Court is another reason why he is a democratic, not an elitist, defender of fundamental rights. During the first year of his appointment, he made a bold claim about the Court, saying 'all Justices now reveal an awareness' of international human rights and 'a new sensitivity to the position of the indigenous peoples of Australia' (Kirby 1996a: 1102). After the 1996 *Wik* case marked the high point of native title in Australia, such awareness and sensitivity diminished. The bold claim was removed when the lecture containing it was reprinted in *Through the World's Eye* (Kirby 2000b: 124). The conservative trend has continued in other human rights cases resolved by the High Court for most of the past decade (Kirby 2005j: 10).

When speaking to audiences abroad, Kirby (2005c: 8) has said that, compared with the USA, 'enlightenment in Australia has been slower in coming' to the highest court.

Nonetheless, Kirby remains optimistic about Australians as a people who listen to alternative views, despite living in a conventional society. He thinks the eventual acceptance of his global outlook is inevitable, although, as Dr H. V. Evatt once observed, inevitability often means 'extreme gradualness' (Kirby 1997c: 230). Yet, waiting on the future does not satisfy Kirby, who once wrote (1980b: 69) that 'it is cold comfort to say that good ideas will triumph in the end'. His judicial isolation on the High Court (Kirby 2007c: 10–13) reinforces his public defence of human rights as a democratic citizen of the world, not as an elitist judge.

Conclusion

Kirby's cosmopolitanism has informed his work as a judge, and his role as a liberal intellectual. His practice of global citizenship involves three basic commitments: to global responsibility, to the value of diversity, and to judging Australia through the world's eye. For Kirby (2000b: 13), being a citizen of the world means accepting a responsibility to oppose injustice and to uphold the dignity of all human beings. This commitment is based on an acute awareness of how people throughout the globe are joined transnationally in a variety of ways, and not merely through their governments. Kirby's position as a judge has given him opportunities for overseas involvement, through organisations like UNESCO, which are not available to most people. Yet his vision of global responsibility does not depend on his judicial role. It can be shared by Australians who value human rights and respect for human dignity, regardless of how well their government acts as an international citizen.

Kirby's second commitment, to the value of diversity, has been very important in the development of his dynamic approach to the global context of law. Kirby (2005b) has described his approach to legal interpretation as being 'a new paradigm' for lawyers, which requires 'an expansion of the mind'. His adoption of the Bangalore Principles showed his openness to other views. By articulating those principles, he contributed to the High Court's decision in the *Mabo* case, where the judges acted to help overcome a serious logjam within Australian democracy. Since joining that court, Kirby has applied his approach to the interpretation of Australia's Constitution. He sees it not as a nationalist icon or a colonial relic, but as a text that needs to be understood as speaking to the wider world of humanity. This view informs his conclusion that racial discrimination has not been permitted by the Constitution since the 1967 referendum on rights for Aborigines (Kirby 2007a). He claims that Australian law and society has already been transformed by the practice of global citizenship, more than his colleagues are prepared to admit.

This leads to the third commitment, which is to seeing and judging Australia through the world's eye, not in isolation from other countries. For Kirby, a global citizen must engage in a double process of overcoming parochialism. They must look out beyond Australia to see what is happening in the wider world, and also assess their country in terms of common global interests and commitments, not narrow nationalist ideas. It is through the activity of global citizens involved in such a process that Kirby believes Australia can become a society that is more inclusive, open to renewal, and committed to achieving progressive change.

Kirby remains remarkably optimistic about the future, thinking that Australians can continue to overcome prejudice and oppression. He urges victims of discrimination to see their plight within a broader picture of a common and diverse humanity. His vision for Australia is of an inclusive society that shares this country with its first owners, as part of a larger, dynamic world. That view once led him into an unusual joy, during the Sydney Olympic Games. Previously, Kirby (1991: 532) had said that: 'If we are to survive, we have to be worthy of survival. We will not prove ourselves worthy simply by more football, cricket and sunny days at the beach'. Yet, in 2000, he experienced something else. He had neither the time nor the inclination to attend the events, but he was 'on the edge of my seat in front of the television as Cathy Freeman made her run' (Kirby 2001a: 1). He was moved in a new way, seeing that, sometimes, sport can unite people in their humanity. For Kirby, Freeman's triumph was not just a win for Australia, but a win for a new and enlarged Australia, open to the world's eye. That it occurred during a decade of reversals for the recognition of Indigenous rights in Australia made it symbolically more important. Like Kirby's exposition of cosmopolitan reasoning in his crucial judicial dissents, it was a powerful way of interpreting the future to the present.

Note

1 I would like to thank particularly Justice Michael Kirby for his feedback and advice on this chapter, and also Robert Cavanagh, Lucinda Horrocks, Mike Leach, Gary Smith, Geoff Stokes and Bruce Stone for their comments, and Lucinda Horrocks for her research assistance.

References

Charlesworth, H., M. Chiam, D. Hovell and G. Williams 2003. 'Deep anxieties: Australia and the international legal order.' *Sydney Law Review* 25(4):423–65.

Durie, E. 2000. 'Te Hono ku Hawai'iki: The bond with the Pacific.' In M. Wilson and P. Hunt (eds) *Culture, Rights, and Cultural Rights: Perspectives from the South Pacific.* Wellington: Huia, pp. 47–55.

Galligan, B. 1995. *A Federal Republic: Australia's constitutional system of government.* Melbourne: Cambridge University Press.

Head, M. 2005. 'Detention without trial: Is there no limit?' *Alternative Law Journal* 30(2):63–8, 96.

Heater, D. 2002. *World Citizenship: Cosmopolitan Thinking and Its Opponents.* London: Continuum.

Horner, J. 2004. *Seeking Racial Justice.* Canberra: Aboriginal Studies Press.

Hovell, D. and G. Williams 2005. 'A tale of two systems: The use of international law in constitutional interpretation in Australia and South Africa.' *Melbourne University Law Review* 29(1):95–130.

Johns, L. 2001. 'Justice Kirby, human rights and the exercise of judicial choice.' *Monash University Law Review* 27(2):290–318.

Jones, B. 2003. Interview with Roderic Pitty. Melbourne, 7 July.

Kirby, M. 1980a. 'T. G. H. Strehlow and Aboriginal customary laws.' *Adelaide Law Review* 7(2), January:172–99.

——1980b. 'Reforming the law.' In Alice Erh-Soon Tay and Eugene Kamenka (eds) *Law-making in Australia.* Melbourne: Edward Arnold, pp. 39–76.

——1983a. *Reform the Law: Essays on the renewal of the Australian legal system.* Melbourne: Oxford University Press.

——1983b. *Morality and Law: Old Debate, New Problems.* Tenth Walter Murdoch Lecture, Murdoch University, Perth: 13 September.

——1987. *Murphy: Bold Spirit of the Living Law.* Inaugural Lionel Murphy Memorial Lecture, Sydney University Law School, October 1987.

——1988a. 'The role of the judge in advancing human rights by reference to international human rights norms.' *Australian Law Journal* 62, July:514–32.

——1988b. 'Interview with Garry Sturgess and Philip Chubb.' In G. Sturgess and P. Chubb, *Judging the World: Law and Politics in the World's Leading Courts.* Sydney: Butterworths, pp. 366–71.

——1988c. 'Human rights and technology: A new dilemma.' *University of British Columbia Law Review* 22(1):123–45.

——1991. 'The intellectual and the law: A personal view.' *Meanjin* 50(4):523–32.

——1993a. 'The Australian use of international human rights norms: From Bangalore to Balliol – A view from the Antipodes.' *The UNSW Law Journal* 16(2):363–93.

——1993b. 'In defence of Mabo.' *Australian Quarterly* 65(4):67–81.

——1995. 'The impact of international human rights norms: "A law undergoing evolution."' *University of Western Australia Law Review* 25(1):30–48.

——1996a. 'A. F. Mason – from *Trigwell* to *Teoh*.' Sir Anthony Mason Lecture 1996. *Melbourne University Law Review* 20(4):1087–107.

——1996b. Swearing in and welcome speech, High Court, Canberra, 6 February. *Australian Law Journal* 70:274–7.

——1996c. 'A perspective on civil liberties: Early days and days ahead.' *Law Society Journal* 34(10):44–7.

——1997a. 'Lord Cooke and fundamental rights.' In P. Rishworth (ed.) *The Struggle for Simplicity in the Law: Essays for Lord Cooke of Thorndon.* Wellington: Butterworths, pp. 331–54.

——1997b. 'Reasons for judgment in *Green v The Queen.*' 191 *Commonwealth Law Reports* 334, pp. 387–416.

——1997c. 'The Australian Constitution – A centenary assessment.' *Monash University Law Review* 23(2):229–47.

——1998a. 'Reasons for judgment in *Kartinyeri v Commonwealth.*' 195 *Commonwealth Law Reports* 337, pp. 386–422.

——1998b. 'P. N. Bhagwati – An Australian appreciation.' In *Collected Speeches of Justice P. N. Bhagwati.* In *Justice Kirby's Papers.* Sydney: Law and Justice Foundation of New South Wales, viewed 31 January 2007, http://www.lawfoundation.net.au/resources/kirby/papers/19981220_de.html

——1999a. 'UNESCO, Human Rights and Courage.' Speech at the Award of the UNESCO Prize for Human Rights Education. Paris, 7 June 1998. In *Justice Kirby's Papers.* Sydney: Law and Justice Foundation of New South Wales, viewed 31 January 2007, http://www.lawfoundation.net.au/resources/kirby/papers/19981220_de.html

——1999b. 'Domestic implementation of international human rights norms.' *Australian Journal of Human Rights* 5(2):109–25.

——1999c. 'Law at century's end – A millenial view from the High Court of Australia.' Address to the Monash University Law School Foundation. Melbourne, 22 November. In *High Court of Australia – Publications.* Canberra: High Court of Australia, viewed 31 January 2007, http://www.hcourt.gov.au/speeches/kirbyj/kirbyj_century.htm

——2000a. 'An interview with Justice Michael Kirby.' Video. Justice Kirby interviewed by Professor Ralph Simmonds. Murdoch University, School of Law, 15 March.

——2000b. *Through the World's Eye.* Federation Press: Sydney.

——2000c. 'Constitutional interpretation and original intent: A form of ancestor worship?' *Melbourne University Law Review* 24(1):1–14.

——2000d. 'Reasons for judgment in *Eastman v The Queen.*' 203 *Commonwealth Law Reports* 1, pp. 65–96.

——2000e. 'Reasons for judgment in *Grain Pool of Western Australia v Commonwealth of Australia.*' 202 *Commonwealth Law Reports* 479, pp. 514–33.

——2000f. 'The Law Reform Commission and the essence of Australia.' *Reform* 70: 60–1.

——2000g. 'Protecting cultural rights: Some developments.' In M. Wilson and P. Hunt (eds) *Culture, Rights, and Cultural Rights: Perspectives from the South Pacific.* Wellington: Huia, pp. 145–61.

——2000h. 'The Australian Republican Referendum 1999 – Ten lessons.' Address to the Law Faculty. University of Buckingham, 3 March. In *Justice Kirby's Papers.* Sydney: Law and Justice Foundation of New South Wales, viewed 31 January 2007, http://www.lawfoundation.net.au/resources/kirby/papers/19981220_de.html

——2001a. 'Who cares about human rights anyway?' Speech launching June 2001 issue of the *Alternative Law Journal.* In *High Court of Australia – Publications.*

Canberra: High Court of Australia, viewed 31 January 2007, http://www.hcourt.
gov.au/speeches/kirbyj/kirbyj_alternative.htm

——2001b. 'Interview with Justice Michael Kirby.' Community Leadership Centre, viewed 10 January 2008, http://www.ourcommunity.com.au/leadership/
leadership_article.jsp?articleId=1039

——2002. 'Surface Nugget.' *Quadrant* 46(10):53–6.

——2003a. 'More Indigenous lawyers – Making a difference.' Address to the
UNSW Indigenous Pre-Law Program, Sydney, 31 January. In *High Court of
Australia – Publications*. Canberra: High Court of Australia, viewed 31 Jan-
uary 2007, www.hcourt.gov.au/speeches/kirbyj/kirbyj_UNSWIndigenousPreLaw
Program.htm

——2003b. 'Genomics and democracy – A global challenge.' *University of Western
Australia Law Review* 31(1):1–18

——2003c. 'Interview with Justice Kirby.' Interviewed by Jordan Tilse, 28 April. In *High
Court of Australia – Publications*. Canberra: High Court of Australia, viewed 31
January 2007, http://www.hcourt.gov.au/speeches/kirbyj/kirbyj_28apr.html

——2003d. 'The High Court of Australia and the Supreme Court of the United States –
A centenary reflection.' *University of Western Australia Law Review* 31(2):171–201.

——2003e. 'The High Court and the death penalty – Looking back, looking forward,
looking around.' Address to the Criminal Law Association (Vic) and Reprieve
Australia. Melbourne, 6 October.

——2003f. 'Record of Interview of Justice Michael Kirby by Monica Attard on Sunday Profile.' ABC Radio, 16 November. In *High Court of Australia – Publications*.
Canberra: High Court of Australia, viewed 31 January 2007, http://www.hcourt.gov.
au/speeches/kirbyj/kirbyj_16nov.html

——2004a. 'God and the Judge.' Radio program. Justice Kirby interviewed by David
Busch and Rev. Ian Pearson. *Encounter*. ABC Radio National, 28 March, transcript
viewed 31 January 2007, http://www.abc.net.au/rn/relig/enc/stories/s1071895.htm

——2004b. 'Interview with Justice Michael Kirby: Leadership.' Justice Kirby interviewed
by Michelle Boyle. Canberra, 29 March. In *High Court of Australia – Publications*.
Canberra: High Court of Australia, viewed 31 January 2007, http://www.hcourt.
gov.au/speeches/kirbyj/kirbyj_29mar04.html

——2004c. 'Are we all nominalists now?' Speech at the Leo Cussen Institute, Melbourne, 30 April. In *High Court of Australia – Publications*. Canberra: High Court
of Australia, viewed 31 January 2007, http://www.hcourt.gov.au/speeches/kirbyj/
kirbyj_30apr04.html

——2004d. 'Patron's perspective: The judicial life.' In *High Court of Australia
– Publications*. Canberra: High Court of Australia, viewed 31 January 2007,
http://www.hcourt.gov.au/speeches/kirbyj/kirbyj_judicial life.htm

——2004e. 'Reasons for judgment in *Al-Kateb v Godwin*.' 208 *Australian Law Reports*
124 pp. 161–74.

——2004f. 'Deep lying rights – A constitutional conversation continues.' The 2004
Robin Cooke Lecture. Wellington, 25 November. In *High Court of Australia –
Publications*. Canberra: High Court of Australia, viewed 31 January 2007,
http://www.hcourt.gov.au/speeches/kirbyj/kirbyj_25nov04.html

——2004g. 'A blaze in the sky – The centenary conference of the High Court of Australia.'
University of Notre Dame Law Review 6:1–20.

——2005a. '"Judicial activism"? A riposte to the counter-Reformation.' *Otago Law Review* 11(1):1–16.

——2005b. 'International human rights law in the legal systems of the Commonwealth of Nations.' Lecture at ANU, Canberra, 8 March. In ANU Law School Archived Downloadable 2005 Past Events, viewed 17 January 2008, http://law.anu.edu.au/cipl/Archived%20Downloadable%202005%20Past%20Events.htm

——2005c. 'International law – the impact on national constitutions.' American Society of International Law, 7th Annual Grotius Lecture, Washington DC, March 30. In *High Court of Australia – Publications.* Canberra: High Court of Australia, viewed 31 January 2007, http://www.hcourt.gov.au/speeches/kirbyj/kirbyj_30mar05.html

——2005d. 'International human rights and constitutional interpretation.' Philippine Judicial Academy, Chief Justice Hilario G. Davide Jr Distinguished Lecture Series, Manila, April 15. In *High Court of Australia – Publications.* Canberra: High Court of Australia, viewed 31 January 2007, http://www.hcourt.gov.au/speeches/kirbyj/kirbyj_15apr05.html

——2005e. 'Tribute to the Right Hon Harry Gibbs GCMG AC KBE.' University of Queensland, 10 October. In *High Court of Australia – Publications.* Canberra: High Court of Australia, viewed 31 January 2007, http://www.hcourt.gov.au/speeches/kirbyj/kirbyj_10oct05.pdf

——2005f. 'Law in Australia – Cause of pride; source of dreams.' *Flinders Journal of Law Reform* 8(2):151–71.

——2005g. 'The Commonwealth Star of Liberty.' Speech to The College of Law, Sydney, 23 November. In *High Court of Australia – Publications.* Canberra: High Court of Australia, viewed 31 January 2007, http://www.hcourt.gov.au/speeches/kirbyj/kirbyj_23nov05.html

——2005h. 'Are we there yet?' In B. Opeskin and D. Weisbrot (eds) *The Promise of Law Reform.* Sydney: Federation Press, pp. 433–48.

——2005i. 'Interview of Justice Kirby by Claire Low.' Canberra, 5 September. In *High Court of Australia – Publications.* Canberra: High Court of Australia, viewed 31 January 2007, http://www.hcourt.gov.au/speeches/kirbyj/kirbyj_cl0905.pdf

——2005j. 'Ten years in the High Court – Continuity and change.' Talk to Bar Readers course, NSW Bar Association, Sydney, 17 October. *Australia Bar Review* 27(1):4–24.

——2005k. 'Globalizing the rule of law? Global challenges to the traditional ideal of the rule of law.' In S. Zifcak (ed.) *Globalisation and the Rule of Law.* London: Routledge, pp. 65–80.

——2006a. 'Take heart – International law comes, ever comes.' In U. Dolgopol and J. Gardham (eds) *The Challenge of Conflict: International Law Responds.* Leiden: Martinus Nijhoff, pp. 283–98.

——2006b. 'Law reform and the trans-Tasman log-jam.' Speech to the Law Commission of New Zealand, Twentieth Anniversary Conference, Wellington, 25 August. In *High Court of Australia – Publications.* Canberra: High Court of Australia, viewed 31 January 2007, http://www.hcourt.gov.au/speeches/kirbyj/kirbyj_25aug06.pdf

——2006c. 'Change through dissent: Disagreement in the High Court and beyond.' In T. Wright (ed.) *Time for Change.* Melbourne: Hardie Grant Books, pp. 17–25.

——2006d. 'Reasons for judgment in *NSW and others v Commonwealth of Australia.*' 231 *Australian Law Reports* 1 pp. 111–65.

——2007a. 'The 1967 referendum: Don't get carried away.' Speech in Melbourne on 1 June, published in *Lawyers Weekly Online*, viewed 10 January 2008, http://www.lawyersweekly.com.au/articles/The-1967-referendum-don-t-get-carried-away_z69652.htm

——2007b. 'Reasons for judgment in *Thomas v Mowbray*.' 237 *Australian Law Reports* 194 pp. 237–302.

——2007c. 'Consensus and dissent in Australia.' Tenth Annual Hawke Lecture, Adelaide, 10 October, viewed 10 January 2008, http://www.unisa.edu.au/hawkecentre/ahl/2007ahl_Kirby.pdf

——2007d. 'The great dissenter: Justice Michael Kirby.' Interviewed by Monica Attard on *Sunday Profile*, ABC Radio, 25 November, transcript viewed 10 January 2008, http://www.abc.net.au/sundayprofile/stories/s2100123.htm

——2007e. 'Bold enough: Justice Michael Kirby.' Interviewed by Monica Attard on *Sunday Profile*, ABC Radio, 2 December, transcript viewed 10 January 2008, http://www.abc.net.au/sundayprofile/stories/s2106109.htm

Koskenniemi, M. 2003. 'Legal cosmopolitanism: Tom Franck's messianic world.' *New York University Journal of International Law and Politics* 35(2):471–86.

Marr, D. 2005. 'Liberty is left in shaky hands when the High Court no longer defends it.' *Sydney Morning Herald* 31 March.

Mason, A. 2001. 'Deakin's vision, Australia's progress.' In *The Alfred Deakin Lectures: Ideas for the Future of a Civil Society*. Sydney: ABC Books, pp. 8–22.

McHugh, M. 2004. 'Reasons for judgment in *Al-Kateb v Godwin*.' 208 *Australian Law Reports* 124 pp. 133–45.

Murphy, L. 1986. *The Judgements of Justice Lionel Murphy*. Edited by A. R. Blackshield, D. Brown, M. Coper and R. Krever. Sydney: Primavera Press.

Oldaker, A. 2003. 'Communist hype: Evatt opposes Menzies' "red herring".' *The Advocate* (Devonport) 27 September:30.

Pitty, R. 2003. 'Assorted recollections of an interview with Justice Michael Kirby.' Melbourne, 15 October, approved as an accurate record by Justice Kirby in an email, 2 December 2003.

Thao Nguyen

Thao Nguyen was Australia's Youth Representative to the United Nations in 2004. She was born in a refugee camp on the Thai–Cambodian border in 1980. She grew up in Bankstown, Sydney. Witnessing her parents struggle to raise their family in Australia, battling hardship and discrimination, sensitised her to the plight of marginalised people in Australia and around the world. In 2001 she became active in the Vietnamese community, working on drug education and youth issues. As Australia's Youth Representative to the UN in 2004, Nguyen lobbied for more youth representation there, and negotiated a resolution on behalf of Australia. She has been the Youth Chair of the Ethnic Communities' Council of NSW, and was Bankstown City Council's Young Australian of the Year in 2003. Since completing her commerce and law degree at Sydney University, she has worked in Vietnam.

Thao Nguyen, Vietnamese-Australian writer and lawyer. (Courtesy Thao Nguyen.)

10

Young Australians as Global Citizens

Thao Nguyen, interviewed by Gary Smith and Roderic Pitty[1]

Each September, a young Australian makes the long journey to the United Nations, not as a tourist but as a specially selected diplomat. For one year, she or he is Australia's official Youth Representative to the UN. The high point is speaking and lobbying at the Third Committee of the UN General Assembly. But the Youth Representative is required to do much more than be a temporary diplomat. She or he must try to inform the UN about key issues of concern to Australian youth, and report back to youth meetings around the country about what happens at the UN, and what it can achieve in today's conflict-ridden and often depressing world. Since there is only one youth position on offer each year, the job is a privilege that is competitively sought after by young people across the nation. Applicants who reach the final round of the selection process sit a video-recorded interview in which they demonstrate that they have the skills and ideas to do this special diplomatic task proficiently.

The Youth Representative for 2004 was Thao Nguyen, a young woman who arrived in Australia in November 1980, a few months after being born in a Red Cross tent for Vietnamese refugees in a camp on the Thai–Cambodian border. Her family had a 'bourgeois' background in South Vietnam, with her father being a banker, and other relatives holding top positions in the judiciary and military. After the fall of Saigon, some family members, including her father, were imprisoned. After his release, he fled from a threat of being sent to remove land mines in fields riddled with them, and walked with his family to Thailand. One of Thao's uncles was captured by the Khmer Rouge in Cambodia, and never seen again.

Thao's family arrived at Villawood hostel in Sydney when it was a place for helping refugees, not the immigration detention centre it later became. But working life for her parents was hard in Australia. Her mother started sewing in 1985 as a sweatshop worker, being paid below $1 per garment; twenty years later the rate was roughly the same. Her father coped with regular abuse working as a machinist for a subsidiary of a whitegoods company, at a time when the family could not afford a washing machine. It was from this newly marginalised background that Thao rose to become the 2004 Youth Representative, partly because of one incident that occurred when she was studying at high school.

Acquiring a voice for marginalised people

Gary Smith: So how did you become Australia's Youth Representative to the UN? What's your story?

Thao Nguyen: I often get asked 'What got you involved in community development?' and similar activities, and a contributing factor is my personal story. There was a defining moment in my life when I was sixteen and I came home to find my father on the verge of tears. My father is a typical Vietnamese/Asian male patriarch who represses things and separates his own suffering from the family. On this particular day he was really bad. I'd never seen my father cry before, and he could hardly hold back the tears. I asked him what was happening, and he said that everyday at work he would get abused, and picked on. There had been an incident that day when he was manning a multi-million dollar machine, and a few of his co-workers got screws and threw them into the machine to sabotage it on his shift. They had also slashed tyres, and done all these other terrible things, and he would just take it. I think it was because of twenty years of just being suppressed. In the re-education camp back in Vietnam he had to get up every day and say that he was worthless, a traitor to his country.

Now, on the factory floor he would be reading *Les Miserables* in French during the morning tea break, and he was subjected to routine forms of abuse. So he got this stick, and he was going to kill the men who were taunting him, because he'd had enough. At that moment, however, he realised that with my mother and the kids it would be too much of a cost and he stopped. He decided then that he would never be violent again. That day he came home, and he said to me: 'I have a mouth to eat with but I don't have a mouth to speak with. I'm working, and you are the only way that I can have a voice. It's not just me. There are a lot of other marginalised people in this country and around the world, and unless you can do something about it we'll be silent forever'. Hence my life of social justice! I think a reality for me was witnessing social injustice for all of my life, with that being a norm. Then I stepped outside of that reality and went to university where I realised that not everybody's mother is a sweatshop worker, and that this wasn't normal.

GS: What were the first things that you did to respond in your own behaviour?

TN: The basic motivation was to study, which was what my family kept pushing. But together with this, I'd always noticed the marginalised people. During my Year 11 at high school, Pauline Hanson rose to public prominence and I became preoccupied about the need for students to protest, to walk out of class. I thought we needed to do something. So I wrote a letter to *Time* magazine. They published it, along with some other pieces I wrote about leadership, and how John Howard didn't stand up and say anything in the face of this, and how it was unacceptable. I had a day to get as many people in my school as possible to walk out. I found a photocopier that night, and copied a thousand flyers and stood at Punchbowl station at 6 am by myself, handing all this stuff out, and getting abused by suspicious people. Then I went to school and got into trouble, and then just walked out. That was at St George Girls' High, and I got a few other students to come with me from other schools as well. Those kids wouldn't have done anything politically engaged or active at all. These were MTV-watching kids. But I didn't feel that this was a political act. I had no concept of this as activism or doing anything of that nature. I just felt you need to do something, and I couldn't be violent.

GS: So that was in your school days. You obviously did well with your school results, and went on to university. Did anything else happen then that influenced your activity?

TN: Yes, when I went there I was completely lost. I did extremely well in the NSW Higher School Certificate, almost topped the state in English, and then I handed in a university essay that barely passed. I recognised that something was really wrong, and something *was* wrong. I was focused on a lot of issues surrounding growing up, about my cultural identity, who I am, and where I come from. All these matters started to affect me in a really big way. So I took the year off and went to Vietnam. That was really life-changing for my identity, and how I saw myself.

Roderic Pitty: When was that?

TN: That was 1999.

RP: How did going back to Vietnam change your life and your identity as an Australian?

TN: I think previously I didn't feel like I was a real person. I didn't have any ancestry or heritage here. It was as if I was plucked from some bizarre place and just planted here. All the stories that my parents told me were so intangible that they were like fantasies from a dream world. When I went back to Vietnam it was like, this is real, and I have some heritage and ancestry. I felt that I was actually alive, and that I was real. So I went to where my father was born, and touched the trees there. Once in Saigon I felt an instantaneous moment of belonging and connection, but I knew that Vietnam was not really my space now. When I came back to Australia I felt even more isolated, feeling I still didn't quite belong here as well. So in 2001 I got involved in the Vietnamese Students' Association, and through that I got involved working with the Vietnamese community in Australia on various social issues, such as drug education and youth issues. That led me to get involved in the National Youth Roundtable.

GS: So you were having to find out about youth issues, and get access to those networks?

TN: I was doing casework with young drug-affected kids, and doing projects in the Vietnamese community. My friend, a fellow student who was involved in mental health work, just sent me a form for the National Youth Roundtable, and I was surprised that they accepted me. Then the main step from that was being involved with the Ethnic Communities' Council of NSW, among lots of other groups.

RP: So you've changed from being very isolated here to becoming an Australian representative?

TN: Yes, and being a voice for marginalised people has helped enormously in achieving that.

Diplomatic involvement with the United Nations

GS: So how did the UN side start to come into the story, and becoming an international representative?

TN: When I was President of the Vietnamese Students' Association at Sydney University I had the opportunity to go to an international conference in Paris. This was an international Vietnamese youth conference, at which there were 400 Vietnamese young people from sixteen different countries, talking – all with different accents, which was strange – about things like democracy,

185

the pro-democracy movement in Vietnam, human rights, and what does being Vietnamese mean. Coming back I switched majors, from commerce to doing international relations, and government, and economics. So I started studying things like human rights, and comparative social policy, while always being drawn to thinking in terms of ideals. I had known about the UN Youth Representative position for a couple of years, but decided to apply when I looked at the criteria. Reviewing all the projects I had been involved in, the criteria pretty much defined all the things I had done, including youth advocacy and representation, working with communities and local government, knowledge of international relations and the UN, and also appropriate life experience skills in order to be successful in that diplomatic role.

RP: What goals did you have at the UN?

TN: I had to write a statement, to be delivered in the Third Committee of the UN General Assembly, which had to put key youth issues on the UN agenda. My statement was based on my consultations with communities around Australia before going to the UN. But my main goal was to lobby other countries to send more youth representatives to the UN. Thirty years after these youth representatives had begun, there were only eleven representatives. So I negotiated a resolution on behalf of Australia, which was unique because no other youth representatives were allowed to sit at the negotiating table on behalf of their countries. Of those eleven I was the only one allowed to do that, to actually support a resolution (moved by Portugal calling for more youth representatives), at a table where everyone except for me was not a young person. It was bizarre because if you talk about democracy, where's the voice of young people on an issue which is supposed to be about young people? I found that my position there became really invaluable, because I had the expertise about youth issues and youth organisations, how young people are active in the world today, and I became that fluid link with the diplomats who were formally creating this resolution. I was having to tell, for example, the delegate from China that this resolution was necessary because the UN must reflect the reality of how young people really organise around the world today, which is now by participation in non-governmental organisations (NGOs) more than by state alignment.

RP: Did the other youth representatives see you as a voice because of the position you had attained?

TN: Not only the other youth representatives, but even the UN Secretariat did so. Because of how the UN works in such a formalised way, the other youth delegates who had all the expertise couldn't even say anything. So what I did was to have strategic meetings with them to work out what we needed to push most, and also with people in the UN Secretariat. So my presence became really invaluable.

GS: I think that's a really interesting statement that you've just made, that young people are affiliated more with non-governmental bodies than to their states. That's a powerful message, but hard to get across to government representatives, since it's coming from an angle they don't really understand.

TN: That's why the main political problem we had with the 2004 resolution was the section on NGO participation. The 2004 resolution was about the 2005 UN General Assembly meeting, which would include a ten-year review of the World Program of Action for Youth that was adopted in 1995. So across the world they were looking at what's been done for young people. At the negotiations, Australia and Portugal were pushing for NGO participation at this event, but because we needed other support this was completely watered down just to NGO access. This was because certain states didn't want NGO involvement, because NGOs say 'governments are doing the wrong thing'. That's why it was fought very vigorously. But if you look back over the last ten years, since the 1995 adoption of that program, there's been a great increase in the number of international networks involving young people, which now have millions and millions of members across the world.

RP: In your lobbying at the UN were you able to cross the boundaries that are conventionally set up by the way diplomats lobby and interact?

TN: Yes, after a negotiation you would approach certain diplomats informally and ask them to support something. That's how it works, even in the toilets. The youth representatives worked together to try to get more representatives by setting up an information session which was held at the General Assembly. We particularly focused on any state that had mentioned youth in their statement, and we got forty-five people there. Then we highlighted individual diplomats for lobbying informally. That's really how we did it.

RP: So you were there in an arena where you were representing non-Australians, as well as Australians, and you were also speaking for much more than Australia?

TN: Yes! I think that is how I operated when I was there. Sure, I had my red diplomatic pass identifying me as Australian, but I felt that I was more pushing the agenda of young people for increased representation and participation in decision-making processes, and the issues of world youth in general.

RP: So you were pushing a universal agenda?

TN: Yes, for sure. That's why it was so easy to work with the other youth representatives from all the other different countries, because we had the same concerns.

RP: What were some of the issues that comprised your agenda?

TN: Obviously there were different issues mentioned in particular presentations, such as high youth unemployment, and I mentioned mental health as a big thing, but the overall thing that united us, and gave us a common agenda, was the fact that young people's voices need to be heard because we're going to be inheriting the consequences of the decision-making process right now. Unless we're in that process, we won't really have more democracy since youth are a very important group in world society. We had that broad agenda, we all believed in stronger youth participation as a core belief, so we could lobby effectively for more youth representatives.

RP: You were there as government representatives, but you saw yourselves beyond that, as human beings articulating a common interest?

TN: Yes, if I compare how the youth representatives worked with how the UN General Assembly Third Committee official delegates worked, it was really different. This was because they would do their job in their roles and would just see the other diplomats as only from other states, whereas we were a team of young people working against established orders denying young people access, whatever our economic and political heritage. I understood that the diplomats were politically restricted as state representatives and we were lucky in a sense to share such significant objectives.

RP: Does that link in practice with the idea of global citizenship?

TN: Yes, definitely. I think after that experience it confirmed it more for me. This was because I went to that environment and worked with the youth representatives of different countries, but completely in a fluid fashion, but also completely united with our agendas. Although we obviously had our differences, really we were speaking exactly the same language. We all had the same sort of talk, we knew the same issues.

Dynamics of global youth political action

GS: Are there tensions within the global youth movement, or does everyone basically agree?

TN: There certainly are tensions, for example between the European Youth Forum and the Global Youth Action Network. Essentially it was this: the European Youth Forum claims the Global Youth Action Network (GYAN) is totally undemocratic, and that its membership base is questionable because it's all online. The GYAN's stance is: 'we have millions of members across the world, we are actually doing incredible work'. And they are. They've been asked by the UN to do Millennium Development Goals work and youth work. Within the European youth representatives we have a big divide: some of them are very open to the GYAN and getting involved in this process, while others are totally against it.

GS: So there's a lot of growth happening, and tensions within this movement. How do you see this moving in the next few years? Do you see a direction coming out of this growth?

TN: I see there is going to be exponential growth actually. It seems that there will always be tensions between similar institutions. But I think this generation of young people have a great capacity to be malleable in the face of these tensions so that they do not become inhibiting. Many of the young people like those I've been speaking to at the moment have this mindset that we need to participate, but we just don't know what the first step is. I have just completed a workshop with Oxfam, and their International Youth Parliament. This is an international network that meets every couple of years, where they look at projects for development and social justice and social change across the world that are initiated by young people. Essentially it's a network which offers a linking of resources. It facilitates young people working together. Someone from Somalia can say 'I'm working on this project around water issues', and the Oxfam International Youth Parliament Secretariat, which is based in Sydney, will say 'OK, someone from your area is doing this and they've got these things they can offer'. So it's the idea of social change within a global network of young people. A lot of young Australians in particular are getting involved, and developing their own organisations. I just found out about this new organisation of Australian Youth Against Landmines. There are more and more of these activities growing up.

GS: That's interesting. It's been said that today, globally, you have youth in quite different societies. First you have youth in developing societies that are quite young demographically, and also you've got youth in other places, particularly European societies, living in rapidly ageing societies. It's almost like there's a global division between these two types of societies; those with very high birth rates over the last twenty years, and societies with an ageing pyramid. So you have youth in some societies positioned as a shrinking minority, and in others they are at the crest of a wave that is moving through society. Has that been expressed yet in any of the youth dynamics that you've seen?

TN: That's a really good point, and I think it's reflected in the level of political engagement within those countries by young people. There's an accusation, which is that Australian youth are really just politically apathetic. Compared to other countries like Indonesian youth, or what have you, they might seem apathetic, but I think it's more the case that, because we are such a minority, there is a sense of disillusionment, and disempowerment. Young people often ask what can we do really? So there's a new divide in Australia among youth. In one group there is just that disillusionment and disempowerment, and in another group, because of that, there is a willingness to do more, and to overcompensate. I think that in countries where young people are almost a majority or a third of the population, there is more of a sense of momentum, and getting involved, and doing things because they actually have strength in numbers and are visible majorities.

Bypassing marginalisation in Australia

RP: Does the difficulty for youth to get a space in formal Australian politics lead them to seek a broader horizon?

TN: Yes, in many cases it does. One group of youth just bypasses the formal political process. In 2004 I spoke at a first-time voters forum before the federal election. Essentially I was saying that, because young people aren't the majority in the population, then logically why would the parties address themselves to a minority in order to win their votes? They just wouldn't do that. So their policies don't reflect a long-term investment, they are just capturing the generational majority. So there's a sense, on the part of some youth, of retreating, saying 'this is all crap', and 'I can't see myself in the political landscape at all'.

RP: Even with all your experience over the last few years? There's no opening for your viewpoints to be heard?

TN: Exactly. I really don't think so. And I think it is especially so for doubly marginalised people. If you're young, you are usually marginalised, but if you are of an ethnic background or of an indigenous background, or if you're disabled, then you are excluded. Anything the government does to give young people a voice is all a token gesture, because they believe that youth don't have the capacity to make meaningful changes. So you either don't do anything, and just concentrate on interest rates, or you just bypass it and get involved in global organisations or networks where you actually feel you are making a difference.

RP: You can have more influence globally . . .

TN: But back in your own country. That's really true. So right now I'm on the Australian non-governmental delegation which will present a shadow report to the UN Committee on the Rights of the Child in Geneva. We're going there soon, and that's one reflection of that approach. In order to get policy change in Australia you have to get some exposure overseas. I think the reality is that at home we don't really have a voice, especially under the Howard government. Advocacy for youth has been straightjacketed, and advocacy bodies are essential for minorities. If we see that limitation happening, there is really no point in us focusing our resources on something that is really restricted at home. So the other avenue is to really bypass that by acting beyond Australia in areas that can affect the home situation.

GS: The disappointment with the [Howard] government might extend to its lack of interest in international fora as the place where norms are set, so you've had a government in the last ten years that's been trying to build a nationalistic barrier against the idea of listening to the UN. And the UN's been criticised in a number of government statements, especially with regard to international law. The big exception was joining the International Criminal Court, and they nearly didn't join that. There's a sense in which for a decade, which is a long period in a young person's life, it's hard to have any sense of another tradition of the state doing things differently, usually under Labor governments. But that tradition of acting and listening in an internationalist way is always there waiting to come back.

RP: When that tradition comes back it will be in a different political environment because of what you have described, where there are new generations of young people who are thinking and acting as global citizens in Australia, and who have started to create a new agenda and new networks.

TN: Exactly. You can talk about this in terms of generation Y, which is my generation, born around 1980. Now this generation, who are potentially people of formal political decision-making capacity in the next twenty years or so, this is quite a unique generation. Because for them, communications technology is the norm, as is cross-border travel for many. I know that many young Australians don't have net access, a personal computer, or the chance to travel. But there is a higher level of engagement with these things than previous generations – that's the difference. For many of us,

191

experiences like the internet and information globalisation have occurred during our childhood. We've grown up with it, and so that will affect how we engage with the world outside of Australia. Right now there are international youth conferences on almost every week around Australia, on social justice, the environment, on mental health or whatever. So it's a huge potential movement.

I'm on an e-list called Youth Gas and it's a national e-list which has youth projects on anything from arts to health and so on, and there are common themes that you can get every day. You don't even need to travel outside of Australia to get the influences of different cultures and different young people. When you get to a space, like an international conference, and you're talking to another young person, say from the Philippines, you're already sharing with them common ideals like greater participation. The important thing to note is that international borderless interaction is absolutely sub-conscious, and it's normal. That has the potential to introduce ideas of global citizenship. If we are talking about global citizenship in terms of a moral community then most of my generation and those younger would probably not yet identify fully with that, but if you're talking about global citizen-ship as being not just entrenched in your own state, but being completely comfortable in a global space, perhaps that fits.

RP: And you've got a common language that has been created?

TN: Yes, and this is a culture. We're growing up in an environment of international engagement, be it arts and music like hip hop, or political ideas, even on a very personal level in terms of relationships, friendships, e-groups and that sort of thing, so it's going to change the political landscape in the future.

GS: Just how the political landscape will change is hard to determine at this point, because, with all this activity going on nationally and internationally, state structures can still make things difficult. It depends on the context. You can get into international institutions, such as into the UN, but it requires quite hard work. What about the younger generations, those much younger than you, what do you think about them?

TN: I don't want to sound pessimistic, but it's very hard for that generation to be engaged in terms of social responsibility, especially if we are talking about middle class Australia. They are a generation that's said to be over-indulged, because their parents are in blended families, with single parents, and also mothers and fathers are working a lot more. All these things that are happening mean that the parents are guilty, and what do they do when they feel guilty? They don't try to change their lifestyle in order to spend more time with the kids, they overindulge them by giving them everything that they want. When you do that you spawn a generation that is apathetic and, well, self-interested, as opposed to being more open to social responsibility.

GS: But because we're still talking about a young group, it might be a bit early to determine what's going to happen to them as they get older, into their twenties.

TN: As they see the consequences of what's happening now, we and particularly they are going to be at the height of environmental changes that we are just starting to see now. So they're going to be at the point where it happens.

RP: In terms of your experience representing Australia internationally as a young person at the UN and at other conferences, what has been the response from people outside Australia to what Australia's reputation has been in the last few years with regard to human rights, and the treatment of refugees?

TN: Bewilderment! They're not hostile but they're just confused. They are asking: 'Well, what's going on here? You guys were really progressive, and we don't know what's going on'. People are actually really bewildered. Yet the youth representatives from Australia have taken a particularly strong lead in doing really good work within the youth representatives group. This is what the UN Secretariat has said: the Australian youth who have been selected for this role have been particularly strong and effective lobbyists, apart from all the other things they've done. This has occurred despite the very difficult situation with the Howard government. So this shows some potential for change. But we need also to make more representations to the Australian Government.

Cosmopolitanism and Australian youth

GS: For your peers, are there three or four issues that will engage the kind of youth organisations that you are involved in? Are there some that really stand out as the long-term issues?

TN: The environment is definitely up there. Just living in Australia, reconciliation with Indigenous peoples, and all of the issues linked with that. The immediate situation with regard to refugees and immigration detention is important. There is also the curtailment of civil liberties, with all these laws that are being passed, and that reflects on how we as a country look at the international arena. So I would say those are all seen as key long-term issues.

193

GS: I'm just wondering about the divide between Islamic and non-Islamic cultures that has grown in the world since 9/11. Has there been much work among youth organisations to address this apparently widening divide? There are very big Islamic NGOs in the world, but I'm not sure what role they allow for youth representation. Does that come up much at all?

TN: Yes, it does. I grew up in Bankstown, so I had experienced everything there in terms of cultural diversity. There's the Australian Muslim Students' Association, the Islamic Youth Council, and lots of those sorts of organisations. But I think for us, as young people, we are a lot more open to other cultures than the previous generation.

RP: Not as fearful or parochial?

TN: There is still some of that, but not as much as before. So it does come up, but we're tending more toward looking at what are the root causes. So we look back to inequalities in the world in terms of wealth and colonisation. We're not as simplistic in our analysis of it, just like saying: 'Let's go to war – great!' So it does come up but we're not simplistic about how we see it.

RP: Gary's question is part of a broader agenda about the potential that exists for inter-cultural dialogue. The UN has talked about a dialogue between civilisations.

GS: Is dialogue across cultures amongst young people relatively easy? Is it just assumed that it's easy so there isn't a lot of work that has to be done?

TN: It's so, because in the 1970s cross-cultural awareness training was something new, and it was done in an institutionalised, formal way. But for the generation that has grown up with cultural diversity being a norm, and for me in particular, and for my peers, I have been really blessed growing up in Bankstown. This is because I've been exposed to all these different cultures and different people, and so how I'm able to relate and interact is just completely normal. Whereas I have gone to places like Tasmania, and spoken to some people there, and been told: 'we've had exchange students over and our students are in a very homogenous form and they don't know how to react or relate'. It's not anything hostile in terms of an attitude, it's actually a skill that you develop. If each particular generation has grown up with cultural diversity more so than other generations, then for us it's quite an inherent skill that we are able to speak on human terms without these barriers. So there is a greater potential for real engagement and dialogue, beyond just looking at the first thing you see.

GS: Coming out of the global city of Sydney, or to some extent Melbourne, makes that easier than coming out of the more provincial parts of Australia, where Hansonism was strongest?

TN: Yes, even now. Viewing the events of the race riots in Sydney was utterly debilitating for me. For those of us who are Australian-born, or who have grown up here, and are of migrant backgrounds, we don't know any other home. Where can we feel a sense of belonging if not in our birthplace, if not in the places of our childhood? The xenophobia still exists and I believe it is in places of greater homogeneity, where people of difference do not interact on a day-to-day human level. Instead of seeing a mother who has fled torture, her nameless son is seen as a potential terrorist. A couple of days later, I was at Bankstown with a friend of Greek descent buying ice cream. An older Anglo man smiled at us and he said, we don't have a problem here do we? The impact from the riots on the idea of global citizenship for me is twofold. On the one hand it is threatened by homogenous communities that are unable to engage with diversity. On the other hand, global citizenship and global ideals may be reinforced for groups and individuals like me whose reaction includes further alienation from identifying as a member of this nation-state.

RP: Looking at your experience reporting back on being the youth representative, you've not only gone to big cities, you've gone to small towns as well, so how have people responded in various places?

TN: They have reacted differently, and that is evident from the questions that they ask. For example, in Adelaide a lot of the questions they asked were about multiculturalism and refugee policy, and 'what are your thoughts on that situation' and about relations with Indigenous peoples. In Tasmania they asked 'how do we start getting involved?', 'do you think that the UN is worthless?', and 'is there hope for us?' So there are a lot of different questions that people ask, like 'how did you feel being an Asian person as the Australian representative?' But everywhere I've been there's been an openness about wanting to get involved and make a difference, and that's something that's really important overall. Even if you go to a homogenous type of place, there's still interest in broader issues like what it is like in the UN.

RP: Does that suggest an openness to a cosmopolitan global agenda?

TN: Yes, definitely. Even if they're not an activist, there's still that sense of openness to it.

RP: You mentioned how important cultural diversity is as a normal social fact for your generation. Is there also a movement towards the norm or value

195

of global equality, in that people would feel a responsibility to other human beings in the world?

TN: I think with us it's because we receive people, as migrants and refugees, and we receive their stories, and we receive their memories, and that becomes a part of our fabric almost. That's why I think that these people, people like me, are able to create those links that are strong across borders. When I speak to someone personally, and they know I'm from a refugee background, then they will think about the refugees from Afghanistan differently. I think that the more we are endowed with these communities and these people, then the more we are open to our fellow citizens, in Australia and beyond. As for me, I don't feel that I belong completely within Australia, but this is no longer a problem for my identity. And if we look at children from cross-cultural marriages, those children who grow up don't identify themselves in terms of cultural pockets, or just a state. They are more interested in ideas that are global, and they travel more. That's across a number of young people [of] mixed background who I've spoken to.

RP: So there's a broader identity?

TN: Definitely a broader identity than anything that is state-based.

RP: This gets back to the point you made earlier about youth participation and activity being across state boundaries and through non-state organisations?

TN: Yes.

GS: There are lots of people like those you are describing in Australia, who no longer belong to only one cultural arena, who have a perspective that takes them out to other arenas and the global environment much more easily than for people who come from within a homogenous cultural group. I'm wondering whether the youth organisations in such inter-cultural societies are better at engaging in global politics than those from more homogenous societies?

TN: Yes, I think they probably are.

RP: So did your background assist you in the lobbying that you were able to achieve?

TN: Yes, I definitely believe so. It's not just those from inter-cultural marriages, it's also those from a second-generation refugee or migrant background who occupy that same space. So for me I had all this angst, worrying about whether I really belonged anywhere, and I found my sense of belonging through broader concepts such as art, international arts and politics, and that sort of thing. Compared to other youth representatives, say from Sweden and other European countries, I felt I was much more malleable and took to the system really quickly. I therefore spearheaded the work of the UN youth representatives as a group, which was really interesting because the European youth representatives are the dominant group, they are the dominant group of seven out of the eleven representatives. They hold a working meeting beforehand and come with a working agenda. But they couldn't really execute it because a lot of them came from a privileged background in very homogenous societies. They couldn't interact well with people from other backgrounds. It just came naturally for me, and I was able to engage with both the European and non-European delegates, whereas the Europeans had some hesitation in approaching someone who was outside of the group of youth representatives.

RP: Do you think you could articulate the common concerns there at the UN precisely because of your experience here, and perhaps ironically because of your experience of exclusion within Australia?

TN: Yes, it is very ironic. I could just move beyond the externals of the tag that said the country or religion the person was from, to seeing them as a fellow human being.

Conclusion: resources for hope

RP: When did you become conscious of the language of global citizenship, as well as the practice you have described that was developing? When did you first think of yourself in those terms, even if not using the actual phrase; that is, as having those universal commitments, and an openness to sharing a cooperative agenda with people beyond Australia?

TN: I think it emerged, although not as a conscious term, but as a reality when I didn't feel as if I belonged in places that I was supposed to, in traditional places of belonging.

RP: You're talking now of your place within Australia, of the exclusion that you felt, of not having a voice, which has led you to find a voice which is a much broader one?

TN: Yes, it came out of my trip to Vietnam and feeling that was not really my space either. But then studying things like human rights, looking at the UN system and international organisations also helped. That was around

2002. That was when I started to feel that these universal commitments really expressed what I felt was important. They are my values that transcend boundaries that separate peoples and states. This was also affirmed by a conversation I had with a senior UN official, Shashi Tharoor, when he visited Sydney in early 2003. I told him about my despair regarding the UN's apparent failure to realise its worthwhile objectives, and fulfil the hopes so many people, including young people, have in it. I told him how disillusioned I felt as a young person growing up in this world. He took my hand and said: 'Don't lose faith. We must maintain hope that our goals can be realised'. The last image I remember from that conversation was the UN pin on his jacket. At that time, little did I know that within a couple of years I would myself be working and lobbying at the UN, holding the same UN pin in my hand, and trying to extend those hopes to this generation of young people.

RP: What do you think about that now? What lessons would you draw from your experiences, both at the UN and more broadly with organisations like the Global Youth Action Network?

TN: I've been honoured to have met so many incredible people, from teenage mothers in Central Australia, to activists in South America, and young farmers in Africa. People all across the world face struggle. In many situations, I have been inspired to learn that often human beings just find a way. My experiences with global organisations, networks and the UN utterly affirmed my belief in the power of communities and individuals for international social development. Armed with communications technology, international linkages and networks are burgeoning everyday. From trans-atlantic hip hop projects, to youth film projects exploring the territorial violence in the Middle East, to hearing speakers who have travelled from faraway continents, the proliferation of shared global ideas helps to cement ideas of global citizenship. I usually detest clichés, but it is my honest belief that it is through NGOs and community development projects that the people of the world will indeed bring about the changes we dream of.

RP: Do you see a lot of your fellow human beings thinking and acting in the same terms?

TN: I see a lot of my peers thinking and acting along the same lines, although not articulating it with that sort of theoretical concept, or naming it as global citizenship for that matter. In many ways, for those of us who feel excluded from the mainstream political agenda, this is all we have left. By being aligned in practical ways in activist types of roles in various different organisations, we really are becoming global citizens. I think there's hope for us yet.

Note

1 This interview was originally conducted in Melbourne on 21 May 2005, and edited in consultation with Thao Nguyen during 2006. Since then, Thao has completed her law degree and continued her involvement in transnational politics. For her essay about her experiences working as a 'foreign lawyer' in Vietnam, see Nguyen (2007).

Reference

Nguyen, T. 2007. 'Finding the way home.' *Sydney Morning Herald* 7–8 July:31.

11

Globalisation and Cosmopolitanism: Beyond Populist Nationalism and Neoliberalism

Roderic Pitty, Geoffrey Stokes and Gary Smith[1]

Since the early 1970s, social and political commentators have deployed the term globalisation to identify what they see as far-reaching and complex changes occurring across the world. There is much debate, however, over how to define globalisation. For our purposes, the term globalisation signifies the growing interdependence and interconnectedness of states, peoples, economies, and cultures, as well as a public consciousness of that process.[2] Referring to the latter dimension, Pierre Bourdieu (1998: 34) calls globalisation a myth, 'a powerful discourse, an *idée force*, an idea that has social force, which obtains belief'. In its different forms, the discourse of globalisation offers an account of both the problems and possibilities confronting human beings in their diverse communities and polities. For some people, the globalisation discourse has become a way of understanding and explaining not only the historical evolution of the world, but also its future direction.

Yet simply describing the process does not tell us what we should do about it, or how we should act when confronted with globalising tendencies.[3] Should we just accept the process and ride the waves of globalisation to wherever they may take us? That is, ought we submit to the inevitable? Alternatively, should we try to resist the process and reaffirm our perceived national political sovereignty and culture? Or, rather than either submit or resist, should we try to shape or transform the process, and bend it towards what we consider to be our needs and interests?[4] Such questions raise issues for individuals, citizens and governments about the rationale for deciding to take one path rather than another. Centrally, the question is one of whether there are any defensible principles that are applicable to political action in a globalising world. This chapter discusses the main

200

types of Australian responses to globalisation, which we categorise here as neoliberalism, populist nationalism, and cosmopolitanism.[5] A case is made for cosmopolitanism providing a significant intellectual and political alternative for guiding individual responsibilities under the conditions of globalisation. Further, it is argued that the practices of global citizenship emanating from cosmopolitanism offer the basis for a new transformative politics.

Neoliberalism, nationalism, and cosmopolitanism

Currently, the most dominant form of political ideology in Australia is that of neoliberalism, which gives primacy to the promotion of capitalism by creating free markets, and reducing direct government intervention in the economy. For neoliberalism, contemporary economic history complements a preferred ethical standpoint. Global trends towards open economies and freer markets are often portrayed as inevitable, and they are also endorsed as necessary because they are considered to increase individual choice and overall wealth.[6] In this neoliberal philosophy, the ownership of private property is both a primary good and a means to greater individual autonomy and wellbeing – for everyone. For many critics, globalisation and neoliberalism are identical. Limiting the understanding of globalisation in this way, however, also constrains the imagination of responses.

Australian governments have been among the most enthusiastic advocates of neoliberal globalisation. From the early 1980s, they have 'opened up' the country to the forces of economic globalisation. Labor and Liberal– National Party governments have lowered tariffs, privatised public sector corporations, corporatised public services, and deregulated the financial system and other national markets, such as the labour market. Although some neoliberal critics (e.g. Norton 2007) do not consider that governments have gone far enough along this path, and think that the size of the public sector is still too large, it is clear that a major change in the culture of public policy has occurred. Market principles, such as consumer choice, profitability, competitiveness, and so on, which are all internal to neoliberalism, have become the sole criteria for evaluating whether any policy is defensible or not. Furthermore, these criteria are staunchly defended in the mass media, and other forums.[7]

This shift in ideology and practice has provoked a second response to globalisation, emanating from nationalistic and populist forms of opposition to neoliberalism. Where the neoliberal advocates brook no criticism of the globalising tendencies in the Australian economy, the populist nationalists would like to restore the previous political arrangements in economic and social policy.[8] For supporters of the One Nation movement, for example, government decisions to open the Australian economy to greater international trade have brought damaging consequences to many industries, employers, and employees. Such populist nationalists also tend to see Australia's relatively open immigration policy as problematic because it does not discriminate on the basis of race and culture. Where newcomers from Asia are perceived to be flourishing, and the Anglo-Celtic and European Australians are seen to be undergoing hardship, there are increasing expressions of ethnocentrism and racism. For the populist nationalists, the Australian state has not only abandoned its previous protective role, it has also been undermining Australian culture and identity. Such dichotomous views necessarily oversimplify and distort the complexity of economic and social life in Australia.[9] Furthermore, and paradoxically, even these nationalistic responses lend support to neoliberal ideas. This is because such reaction appears to offer a crude choice: either one favours an economically open and increasingly unequal Australia, or one must support a narrow and isolationist view.

Yet, these are not the only political options. Neoliberalism is not the only ideology that seeks to transform Australia by exposing it to changes in the wider world. Nor is a reactionary nationalism that wants Australians to return to an era of social and cultural, if not economic, isolation really a viable alternative to neoliberalism. This kind of nationalism has had little success in challenging the hegemony of neoliberalism because it has largely focused on internal factors, and maintained a simple opposition to outside trends and influences. That is, it has offered no vision of how Australians might respond creatively to the rapidly changing conditions of a globalising world.

There is, however, another perspective that *does* take account of global challenges, but which emphasises the crucial principles of universal human rights and social justice. That perspective is one of cosmopolitanism, and it is represented by the diverse group of Australian global citizens whose thought and action we have examined in this book.

Australian activists as cosmopolitans

This book is therefore first an exercise in recognition and recovery. It has sought to give larger meaning to the work of an array of thinkers, activists, and social movements. By refining and applying the terms cosmopolitanism and global citizenship, we have given an organising principle to a disparate history of ideas, and of political and judicial action in Australia. Our conclusion is that there is an important tradition of Australian political thought and action oriented to, or informed by, cosmopolitan values. This tradition is not just an abstract one, articulated by intellectuals, but one that is expressed and practised by a range of politically active Australians. The utility of the term 'cosmopolitan' was also endorsed by most of those interviewed, who, when presented with its chief characteristics, agreed that their views could be categorised under the terms cosmopolitanism and global citizenship.

It is important to note that the universalism espoused by global citizens does not imply any diminished commitment to Australia and its peoples. Instead, it involves a redefinition of Australian patriotism that reaches beyond the limits of what the state or the dominant political elites, or their populist protagonists, may deem appropriate. Although the global citizens discussed in this book are not nationalists, and are very sceptical of nationalism, they retain a strong allegiance to Australia and its people. Indeed, it is often the strength of their concern for Australians that helps explain why they have sought, in innovative ways (which differ substantially from those of the neoliberals), to 'open up' Australia to global influences. These global citizens, by applying universalist ideals in an effort to reshape Australian institutions and policies, have demonstrated the practical possibilities of global citizenship in action. Faith Bandler, for example, used the court of world opinion to help change Australia's 1901 Constitution by popular vote, thus transforming a racist clause (51xxvi) into one that created the possibility for the Commonwealth Parliament to pass special laws for the benefit of Aborigines, and offered the further potential to recognise Indigenous rights. Bob Brown helped establish the Greens as a third force in Tasmania, and then brought them into national politics. By helping create a new political party, Brown has provided an effective political forum for those wanting serious environmental reforms in Australia, and in so doing he also linked them to a broader global movement for a sustainable planet.

None of the nine figures discussed in this book have followed the same path, but they all form part of a distinct group. Because this group is not based in a single organisation or institution, it is not accurate to define it as a movement, although all of those considered here have been active in a range of social and political movements. These Australians subscribe to a way of thinking about Australia and its place in a wider world that is both global in outlook and more inclusive in its approach to politics and citizenship. What unites these Australians as global citizens is a normative vision of how Australia ought to respond to local and global challenges. This vision comprises no less than a new moral community that redefines the boundaries of belonging for Australians, and their resultant individual and social obligations. By distinguishing between cosmopolitanism and internationalism, we have also marked out the different fields of *global* citizenship and *international* citizenship. Given the diverse and often conflicting ways in which the terms are used, such conceptual clarification is crucial if misunderstandings are to be avoided, and political critique to be enhanced. For example, Singer and Gregg's (2004) assessment of Australia's record as a 'global citizen' is really about Australia's official policies as an 'international citizen' in the world of foreign affairs, overseas trade and aid. Singer and Gregg's own critique, however, could be categorised as the product of global citizens applying cosmopolitan principles to the state's external practices.

For a different purpose, and with reference to the internal politics of Australia, Judith Brett contrasts 'cosmopolitans' with 'locals' or 'national patriots'. Brett (2004: 5) explains:

> Cosmopolitans have the social skills and attitudes that enable them to move amongst people of different cultures with confidence and purpose, whereas locals, even when they travel, are more attuned to the familiar than the different. For Australian cosmopolitans, it is their interest in and skills with cultural differences that most distinguishes them from their parochial compatriots.

Although Brett's distinction provides an insight into the character of contemporary Australian political debate, its sociological dichotomy between cosmopolitans and locals suggests that this is the only normative or political option. In reproducing the older image of the rootless cosmopolitans, primarily intellectual elites, whose defining feature is their familiarity with different cultures, the distinction is also too narrow. In our view, the concept of cosmopolitanism indicates a commitment to universal values, *and* to taking civic action to protect them at local, national, and global levels.

This conceptualisation also enables a better understanding of the emergence of an alternative notion of Australian citizenship that complements but also transcends the official, legal meanings. Not only do the cosmopolitans discussed in this book maintain a more inclusive notion of Australian citizenship, they also recognise both a citizen's universal human rights and a citizen's responsibilities beyond the nation-state. Such a global awareness is not just confined to the older age groups. As Thao Nguyen avows, global citizenship has become a practice, often unconscious or unreflective, among many young people. Their practice of global activism often grows out of experiences of discrimination, and is founded upon an appreciation of the power of political cooperation. This is not simply the lifestyle commitment of a certain younger generation, but one that has continuity over a number of generations. Nor is it confined to those people featured in this book. There is a longer tradition of cosmopolitan thought and action in Australia that extends back to the colonial period, and includes liberals, socialists, and feminists.

Making global citizenship practical

One query that is often raised about the ideal of global citizenship is how it can be realised in a world where there is no support for a world government.[10] Our response again is that citizenship is more than a legal or administrative category used by state officials to determine membership in a political community. Citizenship is crucially about the quality of participation in public life, the boundaries of which are not confined to or defined by the nation-state. Obviously there are great challenges facing anyone who claims the title of global citizen, and seeks to take part in global politics independently of their governments. But such challenges are not insuperable. In recent decades, the phenomenon of global civic action has expanded in size and reach. With the growth of information technology and proliferation of diverse means of mass communication, a global public sphere is now emerging, albeit unevenly accessible under authoritarian regimes. Under such conditions, global citizens can profoundly influence and shape national, international, and global agendas.

These remarks lead directly to further questions about the political significance of cosmopolitanism and global citizenship. Through raising new global issues for consideration, or presenting old problems in a new light, global citizens can help to shift the way in which people perceive their country's relations with the wider world. In the Australian context, cosmopolitanism contributes to that 'enlarging' tendency in Australian society and culture, which was commended by the historian Manning Clark. As John Rickard (1994: 53) presents it, this unashamedly progressive tendency looks outward to 'integrate Australia into the world'. Historians like Clark set out such visions 'not simply for the celebration of some localised sense of national identity, but so that we could recognise our humanity' (Rickard 1994: 54). The political project of enlargement is common to all the Australians considered in this book. It necessarily opposes the other rather cramped project, often referred to as the 'small picture', which argues that Australia should *not* be judged by universal norms. During the years of the

Howard government[11] from 1996 until 2007, such arguments were used to reject United Nations monitoring of human rights abuses in Australia, and provided the grounds for labelling Australia not just as 'isolationist', but as 'exceptionalist' (Otto 2001).

As global citizens, each individual discussed in this book is concerned to move popular and official attitudes about the key political issues for Australia away from narrow nationalist and populist viewpoints. Michael Kirby (2000: xxv), for example, urges us (quoting Shakespeare) to 'see the challenges of our time through the world's eye', and demonstrates the relevance of international human rights law for Australia. Global citizenship, however, is not just oriented to changing perceptions, important as these are. Questions of policy, along with the necessary political decisions and action to implement it, are also central. Herb Feith sought to redefine the sources of Australian insecurity in the region and to strengthen non-military responses. Similarly, Nancy Shelley (1987) spoke of the need for a paradigm shift in conceptualising the nation's security, and for recognising that a peaceful world requires an active practice of non-violence. Jack Mundey has worked assiduously to shift the role and purpose of trade unions beyond their usual preoccupation with wages and conditions. Margaret Reynolds has campaigned to promote respect for refugees, and helped to put in place legislation to ensure that Australian tourists are held accountable for criminal actions abroad, especially the sexual exploitation of children. Keith Suter's mission has been to alert Australians to key international and global problems such as disarmament and poverty, and reframe their responses to them.

These examples indicate the general political significance of a cosmopolitan outlook. Cosmopolitanism provides Australian citizens with an ideological and moral resource that can stimulate political criticism of institutions and policies, as well as orient political action inside or outside the nation-state. For this reason, cosmopolitanism is well suited to fill the political spaces left by the decline in attachment to traditional ideologies, such as those of democratic socialism and social liberalism. Cosmopolitanism offers counterpoint values or 'sentiments' (Appiah 2006: 23) of a universalist kind that can be used to hold governments, communities, and individuals to account for their actions. The political location of much cosmopolitanism is also important. It is often expressed through the voluntary non-governmental organisations of civil society, such as Greenpeace or Amnesty International, as well as political parties like the Greens. Activists in such groups 'gain voice across borders', and create new public spheres for the pursuit of global justice and transnational democracy (Bohman 2007: 189). The practices of global citizenship therefore demonstrate an alternative organisational tradition to both that of the state *and* its methods of cooperation with other nation-states. Accordingly, global citizens are not bound by the usual constraints of the international citizenship of states.

The politics and impact of global citizenship

Given the widespread disillusionment with traditional party politics in Australia, as in other liberal democracies, cosmopolitanism offers the possibility of a new politics of commitment. Whenever governments become paralysed by the fear of losing elections, and resort to short-term survival tactics, or parties are disabled by factionalism, the cosmopolitan alternative becomes more appealing. Cosmopolitanism encourages citizens to focus on long-term problems, such as global warming, global pandemics, particularly HIV-AIDS, and systematic infringements upon human and civil rights, and to formulate strategies for solving them. Such strategies involve intellectual elites, but also require participation by ordinary people, both citizens and non-citizens.

Not only can such a new politics entice citizens away from the confines of their individual private lives, it can also inculcate a new cosmopolitan identity through which people understand both the necessity to claim rights *and* to undertake global responsibilities. There is evidence that, while many younger Australians are increasingly distrustful of major political parties and the mainstream media, they are intent on raising global issues and are committed to new forms of debate and 'participatory deliberation' (Walter and Strangio 2007: 83–4). In this regard, cosmopolitan organisations and activities foster processes of political socialisation that build and reinforce the new civic identities of global citizenship.

What, then, has been the impact of the global citizenship tradition in Australia? The examples of the activists for change analysed in this book enable us to make a preliminary assessment. Global citizens have helped to shape the nature of political discourse in Australia over the past fifty years. They have done this by broadening the language of political accountability to include, for example, human rights and ecological sustainability, as well as keeping alive the values of peace and non-violence. Through volunteering to assist in development projects overseas, many Australians have followed in the steps of Herb Feith, and aspired to foster peace through inter-cultural dialogue.

Most of the subjects studied in this book have contributed to the broad project of making governments and corporations more accountable, particularly for breaches of the principle of non-discrimination.[12] In this regard, the Universal Declaration of Human Rights and other UN covenants have been critical. The language of international human rights has become an important political resource for protecting and advancing the interests of those on the margins of mainstream society. Aborigines and Torres Straits Islanders, for example, are now able to call upon the standards of international human rights, albeit with uneven success (see e.g. Davis 2007).

The discourses of environmentalism and political ecology now provide principles for guiding environmental accountability. Precursors to such ideas were articulated and disseminated by activists like Jack Mundey and Bob Brown and many others who succeeded in protecting both urban and remote environmental heritage areas. This discourse and activism helped set the broader political climate for federal government decisions to nominate particular wilderness places for World Heritage protection, and for Australia's eventual decision in late 2007 to sign the Kyoto Protocol on reducing greenhouse emissions.

As Carmen Lawrence notes in her Foreword, the global citizens discussed in this book have experienced vulnerability not as a threat, but as an opportunity to create a different society in Australia, where violence, injustice, and discrimination are diminished. As a consequence, the values of global citizenship are evident in changing Australian attitudes towards racial discrimination, global warming, violence, and the treatment of asylum seekers and refugees. Nonetheless, the discourses of global citizenship are strongly contested, and holding governments and corporations to account through such values remains a constant political struggle.

Taking a risk

Crucially, the commitment to universalism in the cosmopolitan identity entails a commitment to comprehending and taking risks. This is the opposite of the attitude to risk management that preoccupies much contemporary organisational and administrative practice. Discussing the demands upon intellectuals, Edward Said (1994: xii) explains: 'Universality means taking a risk in order to go beyond the easy certainties provided us by our background, language, nationality, which so often shield us from the reality of others'. Martha Nussbaum (1996: 15) puts the problem another way, saying that becoming a citizen of the world is a 'lonely business', in which one cannot rely on the comforts, warmth, and security of patriotism. But in saying that cosmopolitanism offers only 'reason and the love of humanity', she overly intellectualises the problem. Certainly, individual judgment and decision making are very important, but for the contemporary global citizen, their arena of political thought and action is necessarily cooperative and collective. As all the subjects in this book show, the active global citizen is not self-absorbed, but socially engaged. The global citizen does not just conduct an internal conversation.

Global citizens are encouraged to 'manage' their risk and insecurity with inclusive democratic deliberation and personal judgment.[13] In this way, their practices can be differentiated from the narrow rule following, and prohibition upon, deliberative judgment required by the advocates of 'risk management'. While global citizenship must be instrumentalist in pursuing explicit political goals, this is not its defining feature. In showing their commitment to certain values, especially when the prospects of realising them are slim, global citizens are frequently expressivists. Where the conditions for deliberation and negotiation are absent, global citizenship encourages symbolic protest, and direct action. In this way, issues can be brought into the public sphere, and a political groundswell created for deliberation and negotiation (Carter 2005: 190).

When risk is conceived as inherent to politics, and the subject of judgment based upon deliberation, more imaginative forms of political leadership can become possible. Indeed, it is precisely this sort of politics, political identity, and leadership that forms the basis of movements to shift globalisation away from its neoliberal economic tendencies. Popular globalisation, as Suter (2000: 9) calls it, comprises just this collection of cosmopolitan impulses. By building networks of global civic action beyond direct government control, global citizens are creating a movement of 'globalisation from below' (see Falk 1995). In this way, they have opposed the economic and political forces of 'globalisation from above' that tend to disregard the broader panoply of human rights and ecological constraints. With the recovery of political critique, *and* the evolution of cosmopolitan identities and practices, Australians need not be bound by the dogmas of neoliberalism and populist nationalism. Although such a transition in thinking confronts huge obstacles, the studies in this book suggest that cosmopolitanism and global citizenship can provide a basis for the renewal of Australian politics.

Notes

1 We would like to thank Lucinda Horrocks for her comments on this chapter.
2 For good overviews of the concept of globalisation, and debates over its meaning, see Steger (2003) and Scholte (2005).
3 On this topic, see the essays in Booth, Dunne and Cox (2001).
4 These questions are adapted from the three major patterns of argument in debates over globalisation identified by Held et al. (1999: 2–10).

5 There are, of course, other responses, such as those of a religious nature that propose the adoption of universalist theological principles and global programs, but these are expressed by a tiny minority and have had little impact on public policy.

6 See Steger (2003: 93–112).

7 See Stokes (2006b).

8 These national policies, and institutions are now often referred to as the 'Australian Settlement'. See Kelly (1992) and the critique in Stokes (2004a).

9 See the essays in Leach, Stokes and Ward (2000).

10 See also the discussion in Stokes (2004b).

11 The Howard government was defeated in the federal election of November 2007. Whereas the key election issue was industrial relations, a factor contributing to the government's defeat was the unsatisfactory way that global issues like climate change were handled (Walter and Strangio 2007: 14).

12 The principle of non-discrimination is indicated clearly and comprehensively, for example, in Article 26 of *The International Covenant on Civil and Political Rights*: 'All persons are equal before the law and are entitled without any discrimination to the equal protection of the law. In this respect, the law shall prohibit any discrimination and guarantee to all persons equal and effective protection against discrimination on any ground such as race, colour, sex, language, religion, political or other opinion, national or social origin, property, birth or other status'.

13 See the discussions of deliberative democracy in Dryzek (2000; 2006) and deliberative citizenship in Stokes (2006a).

References

Appiah, K. A. 2006. *Cosmopolitanism: Ethics in a World of Strangers*. London: Allen Lane.

Bohman, J. 2007. *Democracy across Borders*. Cambridge, Massachusetts: MIT Press.

Booth, K., T. Dunne and M. Cox (eds) 2001. *How Might We Live? Global Ethics in the New Century*. Cambridge: Cambridge University Press.

Bourdieu, P. 1998. *Acts of Resistance: Against the New Myths of Our Time*. Trans. R. Nice. Cambridge: Polity Press.

Brett, J. 2004. 'Border control.' *Australian Universities Review* 46(2):3–11.

Carter, A. 2005. *Direct Action and Democracy Today*. Cambridge: Polity.

Davis, M. 2007. 'Arguing over Indigenous rights: Australia and the United Nations.' In J. Altman and M. Hinkson (eds) *Coercive Reconciliation*. North Carlton: Arena Publications Association, pp. 97–107.

Dryzek, J. 2000. *Deliberative Democracy and Beyond*. Oxford: Oxford University Press.

——2006. *Deliberative Global Politics: Discourse and Democracy in a Divided World*. Cambridge: Polity.

Falk, R. 1995. *On Humane Governance: Towards a New Global Politics*. Cambridge: Polity.

Held, D., A. McGrew, D. Goldblatt and J. Perraton 1999. *Global Transformations: Politics, Economics and Culture*. Cambridge: Polity.

Kelly, P. 1992. *The End of Certainty*. Sydney: Allen & Unwin.

Kirby, M. 2000. *Through the World's Eye*. Sydney: Federation Press.

Leach, M., G. Stokes and I. Ward (eds) 2000. *The Rise and Fall of One Nation*. St Lucia: University of Queensland Press.

Norton, A. 2007. 'The PM should think small.' *Weekend Australian* 13–14 January:16.

Nussbaum, M. 1996. 'Patriotism and cosmopolitanism.' In J. Cohen (ed.) *For Love of Country: Debating the Limits of Patriotism.* Boston: Beacon Press, pp. 2–17.

Otto, D. 2001. 'From "reluctance" to "exceptionalism": The Australian approach to domestic implementation of human rights.' *Alternative Law Journal* 26(5):219–22.

Pitty, R. and M. Leach 2004. 'Australian nationalism and internationalism.' In P. Boreham, G. Stokes and R. Hall (eds) *The Politics of Australian Society: Political Issues for the New Century.* 2nd edn, Frenchs Forest: Pearson Education Australia, pp. 93–108.

Rickard, J. 1994. 'Clark and Patrick White.' In C. Bridge (ed.) *Manning Clark: Essays on his Place in History.* Melbourne: Melbourne University Press, pp. 45–54.

Said, E. 1994. *Representations of the Intellectual.* London: Vintage.

Scholte, J. A. 2005. *Globalization: A Critical Introduction.* Revised edn, Hundmills: Palgrave Macmillan.

Shelley, N. 1987. 'Interdependence and common security: A new paradigm.' *Social Alternatives* 6(2):43–8.

Singer, P. and T. Gregg 2004. *How Ethical is Australia? An Examination of Australia's Record as a Global Citizen.* Melbourne: Australian Collaboration with Black Inc.

Steger, M. 2003. *Globalization: A Very Short Introduction.* Oxford: Oxford University Press.

Stokes, G. 2004a. 'The "Australian Settlement" and Australian political thought.' *Australian Journal of Political Science* 39(1):5–22.

——2004b. 'Transnational citizenship: Problems of definition, culture and democracy.' *Cambridge Review of International Affairs* 17(1):119–35.

——2006a. 'Critical theories of deliberative democracy and the problem of citizenship.' In Ethan Leib and Baogang He (eds) *The Search for Deliberative Democracy in China.* New York: Palgrave Macmillan, pp. 53–73.

——2006b. 'Neoliberal hyperglobalism in Australian political thought.' Paper for conference on *Challenges of Globalisation: Indian and Australian Responses,* University of Hyderabad, India, 7–9 December.

Suter, K. 2000. *In Defence of Globalisation.* Sydney: UNSW Press.

Walter, J. and P. Strangio 2007. *No, Prime Minister: Reclaiming Politics from Leaders.* Sydney: UNSW Press.

Index

214